# DECISION MAKING IN MEDICINE AND HEALTH CARE

# DECISION MAKING IN MEDICINE AND HEALTH CARE

PATRICIA C. TOLANA
EDITOR

**Nova Biomedical Books**
*New York*

For permission to use material from this book please contact us:
Telephone 631-231-7269; Fax 631-231-8175
Web Site: http://www.novapublishers.com

**NOTICE TO THE READER**



**LIBRARY OF CONGRESS CATALOGING-IN-PUBLICATION DATA**

Decision making in medicine and health care / patricia C. Tolana (editor).
p. ; cm
Includes bibliographical references and indez.
ISBN-13: 978-1-60021-870-5 (hardcover)
ISBN-10: 1-60021-870-9 (hardcover)
1. Medicine--Decision making. 2. Medical care--Decision making. 3. Informed consent (Medical law) 4. Patient participation. 5. Physician and patient. I. Tolana, Patricia C.
[DNLM: 1. Diagnosis. 2. Decision Making. 3. Informed Consent. 4. Physician- Patient Relations--ethics. 5. Physicians--Paychology. WB 141 D2958 2007]
R723.5.d423 2007-11-07 610--dc22
2007026604

*Published by Nova Science Publishers, Inc. ✦ New York*

# CONTENTS

# PREFACE

In a fast-moving world, the necessity of making decisions, and preferably good ones, has become even more difficult. One reason is the variety and number of choices perhaps available which often arenot presented or understood. Alternatives are often unclear and complex paths to them confusing and misleading. Thus the process of decision making itself requires analysis on an ongoing basis. Decision making is often made based on cultural factors whereas the best alternative might be quite different. The subject touches ethics aspects as well as psychological considerations. This new book presents important research on the psychology of decision making related to health care and medicine.

Chapter I - The central purpose of the study was to examine differences between women and men, ages 30-50 years, in their responses to heart disease, and to identify the factors influencing them in the fields of health and illness. The study was conducted using a qualitative method. The participants in the study included 30 men and 30 women who suffered from coronary heart disease. The study findings suggest that women delayed seeking treatment and that when they did seek treatment they were not initially diagnosed as suffering from heart disease due to physicians' perceptions that heart disease is a men's disease. The recovery period for women was characterized by their quick return to daily home making before their physical condition permitted it. Conversely, the men extended their recovery period and received support from their families. As part of the return to normal life, the men were strict in following the instructions of the health regimen, whereas most of the women ignored it. The women, compared to the men, received less support from their spouses and families, and they noted that social expectations concerning their role were high. Our study concludes that heart disease varies between men and women in the characteristics of its symptoms and in the attitude of medical staff and the public, as well as of patients themselves, towards the disease. The role of the cardiac patient is based on male characteristics and, as a result, men are legitimized and receive social support in all that relates to the disease; consequently, men adhere to the health regimen, whereas women are less inclined to. This study can advance insights on the influence of the gender variable on responses to heart disease, as well as supply information on therapeutic intervention for male and female cardiac patients and the nature of the different measures used for each.

Chapter II - Studies suggest that effective doctor-patient communication is associated with higher levels of patient satisfaction, better treatment compliance, and better biomedical and psychosocial outcomes. Much of this research has been conducted in the field of oncology.

Given that effective doctor-patient communication has been linked to beneficial health-related outcomes, an examination of studies relevant to cardiologist-patient communication appears warranted. As studies focusing on communication in heart failure patients are relatively sparse, this article provides a critical review of the larger literature within cancer on communication interventions and an exploration of lessons that can be learned.

Current empirical evidence suggests the importance of considering both the information needs of patients, as well as preferred decision-making processes. There are several types of methods and tools to promote patient understanding and to facilitate decision making, including patient information aids, techniques to reduce patient anxiety, patient decision aids, and communication training for patients and/or physicians.

While many of the findings in studies of oncologist-patient communication can be applied to the improvement of cardiologist-patient communication, further studies are needed to help cardiologists and other healthcare professionals meet the specific needs of patients with heart failure.

Chapter III - Shared Decision Making (SDM) with regard to diagnostic or therapeutic procedures has to be looked at in the framework of clinical indication (CI). Both, CI and SDM are essential parts of patient-physician interaction.

The following paper concentrates on 5 major aspects of patient-physician relationship which promote (or aid?) mutual participation:

a. alterations in patient-physician-relationship;
b. patient-related determinants of SDM;
c. physician-related prerequisites of SDM;
d. legal problems in SDM;
e. ethical problems / aspects of participative clinical DM;
f. CI as the encompassing dimension of patient-physician-relationship.

Ad (a): The patient-physician-relationship has shifted over the last decades from a paternalistic or parentalistic model towards a client-expert- or a customer-shopkeeper- or, finally, to a more partnership-like relation. This is in favour of SDM. Whatever model, there will always remain an asymmetry of information and concern, of rational distance and emotional burden (affliction), resp.related. Nevertheless, the expectancy of or even the demand for better information and more consequent involvement in SDM is increasing with the shift/alteration mentioned above.

Ad (b) There are certain barriers against the trend towards SDM. Patient-related impediments include the lack of full information about the significance/dignity of clinical findings, the value and risk of diagnostic measures and the possibilities of therapeutic procedures with regard to benefits and risks. It also includes actual or permanent restrictions of the patient's capability to understand and consider the information given and to finally decide and follow the decision. This holds true even for the mentally more or less capable adult patient and of course more for the incapacitated patient. In this case, surrogate decision is necessary (advance-decision/self-determination, tutorial or the supposed wish/will of the patient).

Ad (c) Physician-related barriers include the conceptual or personal mental reservation against the patient's participation in the decision process, lack of time for thorough information and the urgency of decisions, the fragmentation of clinical responsibility to more than one doctor for the patient (not only one each to decide and to perform the procedure bur also for a multidisciplinary task).

Ad (d) Legal aspects of SDM include "informed consent" the doctor is obliges to before carrying out any invasive procedure (except for the incapacitated patient or in life-threatening situations), the right of self-determination even against the doctor's convincement/advice for "better" therapy. As for tutorial decision the problem of priority of a verbal or formal advance-determination, of proxies or common sense judgement arises.

Ad (e) Ethical aspects of SDM: Since SDM is part of the way how patient-physician-relationship is actualized, it is within this framework with it's principles of mutual acceptance of autonomy, beneficence, non-maleficence, confidentiality and justice. Autonomy does not mean arbitrary self-decision regardless human society but it borders/is confined by the fellow-man's autonomy. Beneficence does not warrant socially or individually unacceptable demands but has to take into account human and economic justice.

Ad (f) CI in our opinion encompasses a larger field of the physician's acting for his patient. It is the process of reasoning for any step in the process from the first meeting, the "construction" of the "picture of complaints" to diagnostic, therapeutic procedures and prognostic judgement. They all have to be substantiated on both medical and personal reasons. CI has the pivoting function from "information" and evaluation to the next step: not only from diagnosis to treatment but even in the process of taking the medical history (as that of the disease, the patient and the illness, i.e. historia morbi, aegroti et passionis) and the direct examination of the patient as a person feeling her- or himself in his/her bodily constitution as a subject of bodily self-perception, -experience and -consciousness, of acting and suffering possibly in all dimensions of bio-psycho-social aspects of human life.

Patient-physician relationship has changed considerably over the last two or three decades. Once a paternalistic or parentalistic dyad in which the doctor decided about what to do and how to treat the patient, the relation has become more of a partnership of two equally responsible persons who both share in decision making about diagnostic and therapeutic measures. The alteration does not proceed simultaneously in all social classes. It is more pronounced among "intellectual", self-confident people used to an independent, self-responsible life-style, whereas lower class and elderly people still feel dependent upon the doctor's advice even up to complete refusal to decide any medical decision themselves.

The way both partners act is of course dependent upon the clinical situation: whether an acute, perhaps an even life-threatening disease or a chronic, insidious process, whether it is a doctor's additional advice or his accompanying role or function (i.e. the radiologist who is not in charge of leading a patient throughout the process of his illness). And, finally, the relation is highly influenced by personal, institutional and social circumstances which may change from day to day.

Although in the context of clinical decision making it is mainly the patient-doctor relationship the authors are concentrating on, there is a similar shift in the patient's cooperation with nurses and paramedics.

Chapter IV - The purpose of this chapter is to examine the extent to which patients are involved in making decisions about their medications in hospital. Traditionally, decision-making about medications has involved patients taking a passive and receptive role without active participation. In contemporary health care, there is a focus on self care, shorter hospital stays, treatment of individuals with an increasing severity of illness, and positive benefits of patient involvement in improving health outcomes. Furthermore, patients have complex medication regimens that they are expected to manage when they are discharged home from hospital. It is therefore timely to consider how patients contribute to medication decisions. For this study, a descriptive prospective qualitative design was used, incorporating observations with health professionals and patients. Data collection was undertaken in a metropolitan university teaching hospital in Australia, using a stratified random sampling to recruit patients from 12 ward settings. This sampling method ensured that a broad cross-section of patients with different health problems was involved in the study. A medication decision making model was used as a framework to analyze the data according to four principles: identifying treatment goals, selecting different medication options, determining medication monitoring and evaluation, and identifying patient self care. Data findings demonstrated that patients continued to play a passive role in making decisions about their medications in hospital. On the other hand, there were instances where health professionals assisted patients to decide their own course of action about managing medications. In such situations patients were adequately prepared for their transition from hospital to home. This chapter examines the implications of findings for practice and health care policy.

Chapter V - The UN Conventions on the Right of the Child was adopted in 1989, and efforts have been made to implement the intentions of the Convention. When decisions are to be made in pediatric care, comprehensive collaborative work is involved and multiple confounding factors are included. The area comprises several concepts that may be interpreted in various ways. The results from a systematic literature review including concepts like consent, competence, the child's best interest, knowledge, values and attitudes, roles and partnership, power, and economy are discussed. Furthermore, research projects concerning children's and parents' needs and participation in decision-making are described. To identify everyday situations in medical and nursing situations the authors followed twenty-four children during the course of events during their hospital stay. The aim of the study was to identify needs and various levels of participation, actual and optimal, and to describe the way in which children, parents and staff interact during the decision-making process. The results were analyzed according to the Scale of Degree of Self-Determination, which divides participation into decision-making into five levels. In the article the results are discussed from both a theoretical and a clinical perspective.

Chapter VI - Despite the increased use of substitute health care providers in an effort to save money and fill gaps in physicians shortages, little is known about why people decide to enter such work. Gaining further insight into decisions to enter these occupations may help with recruitment and retention strategies, which is critical at a time when health workforces are facing severe shortages. Most research on the employment of substitute health care providers focuses on career choice among various specialties within an occupation while there has been little exploration of why men and women enter these occupations in the first place. Most of what is known about career pathways for substitute providers focuses on job satisfaction and experiences once in the profession but not why people entered the occupation. This chapter examines three health care professions: physician assistants, nurse practitioners and nurse anesthetists. These domains of health care were chosen because they are among the largest substitute providers in the U.S. This chapter draws on normative decision theory to frame an analysis of how people decided to enter these occupations. This project drew on 53 in-depth interviews with substitute health care providers to gain insight into why men and women enter such areas of work. Findings suggest that for this sample, choosing these occupations was the best decision amongst the alternatives because it offered the most desirable consequences with the minimum loss. Both men and women claimed that role models and exposure to the profession influenced their decision to enter. Many women chose their career because they were in the caring field for a long time and this offered them a challenge. Men, on the other hand, often entered their job as a second career choice as an opportunity to expand their skills and increase their autonomy. Male nurse practitioners often came from diverse backgrounds while many physician assistants and nurse anesthetists had military backgrounds. Men and women both claimed that these occupations offered a comparable alternative to the time consuming and expensive training required to become a physician.

Chapter VII - Given that physicians must subjectively judge their level of explanation in actual practice, and that explanations perceived to be inadequate can lead to patients ceasing to use a particular doctor or to the practice of doctor-shopping behavior, physicians need to accurately evaluate patients' perceptions of the sufficiency of physicians' explanations. The authors studied the association between patient and physician evaluations of the level of physician explanations.

The subjects were 630 physician-patient pairs in Japan. Path analysis was used to reveal the structure of the association between patient and physician evaluations. From a random selection of 190 physicians and 950 patients, 126 physicians and 630 patients returned questionnaires (response rate for both: 66.3%).

The authors found the following: (1) There was no direct association between physician and patient evaluations of the sufficiency of a physician's explanation; and (2) "Improvement in health and anxiety level", "courtesy", and "being rushed" had the strongest influences on patient understanding and recognition of the sufficiency of a physician's explanation.

In order to promote patient understanding and to provide patients with satisfactory explanations, it is important for physicians to alleviate patient anxiety, to be courteous, and to not rush patients while seeing them. Although these findings are useful for improving doctor-patient communication, some are not consistent with previous findings; more research will be necessary to add to these present findings.

Chapter VIII - Decision making in the patient-physician relationship was first addressed by courts in England in 1767. The courts first viewed the issues of decision making under the concept of "consent" and asked whether the profession of medicine held physicians to a duty of securing an individual patient's consent prior to performing a medical intervention. Although there was a presumption that some sort of discussion related to the physician obtaining consent from the patient took place, this first British court focused on whether the profession of medicine held such a duty as an obligation of physicians.

Courts in our four countries of interest—England, the United States, Canada, and Australia—hear cases in consent or informed consent under two different standards. Courts in Great Britain hear informed consent cases under a professional standard. Courts in Canada and Australia hear them under a reasonable person standard. And in the United States, about half of the states hear them under a professional standard and the others hear them under a reasonable person standard.

In court decision making under a professional standard, a physician must disclose to a patient what other physicians with the same or similar training would commonly disclose to their patients. Under a reasonable person standard, a physician must disclose what a reasonable person in the patient's position would want to know.

In their formulation of the concepts of consent (Great Britain and Australia) and informed consent (the United States and Canada), courts have focused on the physician's obligation to disclose information about the risks of physician-recommended interventions. Ethicists and cognitive psychologists have gone beyond court decision making, focusing on forms of shared and participatory decision making in which patients are encouraged to take more active roles.

This paper reviews the challenges patients face as they decide whether to take more active roles in decision making, and the challenges physicians face as non-physicians propose alternative frameworks for the patient-physician relationship. This review examines four perspectives on decision making in the patient-physician relationship: judicial, ethical, decision analytical, and cognitive psychological. Patient challenges include issues of literacy and numeracy, and the level of comfort patients have with the words, numbers, tables, and graphs used to portray scientific evidence in discussions related to their medical care. Physician challenges include following the laws of consent and informed consent in their respective countries. Challenges for both patients and physicians include: (1) deciding which decision making strategy to adopt in the patient-physician relationship—patient-based, physician-based, or some form of shared or participatory decision making, and (2) determining how decisions are to be made in the absence of high quality scientific information.

Chapter IX - The benefits of good quality patient information are now firmly established. Adequately informed patients are able to share decision making with their medical team whilst exercising their own autonomy. Providing higher levels of information and involving patients in their own treatment decisions has been shown to have a protective effect on patients' psychological and physical wellbeing. In both randomized [1-5] and prospective observational studies [6-8] patients with a variety of cancer types offered higher levels of information were significantly more satisfied, had improved compliance, and reduced anxiety and depression. In order to empower patients with enough understanding to have a truly informed input into their management, many oncology units around the world have introduced a wide selection of educational tools, which aim to provide multifaceted education programmes, addressing a range of cultural and educational levels. In order to know whether these manoeuvers are satisfying patient's information needs, as this chapter discusses, the authors need to know what these needs are and how to measure them.

Chapter X - This chapter gives an overview of the literature regarding the ethical dilemmas that are debated in relation to primary care physicians' gatekeeper role. Theories and experiences of policy measures aiming at motivating rationing decisions in primary care are presented with the empirical case of the Norwegian health care system and policy.

Gatekeeping systems are health care systems where access to secondary care is filtered through primary care, as is the case in Norway, the UK, the Netherlands, Denmark, France and within managed care in the USA. One of the dilemmas often referred to in studies of primary care physicians' rationing decisions is how to balance the needs of the individual patient against the needs of the population while securing patient involvement in decision making.

Recent research gives several indications that primary care physicians are avoiding the rationing task. The Norwegian health care sector is one of the most expensive health care systems in the world, and it is almost entirely covered by universal insurance which means that it is practically free at the point of service. While the system is increasingly dependent on the primary care physicians' gatekeeper function for cost containment and fair and effective resource allocation, professional freedom of primary care physicians is extensive.

Finally, the chapter suggests and discusses policy measures to motivate rationing in gatekeeping systems.

In: Decision Making in Medicine and Health Care
Editor: P. C. Tolana, pp. 1-5
ISBN: 978-1-60021-870-5


*Expert Commentary A*

# The Role of Consent in the Relationship between Physician and Patient

***Salvatore Pisu[1], Giovanni Caocci[2], Giorgio La Nasa[2] and Francesco De Stefano[3]***
[1]Department of Legal Medicine, University of Cagliari, Italy;
[2]Bone Marrow Transplantation Centre, "R. Binaghi" Hospital, Departmenf of Hematology, University of Cagliari, Italy;
[3]Department of Legal Medicine, University of Genova, Italy.

Medicine is not simply a science. This may seem to be a rather game affirmation but there is some truth in it. Besides, we are not the only ones to uphold this concept. Pellegrino and Thomasma, reporting the thought of MacIntyre and Gorovitz [1], said that: « medicine, in the strict sense, is not a science, it is rather, a "practical science" with a set of principles that govern the art of healing, it is a "techne iatriké"». In the broad sense, medical science certainly requires a certain amount of scientific knowledge but still medicine cannot be said to coincide with medical science. It combines knowledge and cleverness just as Plato and Aristotle intended *techne*. For this reason it is art. Indeed, medical science is logically related to a series of experimentally validated propositions about health and illness. Yet, medical science is not synonymous of medicine [2]. Medicine is a human practice, based on science, that operates in a world of values. Man being the focus of medicine makes it very different from the other doctrines. The confusion between medicine and science has thrown doubt upon the true assets of medicine. Current reflections on science can be tied down to two basic lines of thought: a – the idea that science purely deals with the enunciations of facts, without any appeal for values; b – the enormous progress persuades us that efficiency is the most important goal. It follows that if medicine is simply a science it needs to have the same characteristics: 1 - to be free of any appeal for values; 2 – to use technological progress to determine what is good for the patient. If medicine is to be considered a science it has to be free of any value and the moral problem must remain external to it. If we add to this the supremacy of the individual, the picture is complete: medical science offers a service that the individual is free to accept or not. Unfortunately, in most cases a good decision does not simply implicate a correct decision based on criterions of scientific nature but rather a decision that has to account for the good of the patient. The good of the patient is not inferred by scientific input alone. It needs to consider the patient as a person. As Shorter said: the progress of medicine in the comprehension of the mechanism of disease must not be disjoined from the good of the patient. In fact, to understand the patient as a whole is the secret of healing [3].

A medical action implies a profound respect for the freedom, dignity and values of a person and at the same time requires sensitivity and compassion, all values that cannot be acquired through scientific training. The emphasis can be put on two fundamental aspects: the existential nature of the illness and the substantial inequality of the relationship between physician and patient. In fact, the patient is a person who needs assistance, whereas the physician is the one to offer help [4].

The contemporary technical approach has too superficially abandoned the ancient conception of the physician, expressed very well by Albert Jonsen in his book *The Birth of Bioethics*, where he underlined his great humanity and moral responsibility: «He was gentle but firm, honest but discreet, a thoroughly trustworthy confidant. He expended energy and time, often compensated only with gratitude. He practiced alone, his medical judgement unfettered by any supervisor. The doctor's ethics, even more than his power to cure, made him, if not an American folk hero, at least a paradigm of moral probity» [5].

This "scenario" has changed. In the modern concept the physician is thought to be a medical scientist with a great amount of knowledge and technological equipment. Technology certainly represents an event of incalculable value for the medical profession, but the patient's perception of this progress is at least ambiguous. The physician-patient relationship has been burdened by the dominion or tyranny of technological tools, tests and procedures that the patient often does not understand. The fear to become slave of the physician sometimes overcomes the trust in him. This points out the right of the person to be free. The autonomy of the patient relates to dignity of the human being which claims the liberty for a person to establish his own values and life plans based on information and reasoning.

The autonomy is a conquest that provides modern liberal philosophy of personal rights and liberties with an important philosophical background. The historical origin derives from the philosophical treatise of the French and English Enlightenment and the emergence of new doctrines of individual and political rights to freedom that characterize modern democracy [6]. But to exert autonomy, the patient needs to be informed and conscious of what he is going to do. The so-called Informed Consent must serve this task and is one of the most important features of twentieth-century health care. It is a personal exchange between physician and patient. The physician provides information so that the patient is informed and can give his or her informed consent. This formula stands in the conviction that information is the most significant attribute of the informed consent. Consequently, many patients and providers alike confuse the signing of this form with the reality of giving consent. The relationship between physician and patient has progressively changed over the last 50 years. The shift was determined by the deep revolution that characterizes technological progress. The fundamental characteristic of the doctor-patient relationship, at least until fifty years ago, has been the absolute authority of the physician. The patient must be obedient. The classical period was characterized by the lack of distinction between the natural and the moral order. The physician-philosopher was similar to God and between medicine and wisdom there was not a great difference, while the habits and customs of the sick were not only pathologic, but even immoral. The Hippocratic oath imposed certain firm duties: the physician was to heal, not harm; if asked to extinguish life, either at its beginning or at its end, he must refuse; he must maintain the strictest confidence. At the same time the patient was treated as a child: only the physician knew what was good for the patient. The approach was called "Paternalism". Gerald Dworkin defined paternalism as the meddling into the freedom of action of the patient justified by his best interest. The relationship was coercive because the physician knew the good, the happiness, and the needs of the patient [7]. But, as Childress said, not always the paternalism was coercive. In many cases the patient himself was convinced that the physician knew better what was in his best interest [8]. The last fifty years have witnessed tumultuous transformations changing the ethical and psychological approach. The most important issue is represented by the awareness that a physician often cannot heal a person just by curing a disease, especially if the physician systematically ignores or disregards the patient's view [6]. Subsequently, the freedom of the patient became very relevant in the relationship. Justice Cardozo's decision (New York 1914) contains one of the most quoted sentences in the history of informed consent: «Every human being of adult years and sound mind has a right to determine what shall be done with his own body; and a surgeon who performs an operation without his patient's consent commits an assault, for which he is liable to damages». The ferocious Nazi experiments gave rise to many codes and guidelines. The first was the *Nuremberg Code*. The first point of this Code stated: «All agree that certain basic principles must be observed in order to satisfy moral, ethical and legal concept. The voluntary consent of the human subject is absolutely essential. This means that the person involved should have legal capability to give consent; should be so situated as to be able to exercise free power of choice, without the intervention of any element of force, fraud, deceit, duress, overreaching, or other ulterior form of constraint or coercion; and should have sufficient knowledge and comprehension of the elements of the subject matter involved as to enable him to make an understanding and enlightened decision». In 1957, the word "Informed Consent" appeared for the first time. In 1964, it was adopted by the *Declaration of Helsinki*. In 1978, the Belmont Report stressed this view and inserted the principle of autonomy as one of the three principles that must be respected in the sanitary setting. In 1979, Tom Beauchamp and James Childress definitively established autonomy as an indefeasible right [9]. The International Ethical Guidelines for Biomedical Research Involving Human Subjects promulgated by *The World Health Organization* in 1993 stated. «Respect for persons incorporates at least two fundamental ethical considerations, namely: a – respect for autonomy, which requires that those who are capable of deliberation about their personal choices should be treated with respect for their capacity for self-determination; and b – protection of persons with impaired or diminished autonomy, which requires that those who are dependent or vulnerable be afforded security against harm or abuse». This is the stand of the Informed Consent. In particular, it is the way of gaining permission from others without harming individual dignity [10]. Hengelhardt's interpretation of informed consent points out the impossibility to reach a morally shared vision and the impracticality to recognize an authority as a reference [6]. Another evaluation considers the informed consent an obstacle to the relationship. It is a legalistic myth where the quality of care becomes questionable and paralyses the conscientious physician. It erects insuperable barriers toward the patient and, in many cases is not applicable. A more convincing interpretation of the informed consent has substantial juridical bases, but, in the end it rests essentially on an ethical imperative. An ethically valid consent consists in a decisional process based on the mutual respect of both parties, and not a bureaucratic ritual. What information must the physician disclose and discuss for the consent to be an aware consent? First of all, the physician must inform patients of their medical diagnosis. He must make sure that they understand what is wrong and what will happen if they are not treated. Secondly, the physician must make sure that the patients understood the information about therapy, particularly the risks, burdens, and benefits associated with each treatment scheme. Finally the physician must give the reasons for which he thinks a treatment plan is best for the patient [11]. Furthermore, consent requires the free will of the patient. To reach these goals, experience has shown that it is not sufficient to speak of informed consent. Often the physician gives a multitude of information but the patient fails to grasp the central point. Sometimes, there is enough information but the involvement of the physician is poor and so on. Hence, the most important goal in the relationship is not the information but rather the understanding. The information is a condition to obtain awareness but it does not coincide. One can give consent without understanding, while the aim is comprehension. Understanding means information, empathy between physician and patient in a situation that is as comfortable as possible. Our proposal is to shift from Informed Consent to Conscious Consent. The pursuit of Conscious Consent is paramount and the physician needs to be educated to learn that to respect the freedom of the patient is part of the goal of his profession. For this reason, we can call this approach: beneficence in trust [6].

## REFERENCES


[1] Gorovitz S, MacIntyre A. "Toward a theory of medical fallibility". *J Med Philos* 1976; 1:51-71.

[2] Thomasma DC, Pellegrino E. Philosophy of medicine as the source of medical ethics. *Metamedicine* 1981; 2:7.

[3] Shorter E. Beside manners. *The Troubled History of Doctors and Patients*. Simon and Schuster, New York, 1985.

[4] Pellegrino E. Humanistic Base for Professional Ethics in Medicine. *NY State J Med* 1977; 1457.

[5] Jonsen A. *The Birth of Bioethics*. Oxford University Press, New York-Oxford, 1998, 3.

[6] Pellegrino E, Thomasma DC. *For the Patient's Good*. Oxford University Press, New York-Oxford, 1988.

[7] Dworkin G. Paternalism. *Monist* 1972; 56:6-84.

[8] Childress JF. *Who Should Decide? Paternalism in Health Care Ethics*. New York-Oxford University Press, 1982, 237-241.

[9] Beauchamp TL, Childress JF. *Principles of Biomedical Ethics.* Oxford University Press, New York-Oxford, 1994.

[10] Engelhardt HT. *The foundations of Bioethics.* Oxford University Press, New York-Oxford, 1996, 300.

[11] Devettere RJ. *Practical Decision Making in Health Care Ethics.* Georgetown University Press, Washington, 2000, 104.

In: Decision Making in Medicine and Health Care
Editor: P. C. Tolana, pp. 7-9
ISBN: 978-1-60021-870-5


*Expert Commentary B*

# Decision-Making and Expert Patients

***Sally Lindsay****
Institute for Social, Cultural & Policy Research,
University of Salford, Salford United Kingdom.

Chronic illness is a cause of poor health and disability and is now one of the leading causes of death. Given the extent of chronic illness where approximately one in three people have a chronic condition, the consequences for health care systems and the burden on patients is great (Department of Health 2005). With the rise of self-care and expert patient initiatives, health professionals are increasingly realizing that the management of chronic conditions is not in the direct control of health professionals but rather, increasingly in the hands of patients. The objective of expert patient initiatives is to encourage patients suffering from chronic conditions to become more actively involved in decisions concerning their treatment. The notion of 'expert patients' is pivotal to government plans to modernise health care systems by linking patient expertise to ideas of empowerment, a better quality of life, self-esteem and a user-driven health care system (Fox et al. 2005).

Shared decision-making between patients and health care providers is often advocated because of its potential to improve the quality of the decision-making process and hopefully, patient outcomes (Gravel et al. 2006). Although much is known about the barriers and facilitators to shared decision-making between patients and physicians (Gravel et al 2006), little is known about the *process* that expert patients go through to reach a decision about their health. Further, little is known about how expert patients influence treatment decisions with their health care providers. Given that most patients would like to be involved in decision-making concerning their health more research is needed into the decision-making process to help them become more involved in the treatment of their condition.

* Correspondence concerning this article should be addressed to: Dr. Sally Lindsay Institute for Social, Cultural and Policy Research, 4th Floor Humphrey Booth House, University of Salford, Salford, United Kingdom M5 4QA. Phone: +011 44 161 295 5029 Email: s.lindsay@salford.ac.uk.

In order to make effective self-care decisions individuals must become skilled at anticipating when difficulties in self-care management might occur and learn how to change their practices to integrate new insights about their body's response to certain situations or interventions (Thorne et al. 2003). Patients then often form judgements related to seeking help or advice and evaluate the decisions that are taken. Self-care decision-making is a complex process and involves assuming control of self-care management, fine-tuning the bases on which self-care decisions should be made and understanding how to judge the quality of decisions (Thorne et al. 2003).

Despite the potential of the expert patient program as a lay-led empowering initiative the program has been criticized as perpetuating the medical model and failing to reach those most in need (Wilson et al. 2007). First, not everyone has the knowledge, resources and social capital to make decisions about their health. For example, the elderly, those who are geographically isolated, ethnic minorities and the deprived may encounter challenges in making decisions about their health. As people age, they are more likely to experience multiple chronic health problems, have changes in living conditions and poorer mental health. Further, the ability to engage in self-care is strongly linked with social class where those with higher incomes often have a better health locus of control and more actively care for their chronic illness (Lindsay & Bellaby 2007). Meanwhile those who are from deprived areas often lack the resources to properly self-manage their condition such as the ability to buy good food (like low fat meats and fruits and vegetables). Health care providers should also be cognizant of geographical barriers to engaging in self-care. Vulnerable groups, such as deprived, elderly heart patients often rely on public transportation and lack the ability to attend cardiac rehabilitation and other health promotion programs because they are not readily accessible on a bus route and a taxi would be too expensive for them (Lindsay & Bellaby 2007). Health care providers may look at such people and think that they simply do not care about managing their health; however, they often lack the resources and social capital to implement effective self-care decisions. Involvement in self-care and expert patient initiatives is socially unequal and further efforts are needed to support those who would benefit from such programs. What we need to keep in mind is who are expert patient and self-care initiatives designed for? And are we doing everything that we can to ensure equal opportunities to participate in such health care initiatives?

Other gaps also exist within this area of expert patients and decision-making. First, although expert patient initiatives have many implications for patients, there has been much less attention given to the impact this is having for health care providers, especially from a decision-making perspective. The introduction of the expert patients program and the rise in self-care initiatives has presented new challenges to health care providers (Taylor & Bury 2007). Most of the research in this area focuses on physicians' and nurses' ability to influence patients and to empower them to become more active in their self-care and not the impact this may have on health care providers themselves. From a health care provider's perspective, encouraging self-care is more than simply providing information to patients. It is also about educating patients about how to take care of their illness (Department of Health 2005). Indeed, patients often want more information from their health providers about how to manage their illness. At the same time, health care providers need to become more informed about the realities of life for their patients, especially those who are from disadvantaged backgrounds (Shaw & Baker 2004).

Most of the research in this area has examined physicians while little is known about the decision-making process between expert patients and other types of health care providers. More focus on a variety of health care providers (in addition to physicians) such as nurses and pharmacists is needed because they have a valuable influence on patient decision-making (Gravel et al. 2006). Second, little is known about the process of decision-making by health care providers and how they incorporate patient's expertise into their decisions of how to treat them. Finally, more research is also needed that examines (and ideally compares) how 'expert patients' use various forms of self-help (e.g., support groups, expert patient programs, Internet, hand held technologies etc.) to help make decisions about their health. Psychology can help shed light on the impact of the expert patient agenda by opening the debate in several key areas.

## REFERENCES

Department of Health. (2005) *Supporting People with Long Term Conditions*. Leeds: Primary Care DOH.

Fox N, Ward K, & O'Rourke A. (2005) The 'expert patient.' *Social Science & Medicine 60*:1299-1309.

Gravel K, Legare F. & Graham I. (2006) Barriers and facilitators to implementing shared decision-making in clinical practice: a systematic review of health professionals' perceptions. *Implementation Science 1*: 1-16.

Lindsay S & Bellaby P. (2007) How and why the motivation and skill to self-manage coronary heart disease are socially unequal. *ESRC Symposium: Barriers and Inequalities in Self-Managing Chronic Illness*. Think Lab, University of Salford, May 11.

Shaw J & Baker M. (2004) 'Expert patient:' dream or nightmare? *British Medical Journal 328*: 723-724.

Taylor D & Bury M. (2007) Chronic illness, expert patients and care transition. *Sociology of Health & Illness* 29(1): 27-45.

Thorne S, Paterson B & Russell C. (2003) The structure of everyday self-care decision-making in chronic illness. *Qualitative Health Research 13(10)*: 1337-1352.

Wilson P, Kendall S & Brooks F. (2007) The Expert Patients Programme: a paradox of patient empowerment and medical dominance. *Health & Social Care in the Community* (in press).

In: Decision Making in Medicine and Health Care
Editor: P. C. Tolana, pp. 11-30

ISBN: 978-1-60021-870-5


*Chapter I*

# WOMEN IN A WORLD OF MEN'S DISEASE – THE CASE OF FEMALE CARDIAC PATIENTS

***Michal Rassin****
Assaf Harofeh Medical Center, Zrifine, Beer- Yakov, 70300, Israel.

## ABSTRACT

The central purpose of the study was to examine differences between women and men, ages 30-50 years, in their responses to heart disease, and to identify the factors influencing them in the fields of health and illness. The study was conducted using a qualitative method. The participants in the study included 30 men and 30 women who suffered from coronary heart disease. The study findings suggest that women delayed seeking treatment and that when they did seek treatment they were not initially diagnosed as suffering from heart disease due to physicians' perceptions that heart disease is a men's disease. The recovery period for women was characterized by their quick return to daily home making before their physical condition permitted it. Conversely, the men extended their recovery period and received support from their families. As part of the return to normal life, the men were strict in following the instructions of the health regimen, whereas most of the women ignored it. The women, compared to the men, received less support from their spouses and families, and they noted that social expectations concerning their role were high. Our study concludes that heart disease varies between men and women in the characteristics of its symptoms and in the attitude of medical staff and the public, as well as of patients themselves, towards the disease. The role of the cardiac patient is based on male characteristics and, as a result, men are legitimized and receive social support in all that relates to the disease; consequently, men adhere to the health regimen, whereas women are less inclined to. This study can advance insights on the influence of the gender variable on responses to heart disease, as

* Correspondence concerning this article should be addressed to: Dr. Michal Rassin, R.N, PhD, Research Unit, Nursing Care Management, Asaf Harofe Medical Center, Zrifinn, Bear Yaakov, 70300, ISRAEL. Tel- 972-8-9779114; fax- 972-8-9779551; Email address: rasinm@asaf.health.gov.il.

well as supply information on therapeutic intervention for male and female cardiac patients and the nature of the different measures used for each.

**Keywords:** gender, coronary heart disease, diagnosis, recovery, health regimen

## INTRODUCTION

Coronary heart disease (CHD) is the leading cause of mortality and morbidity in developing countries (Grace et al, 2002; Weidner, 2000). For many years, coronary heart disease was considered mostly a male illness. However, current data show that it is also the main cause of mortality among women (Efre, 2004; Gottlieb, 2005). Once heart disease reaches clinical expression, the quality of life and prognosis for women are worse than for men (Helitz et al, 2002; Hochner et al, 2002; Lukkarine & Hentinen, 1998). Research indicates that this is due not only to biological and genetic factors but also to gender differences in personal and social responses to the illness (McKinlay, 1996; Weidner, 2000).

Efforts in coping with the illness are especially remarkable among young cardiac patients between the ages of 30 and 50, despite the fact that in these ages there is an increasing difficulty in combining the major tasks of life, such as work and raising children, with the demands of the illness. However, these age groups have been neglected in the sphere of research, in particular women, who have been neglected due to the misguided assumption that heart disease is a disease of elderly men (McKinlay, 1996; Uuskuela, 1996). A comparison of male and female responses to the illness, and identification of the factors affecting them, can contribute to a deep appreciation of the aspects related to quality of life among male and female cardiac patients, as well as provide nurses with information on the necessity of therapeutic intervention and the nature of its specific measures for women and men.

## GENDER DIFFERENCES IN THE RESPONSE TO HEART DISEASE

Studies on the differences between the sexes in the field of health habits suggest that women, more than men, participate in health-promoting activities. Women often seek help from the health system, receive more medical services, and maintain a healthier lifestyle (Courtenay, 2000; Verbrugge, 1985, 1986). However, where heart diseases are concerned, women delay seeking medical services despite the appearance of symptoms, resulting in a worsening of their condition (Ashton, 1999; Evanoski, 1997; Foster & Millik, 1998). In addition, physicians diagnose and treat women less than men for heart disease (Brink, Karlson & Hallberg, 2002; Efre, 2004; Ferrara, Williamson, Karter, Thompson & Kim, 2004). Furthermore, female cardiac patients are less responsive to a health regimen than men, especially among those 55 years of age and younger, and thus have a much worse prognosis (Drori, 1999, Foster & Mallik, 1998; Keller & Lemberg, 2000; King & Koop, 1999; Lieberman et al, 1998; Mark, 2000; Noris, 1998; Remennick & Raanan, 2000)., Among young female cardiac patients ages 50 years and younger, the mortality rates are twice as high in comparison to those of male patients of the same ages (Efre, 2004).

According to the System Contribution Model, which is a model specific to heart disease, women are discriminated against, especially by the medical system. The American sociologist John McKinlay (1996), who developed this model, explains that cardiologic services exemplify markedly the way gender stereotypes turn women into second-rate patients, causing them to further neglect their cardiac disease. McKinlay demonstrates that physicians ignore coronary events among young women due to the common belief that the estrogen hormone has cardiac protective influences. As such, they often do not diagnose cardiac conditions among women, even in the presence of symptoms. When women are eventually diagnosed, they are admitted less to intensive care, are referred less to a cardiologist, and receive less medication and treatment in comparison to men. This leads to the conclusion that physicians make their clinical decisions based on gender biases. This phenomenon is most obvious among patients 30 to 50 years of age, a time of life known to be a person's most productive. The appearance of illness at this time of life makes it difficult to deal with the numerous and demanding tasks of these years such as family, parenting, and employment (Bury, 1982; Verbrugge, 1985). Nonetheless, these ages have been neglected in the research, apparently due to the common belief that heart diseases appear only at older ages. This belief is misguided, as evidenced by statistical data (McKinlay, 1996; Uuskuela, 1996).

Most studies dealing with heart disease have examined its influences mainly on older male patients, and the studies that have dealt with younger patients have examined far fewer women than men (Ashton, 1999; Rosenfeld, 2000). The current study wishes to change this. Up until now, the factors and responses examined have over-emphasized physiological and psychological aspects and have neglected the influences of social factors such as the medical establishment, employers, friends, and family (Brezinka & Kittel, 1996; Ladwing et al, 2000).

All of the above suggests that critical questions concerning gender differences in the diagnosis and treatment of heart disease are still unresolved. The current study wishes to broaden this body of knowledge.

## Purpose of Study

The central purpose of the current study was to examine the differences between women and men, ages 30 to 50, in their responses to heart disease, and to identify the factors influencing them in the areas of health and illness.

## Design

The study used a qualitative design and was conducted using narrative investigation. The illness narratives, gathered using in-depth interviews, were analyzed by thematic analysis. Narrative is especially suitable for studying cardiac patients, while providing a sense of order in terms of causality and direction of progress. The interviewee was asked to reconstruct his/her past by presenting a chronological sequence of events linking the dimensions of past, present, and future as well as body, self, and society.

## Sample

The study included 60 Israeli patients with coronary heart disease, 30 females and 30 males, selected using a convenience-sampling method. Most participants were native Israelis, married and with children (*see Table 1*). The participants were chosen according to the following criteria: 1) patients classified in one of the following states: patients who had undergone myocardial infarction, patients who had undergone coronary artery bypass grafts, or patients suffering from ischemic heart disease; 2) patients within the age range of 30 to 50; and 3) patients with a period of three or more years from the time of diagnosis of the illness, (as it is reasonable to assume that experienced patients can provide much more information than inexperienced patients). For the purposes of comparing the groups of men and women, they were matched according to the variables of clinical status, age, and illness experience (*see Table 2*).

**Table 1. Sociodemographic Variables, Comparison of Women and Men**

| Variable | Category | Women – N (%) | Men – N (%) |
|---|---|---|---|
| Marital Status | Married | 21 (70%) | 25 (83%) |
| | Divorced | 6 (20%) | 5 (15%) |
| | Single | 3 (10%) | ------- |
| Number of Children | Average | 2.8 | 3.3 |
| | Range | 1-6 | 1-8 |
| Country of Origin | Israel | 22 (73.4%) | 17 (56.6%) |
| | Russia | 3 (10%) | 5 (16.6%) |
| | Morocco | 3 (10%) | 3 (10%) |
| | South America | 2 (6.6%) | 5 (16.6%) |
| Education | Average Years of Study | 12.9 | 14.8 |
| | Range of Years of Study | 10-18 | 8-19 |
| Employment | Employed | 24 (80%) | 27 (90%) |
| | Unemployed | 3 (10%) | 1 (3.3%) |
| | Retired (due to illness) | 3 (10%) | 2 (6.6%) |
| Self-Defined Economic State | Very Good | ------- | 6 (20%) |
| | Fair (give or take) | 24 (80%) | 18 (60%) |
| | Not Good | 6 (20%) | 6 (20%) |
| Religious Background | Secular | 17 (56.6%) | 20 (66.6%) |
| | Traditional | 10 (33.3%) | 6 (20%) |
| | Orthodox | 3 (10%) | 4 (13.3%) |

## Methods

Data collection was carried out for 10 months. The participants were located with the help of two senior physicians working in large cardiology clinics in Israel. The physicians contacted candidates who met the criteria for participating in the study. The telephone numbers of suitable candidates who agreed to participate were delivered to the researcher. The researcher met with and explained to the candidates the purpose of the study. Participants were promised complete confidentiality. The meetings lasted for two hours, and when this was not sufficient an additional meeting was held. Meetings were held in the participants' homes when requested. The interviews contents were recorded with the consent of the participants.

**Table 2. The Variables Correlated Between Women and Men**

| Gender | Diagnosis Age Average | Time from Diagnosis Average (years) | Clinical Status in Diagnosis | | |
|---|---|---|---|---|---|
| | | | Myocardial Infarct | Coronary Artery Bypass Graft | Ischemic heart disease |
| Women | 42.8 | 4.7 | 20 | 8 | 2 |
| Men | 40.8 | 5.7 | 20 | 8 | 2 |

Data gathering was conducted using in-depth interviews. The interview started with a general question: "Could you tell me how it all started and what happened later?" The interview included coverage points, topics that reminded the researcher what the question should encompass; for example, "What were your sensations and how did you respond?", "What made you respond?", and "How did the illness affect your function at work and home?" The interview also included probing questions, such as "What do you mean?" and "Can you give an example?" (Berg, 1998). These questions were asked only when the interviewees' answers were superficial and demanded more details, or when he or she digressed.

The interview with the participants was carried out by the researcher using a qualitative method. "The man as a research tool", a term coined by Lincoln & Guba (1985) illustrates the special role of researchers in the qualitative study, seeing human beings as the only "tools" flexible enough to comprehend the complexity of the human experience. Human beings vary from other tools in that humans respond to context, changing their methods according to the circumstances and dealing with and adjusting to various responses.

## Analysis of Data

Findings from the interviews were analyzed using thematic analyses. In the first stage, the recorded interviews were transcribed and the analytic work was begun with a preliminary reading of each interview in order to gain some general impressions.

The second stage consisted of an additional reading of each interview in order to identify themes, or units, which appeared to be the central building blocks of the narrative. Identification of themes in the narrative investigation is particularly characterized by a process termed "over-reading," implying a meticulous, educated, and sensitive reading during which the narrative is examined several times by the researcher in order to identify repetitions; inconsistencies; metaphors; side comments; defensive statements; latent relations; nuances; endings; and silences all of which can constitute an index for interpreting the narrative (Good & Good, 1994; Poirier & Lioness, 1997; Sandelowski, 1991). As is customary in qualitative studies, theme conceptualization is bound to the process of data organization (Berg, 1998); it requires the organization of data in a systematic filing system in which prominent topics arising from the participants' narratives are classified. Each topic in the study was coded on a separate list. Each list, in turn, was related to the original interview material, referencing the number of the interviewee, the page number in the interview, and an abstract of the segment. Similarly, relevant sub-topics were classified according to various themes.

Each theme title chosen was based on what seemed the most logically related to the information it represented; initially, a temporary name was chosen, and only later was a permanent name decided on. Straus and Corbin (1992) claim that theme titles should be related as closely as possible to the expressions the participants used in vivo. These are usually catchy phrases that attract one's attention and embody and summarize the phenomenon. In this tenor, most titles given in the current study were taken from the natural language of the participants.

In the third stage, the themes were reorganized according to the chronological order of events on a continuum, as narratives presented by interviewees are often inconsistent and lack causality. In such cases, some claim it is allowed, and even required, to cut and reorganize the narrative segments, provided the content and meaning of the narrative are not changed (Franzosi, 1998; Kleinman, 1988; Poirier & Lioness, 1997).

In the fourth stage, the themes collected from the male and female groups were compared, and gender patterns were marked in a manner that would demonstrate similarities and differences between the two groups. Similarities and differences between the groups were then identified and explained.

In the fifth stage, occurrences (quotes from the participants) were copied below their respective themes and sub-themes. The themes were characterized by a narrative segment, accounting for a discursive organization of time and causality (Bury, 2001; Riessman, 1990). As the central purpose of the narrative approach is to provide explanations of given descriptions (Franzosi, 1998; Sandelowski, 1991), special attention was given to the detailed explanation of the events, contexts, and comparisons suggested from the study data. Combining these conditions, the thematic framework included a reference to the chronological order of the factors, as well as responses, analysis of the connections between them, and comparison of the files from the women's group to those from the men's group.

In the final stage, as in the discussion section, there was an attempt to link the personal narratives to a broader discourse dealing with themes resulting from the concepts and theories developed (Franzosi, 1998; Silverman, 1993).

Standards of trustworthiness were obtained using peer debriefing, incorporating into the findings an additional study colleague familiar with the qualitative method, as well as peer review. Two interviewees, chosen according to their interest and desire to see the findings, were re-interviewed for their feedback on the study conclusions (Lincoln & Guba, 1985). In addition to standards of trustworthiness, relationships of confidence and rapport formed with the participants during the meetings helped in obtaining authentic reports (Berg, 1998).

## FINDINGS

In analyzing the narratives provided by the female and male participants in the study, eight different themes were identified. The themes characteristic of the women were then compared to those characteristic of the men. Events were classified in terms of causality into three main time periods: diagnosis and hospitalization, recovery, and return to normal life. The study findings point to gender differences in both the nature of some of the responses and the factors that shaped them.

### a) Diagnosis and Hospitalization

#### *--"Young Women Don't Expect to Get a Heart Attack, It Has Always Been a Men's Disease"*

The women who participated in the current study sought help from the health system only after many hours, sometimes days, had passed since the appearance of symptoms. All female participants interpreted the symptoms as originating from logical causes linked to everyday activities, such as muscle aches due to hard work, digestive problems due to spoiled food, etc. Despite the numerous causes the female participants attributed to their symptoms, it never crossed their minds that these symptoms might be related to heart disease. Several factors led to this, including an unrealistic perception of related symptoms and the women's perception that their young age and feminine sexuality protected them from illness

> *(Female, age 38) – It started with aches in my hands and shoulders. I thought it was because of the work, since I had just finished with the Passover Spring cleanings. At first I didn't take it seriously, because I occasionally get an ache here and there. I said to myself, "forget about it, you're young, it'll pass". I took an Acamol here, an Optalgin there. Who would have thought of the heart, because young women don't expect to get a heart attack, it has always been a men's disease... A few days later, when it hadn't passed, I saw my GP. He laughed and said "Passover's a dangerous holiday for women." He gave me Moscul and a Voltaren gel to apply. Meanwhile, several more days passed and the aches didn't go away. One day, I came to work feeling aches in my back and shoulders, dizziness and nausea, and the world around me turned black and white, colorless... A co-worker who passed by was alarmed by how I looked. She asked me "do you feel alright?"... I answered: "I'll rest a bit and it'll pass," but she decided to call an ambulance and they took me to the hospital... My condition was so bad they had to admit me. Then they started talking about it maybe being something with the heart. The EKG showed disturbances, yet they told me, "look, at such a young age we don't suspect

women as having heart problems." The next morning they sent me for mapping. The physician insisted that the mapping showed a shadow on the breast: "We'll have another mapping in three months and see", he said... In the evening my condition deteriorated. They took my right away for catheterization. There they found blocks of 95%. I was operated on within a week...

## --"*Men at the Age of 40 Get Glasses, and at 50 They Get a Heart Attack*"

While it was a noticeable fact among the female participants that none of them related their symptoms to the heart, most of the male participants reported immediately relating their symptoms to the heart. As a result, the time that passed from the appearance of symptoms to their receiving medical help was shorter for the men, and within the time range defined as critical for minimizing damage to the heart. The interviewees' descriptions suggest that the quick diagnosis, which prevented unnecessary suffering, resulted from the legitimacy given to men by health system workers, according to which a man can have a heart attack even if he is young:

> *(Male, age 45) – One day I was climbing up the stairs and started feeling all kinds of recurrent pressures in my chest. I sat on the couch. The A.C. was working full force, and I was sweating buckets and nothing helped... When I saw after half an hour that the pain was severe and would not pass, I realized it was the heart. I called an ambulance, alerted my wife, and arrived at the E.R. There they shocked me, attached me to all sorts of equipment, and sent me right away to the I.C.U... After that, as a present for my 45$^{th}$ birthday, I subscribed to a cardiac patients' service. Well, I'm a man, and a smoker, and you know what they say - men at the age of 40 get glasses, and at 50 they get a heart attack.

## --"*How Come I Got a Heart Attack?*"

Upon receiving their diagnosis, all participants expressed crisis responses, exhibited by shock, mistrust, and denial. However, the women's crisis responses were more noticeable inasmuch as the women, in contrast to the men, had not thought that they might develop heart disease. The shock response was accompanied by feelings of anger, self pity, and an explicit accusation of malpractice on the part of the medical system.

> *(Female, age 34) – The director of the catheterization unit looked at me and said "I want her in my unit." He admitted me to the I.C.U. I was hospitalized at 8:30 in the morning. In the evening, after the blood tests, he talked with me and said I had had a heart attack. I was in shock. I said: "how come I got a heart attack? How come? I'm young and healthy, I never had any problems. All my brothers and sisters are well. And I don't even smoke"... I was shocked; I took it very badly, thinking of my very young kids. I started thinking about what would happen to them, who would take care of them. I felt I was loosing my ability to control my life. I went out and had a good cry. I felt my world come crashing down... I blamed the GP in the clinic for not taking me seriously; maybe if he had done something straight away all of this would've been avoided. When I got to the ward all the doctors and nurses started coming in. They came to see the 'case' and were buzzing around me all day because I was the youngest there and it was very strange to see a woman in my condition. It was very stressful...

The men participating in the study also responded intensely to the diagnosis, even though most saw heart attacks as a part of life for men. The men's shock resulted from the fact that they had not expected heart disease at such a young age, and mainly from a feeling that the illness had cut short their plans and threatened their lives. Unlike the women's narratives, the men chose to concentrate more on facts than feelings in describing the diagnostic process. Another aspect of the men's narratices, noticeable in its absence, was that, despite the fact that the men had children, they did not mention them, whereas in the women's accounts children were a central issue.

*(Male, age 42) – After this, they took me for catheterization. The doctor told me that there were two blocks and they would have to operate. Until I was 44, I hadn't thought about my health. I hadn't thought something would happen to me. My father died of a heart attack when he was 60, but I didn't know what cholesterol and blood-pressure were… So maybe the risk was there under the surface. The crisis was serious because I was in the middle of my plans at work and it cut it all short. I understood I had no choice and needed to be operated on. I tried to focus on the facts…

## b) Recovery

### --*"Women Are Someplace Else in Terms of Home and the Family"*

Although the female participants noted that they had received medical instructions concerning the recommended recovery period, the response pattern characteristic of most of the women was nonetheless a quick return to all of their familial roles and homemaking tasks. A minority of them checked into a rehabilitation center upon discharge, but these were mostly from the group of women who had had surgery. Even these women, however, who suffered from pains due to difficult surgery, waited anxiously for the end of their time in the rehabilitation center in order to return home and continue to function as mothers and wives:

*(Female, age 42) – Before the heart attack I was a healthy, strong woman who worked long hours and worried about everyone. After the heart attack, I felt that everything was difficult for me. I was discharged on Friday and on Sunday I was back working at home. It was hard but I didn't make allowances for myself. I forced myself to do things. I started washing the dishes, dusting, all by myself…

*(Female, age 46) – I quickly returned to functioning because I worried so much about the house. Generally, women are someplace else in terms of the home, the family, the kids, and doing their responsibilities… Ten days after the surgery I was still recovering, and when I returned home after a fortnight I did everything by myself until I felt physical pain… I told them, "Now you have a refurbished maid." At first my daughters told me, "Mom, don't work, mom sit, don't do this," but they sort of enjoyed me doing the work, so that's not much help. Even my husband stopped helping me pretty quickly. So I found myself standing in the kitchen frying his steaks, and preparing sandwiches for the kids in the morning. But then again, that's me. I need to do everything by myself like I like to do. A month after the surgery I even hosted all of our friends and thanked them… When they saw my husband put the dishes in the dishwasher they were

very impressed. I thought to myself, "Do I need to have something like a heart attack to get some help around here?"

The men, in comparison, were using the rehabilitation centers as much as possible, and some even extended their stay beyond the period subsidized by the HMO. Other male interviewees chose complete physical rest at home, during which they received substantial support from wife and family. Support was expressed, among other things, in preparing special foods, administering medication, keeping them rested, and freeing them from all household chores:

> *(Male, age 42) – I stayed a little bit longer at Kfar Hamacabia (a rehabilitation center), and when I returned home I was taken care of. They kept me lying down all the time so that I wouldn't strain myself or lift heavy things. My wife made me special low-fat foods and called me from work to remind me to take my pills...

### c) Normal Life

#### --*"Returning to Living Normally"*

After the recovery period, both female and male participants started dealing with their condition by returning to normal lives. However, the return to normalcy among the women was quick, concise, and more extreme than for the men, in some cases so extreme that they denied ever being ill:

> *(Female, age 43) – In the first few months life revolves around the disease. You invest yourself in how to rebuild your life, doing sports, meticulous tests each month, all those diets, and having intense thoughts. And they help too, with more mapping and more ergometry. So you can't repress the illness. You have to run to your checkup and talk about it with everyone. Then it ended all at once. I stopped going to the institute; it didn't suit me anymore. I returned to the couple of years before the illness, to the routine, the work. I had no time to be ill and forgot about my heart. I asked myself, "Why shouldn't I live normally, why should I eat hard cheese only once a month? Everything is either not allowed or not recommended..." So I decided to return to normal life.

Among the men, the return to normal life was not expressed as succinctly but with gradual and cautious progress. In their narratives, the male participants reported how elements from the sphere of illness penetrated their everyday life, integrating with other aspects to produce a normal life but with a different perspective compared to before the diagnosis:

> *(Male, age 42) – It's safe to say that six months later I returned to normal life, but more cautiously and more aware of my health. Once I used to do what I felt like doing, smoking and eating what I wanted, but all of this changed. I continue as before but with the addition of taking pills, and keeping fit. In short, today I'm more alert and conscious of my condition.

### --*"With Time They Forgot I was Ill and They Don't Give Me Any More Allowances"*

Complete return to normal life and maintaining stability for an extended period of time was made possible due to several factors. The first and central factor was a noticeable improvement in the physical feeling of the participants. The second factor was the message of the physicians that their condition was now good. The third included the expectations of family and other relatives that it was time to return to normal life. The women, in particular, expressed that family expectations of them to return to full function, both at home and work, were tremendous. Moreover, they noted that their family members virtually forgot the fact that only a few months before they had been ill and in grave danger:

> *(Female, age 47) – After a year people forgot I had had a heart attack. All settled back into routine. They were less interested, less caring and less supportive. You no longer carry the "title" of a cardiac patient. Eventually, you are left to face it all alone, by yourself, with no support, as if you are no longer ill. At home I get no allowances. I remain both homemaker and working wife. I live at home with four uninterested people (a husband, two daughters, and one son) and no one so much as lifts a finger around the house. It doesn't seem awkward to them that I pick up after them; if they drop something they won't even bother to pick it up. As far as they're concerned, if the physician said from now on everything's fine and I'm healthy then it's all back to where they left it…

## d) Health Regimen

### --*"You Can't Live Under Constant Warning"*

Most of the study participants reported that they were given medical recommendations regarding a health regimen that included quitting smoking; a low-cholesterol diet; rehabilitative physical activity; medication according to instructions; and being under medical supervision. However, the women dismissed the health regimen almost entirely. While some clearly specified that they were aware of not following physicians' orders, others reported that they were following them. In actual fact, it turned out that these women were only partially following physicians' orders, which usually amounted to taking pills and following up medically. Aside from not maintaining adequate finances, quitting smoking, or exercising, most serious was the issue of discontinuing medication. The women reported various causes for such behaviors, including difficulty following the strict recommendations, a desire to enjoy life without constraints, and a lack of social support. They also mentioned aesthetic and health reasons. Above all, however, the participants demonstrated a strong will to be distracted from the illness and not to dwell on it. Thus, by partially or completely avoiding any illness-related activities, they managed to remain distracted, preserving their inner feeling that they were maintaining ordinary and normal lives like anyone else:

> *(Female, age 45) – I hadn't quite changed my health habits. The sports thing – sweating isn't for me. Besides, you are always warned don't eat, don't smoke, don't, don't, don't! … You can't live under constant warning. So I eat salt, buy cakes and ice-creams, smoke cigarettes, and do as I please…

> *(Female, age 47) – After a year or so, you are left to deal with it alone. There's less support from your surroundings. They're not interested anymore if you've been to your checkups. So I ignore this too, I don't go to checkups or anything. I've become indifferent...

> *(Female, age 38) – After three months they referred me for rehabilitation; I was there one time, and one time only. As I entered I saw they were all old and men. They gave me a look like "what are *you* doing here." So there was nothing for me... Six months after surgery I decided to stop with the medication. The pills stressed me out from the get-go. I used to sit each morning by the pile of pills and cry because of having to take them, because a healthy person doesn't take pills. Taking pills is being sick, and I had never taken a pill in my life. Even when I had headaches I wouldn't...

*--"Perseverance for Me is Like Life Insurance"*

In contrast to the women, most of the male participants in the study adhered to a health regimen and were cooperative with the medical staff:

> *(Male, age 45) – I quit smoking right away, and I used to smoke two to three packs a day. I've been at it for seven years. Every three months I see the GP for a checkup and take the medication that he tells me to. Even my physical fitness has improved because I exercise. All in all, today I live better then I ever did.

> *(Male, age 38) – From that day I quit smoking and stopped eating butter. I went to see a dietitian and I was in a follow-up group. Since the heart attack I practice in the Institute (for Heart Rehabilitation) twice a week. I realize that if I don't have a framework I won't do a thing, so I prefer to pay. I get up everyday at 6 o'clock to practice, rain or shine, and it's not easy. But perseverance for me is like life insurance.

Following a health regimen strengthened the feeling among the participants that they had recovered and were doing their best to stay alive. The men's reaction seems in opposition to that of the women's described above; however, it, too, was aimed at distracting their minds from the possibility that the illness would recur or that their condition would deteriorate. Ultimately, both women's and men's reactions and ways of coping are meant to preserve the "healthy self" with the passage of time.

## Discussion

The study findings suggest that the participants' reactions to the diagnosis of heart disease were particularly influenced by the social legitimacy they are given in assuming the "sick role." Parsons (1951), in coining this term, explained that humans are not to be blamed for their illness and so are exempt from normal social duties. However, they should understand that illness is not a desirable thing and that they are to seek help in improving their condition so that they can return to their normal social role. Thus, the first duty defined by the sick role is to seek appropriate help by turning to the medical system.

Social legitimacy for the sick role requires the seal of approval of a medical diagnosis; however, before this, the individual is required to acknowledge that the symptoms demand help. The findings of the current study showed that women, as opposed to men, sought help much later because they had not thought of the symptoms as originating from the heart, and in most cases they attempted to deal with them on their own. As mentioned, the men did not delay seeking medical treatment, and some immediately attributed their symptoms to the heart.

Seeking immediate medical help during a heart attack has well-known importance, for it improves survival and prevents complications (Clark, 2001). However, some linger and therefore do not receive treatment in time. Numerous studies that examine this phenomenon among young cardiac patients identify that the main causes for this delay result first and foremost from a misinterpretation of the symptoms, attributing them to more familiar conditions such as stomach aches, muscle aches, etc. Secondly, the social image of the heart disease as a disease of the elderly, and myths that relate heart disease to loss of consciousness and sudden death, create disparities between people's expectations and the symptoms they actually experience. However, others who reach the hospital quickly perceive themselves as being at high risk for developing heart disease and so are aware of a wide range of illness-related symptoms (Alonzo & Reynolds, 1998; Clark, 2001; Johnson & Morse, 1990; Maclean & Cockshutt, 1979; Ruston, Clayton & Calnan, 1998).

The symptoms reported by the women in the current study, together with findings from other studies, indicate that in most cases women tend to report pains in areas other than the chest, such as hands; shoulders; neck; jaw; stomach; and back. Men, however, mainly report pain in the chest area (Efre, 2004; McSweeney, Cody & Crane, 2001; Meischke, Larsen & Eisenberg, 1998; Miller, 2002; Philipott et al, 2001). Although evidence clearly points to different pain locations in women and men, the medical textbooks continue to treat these pain locations as atypical. Philpott et al (2001), read "atypical" as relating to "not like men." The failure of the health system in the timely diagnosis of heart disease among women is documented in the current study, as it has been in previously published studies. This failure is illustrated in the careless disregard of women's complaints, even relating these complaints to psychiatric problems. In addition, the medical system still maintains that heart disease among young women is a rare phenomenon, based on the common misperception that female hormones protect against this illness (Efre, 2004; Ferrara et al, 2004; Foster et al, 1998; McKinlay, 1996; Philpott et al, 2001; Rosenfeld, 2000; Van-Tiel et al, 1998).

The conclusion of the current study, which is consistent with that of many previously published studies, is that social legitimizing of the sick role of the cardiac patient is gender related. This is due to the perception of heart disease as a men's disease. This provides the main explanation for the difficulty female participants experienced in achieving personal, medical, and social legitimacy regarding their diagnosis as cardiac patients. It also explains their delay in turning to health services upon the appearance of symptoms.

Another factor to be considered in the sick role is that entering into this role is especially difficult for women, as traditionally a woman's role is perceived as being engaged in helping others; women are not expected to be sick themselves (Johansson et al, 1999; Maclean & Cockshutt, 1979; Miles, 1991). In a survey conducted in Israel among a random sample of 839 women, average age 38, the women were asked to describe how they respond to not feeling well. More than 70% answered that they "ignore" it, that they decide it is "nothing" and wait for it to pass. Avgar and Gordon (1997) explain the findings of this survey in the context of considering the tremendous commitments these women carry; they might not have the time to be sick. However, there still persists the common misperception of women as hypochondriacs, constantly complaining and using health services excessively (Courtenay, 2000; Lorber, 1997).

During the recovery period, the participants in the study reassumed their social functions. Particularly noticeable among the women was the tension between their sick role and their role as woman. The women's families had only partly legitimized their sick role, while their maternal and domestic functions were viewed as superior. A similar picture is reported in numerous other studies, in which women note an early return to domestic tasks during the recovery period. Furthermore, they feel a withdrawal of social support, and in some cases unrealistic expectations are reported by recovering women regarding the extent of their involvement in domestic tasks. In comparison, men assume the sick role perfectly and it is fully legitimized by their family members (Fleury, 2001; Hawthorne, 1992; Johnson & Morse, 1990; King & Koop, 1999; King, 2001; Rose et al, 1996; Uuskuela, 1996).

Factors concerning self were also identified during the current study, prompted by the women's feelings of guilt that, due to their illness and dysfunction, their families were suffering. These feelings served as the main factor in driving these women quickly back to their domestic tasks. Research indicates that women's severe perceptions of their failure to function as mothers and wives drives them back to their domestic tasks, even before fully recovering physically (Brink, Karlson & Hallberg, 2002; Miles, 1991). This, however, is a simplistic perspective, since it ignores the origin of the women's private feelings of guilt – they were brought up with these social expectations. Izraeli (1990) explains that a woman's decision to give priority to the family seems to be her personal preference and will. In effect, this interpretation ignores the power of the subconscious ideology, that which demands that women give precedence to the requirements of family life over anything else. For instance, in all that pertains to Israeli society, Berkowitz (1999) claims that women's position and status were designed during the first decades of the fledgling state, their full citizenship being granted in exchange for their contribution to the collective as mothers and wives. This role has been fixated since then in the national consciousness as the central one for the woman in Israeli society. Izraeli (1990) adds that the family institution is particularly demanding for the women, and that questions about having children or a career are alien to the Israeli cultural milieu, which is dominated by the assumption that career and family will be combined. This perspective can explain why the women in the current study found themselves "trapped" between the sick role and the roles of mother and wife. This can explain also why they did not receive full social legitimacy for their sick role, as was granted the men.

Return to normal life following the recovery period was marked by all the research participants leaving the crisis-response pattern that had characterized their diagnosis and hospitalization. The female participants' narratives generally described a sharper return than the males to life as it had been before the diagnosis.

Miles (1991) states that there are negotiations between the patient, the physician, and the patient's social group, about the period of retirement from social roles. The timing of return to normal life depends, of course, on the absence of symptoms; however, this too, is a consequence both of one's social group's expectations as well as of the patient's commitments to his/her normal roles.

The structure of normal life, and normalcy in general, are the most favorable and dominant social principles in Western society. Being normal means being productive within society (Anderton, Elfert & Lai, 1989). It follows that the role of the norm is to contribute to society, in complete opposition to the sick role, which does not contribute. Therefore, stories of "normalization" are most favorable among the sick and disabled, even when this illusion of normalcy turns out to be counterproductive, preventing them from obtaining support, talking about their problems, or asking for allowances when tired or under the weather (Anderton et al, 1989; Robinson, 1993).

Two variations on the return to normal life were demonstrated by the participants in the current study. Most of the men carried on with the lifestyles that had preceded their illness, incorporating into them their medical regimens, which they perceived would protect and maintain their health. Based on this, they could present themselves as healthy. In contrast, the women employed a different strategy. An examination of their behaviors shows that most of the women ignored the medical regimen and instead reverted to the lifestyles that had preceded their illness. Thus, the women preserved a sense of health and normal life by avoiding any illness-related activities such as taking pills. In relation to this strategy, Bury (1982, 2001) differentiates between normalization and normal life. Normalization, he asserts, is the preservation of the lifestyle preceding the illness by way of maintaining a large proportion of previous activities and minimizing the influences of the illness on life, often by actively denying the illness and by adopting an opposing lifestyle. Conversely, normal life is expressed by redesigning one's lifestyle to accommodate the illness; in other words, it is a combination of the previous lifestyle and the demands of the illness.

In a study conducted among 3523 cardiac patients, it was found that 50% of their mortality resulted from unwillingness to follow their health regimen. The same study also suggested that this unwillingness was particularly marked among the young group, ages 55 and under (Noris, 1998). In another study comparing women and men, it was found that the willingness of female cardiac patients to maintain their health regimen was lower than that of the male patients, thus worsening their prognosis (Keller & Lemberg, 2000; Lieberman et al, 1998). In interviews held with 30 HIV carriers, it was found that women in particular employed the approach of continuing normal life, which revolved around the concept of not needing to change anything because of the illness (Pierret, 2001). Another study, conducted among cystic fibrosis patients, examined why the women's prognoses were much worse than the men's (the men had a life expectancy of 14 years, on average, more than the women). The researchers state clearly that even though it is customary to explain this disparity between the sexes in physiological terms such as women's lower weight, different microbiology of the airways, etc., in actuality, willingness versus unwillingness to follow the recommended health regimens underlies this disparity. In principle, the men in the study incorporated their health regimens into their lives by following recommendations regarding physiotherapy, exercise, diet, and antibiotic courses, whereas the women ignored their regimens completely and were less active physically, less strict with their diet, and in some cases did not take their medications or simply ignored the illness altogether (Willis, Miller & Wyn, 2001).

These findings closely resemble the findings of the current study, even though the patient populations vary. Again, it seems that, in all that relates to the gender variable, there are identical response patterns among same-sex patients, even when they suffer from different illnesses.

The literature, in numerous instances, notes that the willingness to observe, and maintenance of, a health regimen are directly linked to the level of social support a patient receives (Barefoot, Gronbæk, Jensen, Schnohr & Prescott, 2005; Chafetz, 1996; Charmaz, 1991; Twaddle & Hessler, 1987). Sick women receive less social support from their spouses and families compared to sick men. And when a woman does receive support, it is curtailed shortly thereafter, at which point she is expected to resume her previous roles, primarily the role of providing support for her family members (Miles, 1991). Managing a health regimen requires that the family encourage the patient so that he/she can persist in it despite hardships. It is therefore not surprising that women turn less than men to heart rehabilitation programs, and when they do it is only short lived (Drori, 1999). This phenomenon has been found to be significantly linked to a lack of support and encouragement from family members (Lieberman et al, 1998).

In conclusion, heart disease varies between men and women in the nature of its symptoms and the attitudes of medical staff, the public, and even the sick person towards the illness. The role of the cardiac patient is traditionally based on male characteristics, thus offering men social legitimacy and support in all that relates to the illness. Consequently, men are much more willing to maintain a health regimen than women. This finding contradicts the prevalent theories that present women as obedient and adapting to a healthier lifestyle than men.

This study concludes that social factors, mainly the legitimacy of sick roles, is different for men than for women, and specifically that men are afforded much more legitimacy than women regarding sick roles. The findings of this study are very consistent with explanations of the system-contribution approach regarding gender differences in heart disease. This approach states that the reason for under-diagnosis of heart disease among young women results from physicians' perception of heart disease as a male illness. This perception, in turn, creates a societal gender delineation of the illness as a men's disease, leading to social legitimacy of the sick role only for men.

This study, following the qualitative approach, can provide insights into the phenomenon of heart disease among women and men. The qualitative approach hypothesizes that a social phenomenon draws its meaning from the way people who are related to it interpret it. This study provides information on the extent to which therapeutic intervention is necessary for cardiac patients, including specific measures, which differ between women and men. In addition, social factors influencing patients' responses are identified in the study, which could help in locating target populations requiring intervention. While the responses and factors are expressed from the perspectives of both women and men, these personal points of view can bridge the gap between caregivers' and patients' perceptions regarding heart disease. As the current study was based on a convenience sample, which included only 60 participants from one country, it is highly recommended that additional studies be conducted, aimed at exploring further the claim on gender-based differences in diagnosis and treatment among young cardiac patients.

## REFERENCES

Alonzo, A., & Renolds, N. (1998). The structure of emotions during acute myocardial infarction: A model of caring. *Social Sciences and Medicine, 46*, 1099-1110.

Anderton, J. M., Elfert, H., & Lai, M. (1989). Ideology in the clinical context: Chronic illness, ethnicity and the discourse on normalisation. *Sociology of Health & Illness, 11*, 253-278.

Ashoton, K. C. (1999). How men and women with heart disease seek care: The delay experience. *Progress in Cardiovascular Nursing, 14*(2), 53-60

Avgar, A., Gordon, K. (1997). Your health: The results and conclusions. *At, 97*, 62-65 [Hebrew].

Barefoot, J. C., Gronbæk, M., Jensen, G., Schnohr, P., & Prescott., E. (2005). Social network diversity and risks of ischemic heart disease and total mortality: Findings from the Copenhagen city heart study. *American Journal of Epidemiology. 161, 960-971.*

Berg, B. L. (1998). *Qualitative research: Methods for the social science*. London: Viacom.

Berkowitz, N. (1999). A woman of valor who can find? Women and citizens in Israel. *Israeli Sociology, B*(1), 277-318 [Hebrew].

Brezinka, V., & Kittel, F. (1996). Psychosocial factors of coronary heart disease in women: A review. *Social Science and Medicine, 42*, 1351-1365

Brink, E., Karlson, B. W., & Hallberg, L. R. M. (2002). Health experiences of first time myocardial infarction: Factors influencing women's and men's health related quality of life after five months. *Psychology Health and Medicine, 7* (1), 5-

Bury, M. (1982). Chronic illness as biographical disruption. *Sociology of Health and Illness, 4*, 165-182.

Bury, M. (2001). Illness narratives: Fact or fiction? *Sociology of Health and Illness, 23*, 263-285.

Chafetz, L. (1996). The experience of severe mental illness: A life history approach. *Archives of Psychiatric Nursing, 10*(1), 24-31.

Charmaz, K. (1991). *Good days, bad days: The self in chronic illness and time*. New Brunswick, NJ: Rutgers University Press.

Clark, A. M. (2001). Treatment decision- making during the early stages of heart attack: A case for the role of body and self in influencing delays. *Sociology of Health and Illness, 23*(4), 425-446.

Corbin, J. M., & Strauss, A. (1992). A nursing model fore chronic illness management based upon the trajectory framework. In P.Woog, (Ed), *The chronic illness trajectory framework*, (pp. 9-28). New- York, NY: Springer Publishing Company

Courtenay, W. H. (2000). Constructions of masculinity and their influence on men's well-being: A theory of gender and health. *Social Science and Medicine, 50*, 1385-1401.

Drori, I. (1999). Cardiac rehabilitation among women: The desirable and available. *Ha-Rephuah, 137*(e-f), 228-232 [Hebrew].

Efre, A. J. (2004). Gender bias in Acute Myocardial Infarction. *Nurse Practitioner, 29*(11) 42-51.

Evanoski, C. (1997). Myocardial infarction: The number one killer of women. *Critical Care Nursing of North America, 9*, 489-496.

Ferrara, A., Williamson, D. F., Karter, A. J., Thompson, T. J.,& Kim, K. (2004). Sex differences in quality of health care related to ischemic heart disease prevention in patients with diabetes: The translating research into action for diabetes (TRIAD) study, 2000-2001. *Diabetes Care, 27,* 2974-2977.

Fleury, J., Sedikidies, C., & Lunsford, V. (2001). Women's experience following a cardiac event: The role of the self in healing. *Journal of Cardiovascular Nursing, 15*(3), 71-82.

Foster, S., & Mallik, M. (1998). A comparative study of differences in the referral behaviour patterns of men and women who have experienced cardiac related chest pain. *Intensive and Critical Care Nursing, 14*, 192-202.

Franzosi, R. (1998). Narrative analysis — or why (and how) Sociologists should be interested in narrative. *Annual Review of Sociology, 24*, 517-554

Good, B., & Good, M. (1994). In the subjunctive mode: Epilepsy narrative in Turkey. *Social Science and Medicine, 38*, 835-842.

Gottlieb, S. H. (2005). Dose sex matter? Diabetes, heart disease and gender. *Diabetes Forecast, 58*(2), 33-36.

Grace, S. L., Abbey, S. E., Shnek, Z. M., Irvine, J., Franch, R. L., & Stewart, D. E. (2002). Cardiac rehabilitation I: Review of psychosocial factors. *General Hospital Psychiatry, 24*(3), 121-126.

Hawthorne, M. H. (1992). Using the trajectory framework: Reconceptualizing cardiac illness. In P.Woog, (Ed), *The chronic illness trajectory framework,* (pp. 29-39). New- York, NY: Springer Publishing Company.

Herlitz, J., Karlson, B. W., Lindqvist, J., & Sjolin, M. (2002). Prognosis and risk indicators of death during a period of 10 years for women admitted to the emergency department with a suspected acute coronary syndrome. *International Journal of Cardiology, 82*, 259-269.

Hochner-Celnikier, D., Manor, O., Gotzman, O., Lotan, H., & Chajek-shaul, T. (2002). Gender gap in coronary artery disease: Comparison of the extent, severity and risk factors in men and women aged 45-65. *Cardiology, 97*(1), 18-23.

Izraeli, D. (199). Women, work, family and public policy. In Globerzon et al., (Eds.), *Human Resources and Labor Relationships in Israel – New Routes* (pp. 228-232). Tel-Aviv: Ramot (Hebrew). .

Johnson, J. L., & Morse, J. M. (1990). Regaining control: The process of adjustment after myocardial infarction. *Heart & Lung, 19,* 126-135.

Johanson, E. E., Hamberg, K., West, G., & Linder, G. (1999). The meaning of pain: An exploration of women's description of symptoms. *Social Science and Medicine, 48*, 1791-1802.

Keller, K. B.,& Lemberg, L. (2000). Gender differences in acute coronary events. *American Journal of Critical Care, 9*, 207-209.

Kim-Kyungeh, A. (2000). *Gender differences in the associations between anxiety early after acute myocardial infarction and subsequent in hospital complications.* Dissertation Abstracts.

King, K., & Koop, P. M. (1999). The influence of the cardiac surgery patient's sex and age on care giving received. *Social Science and Medicine, 48*, 1735-1742.

Kleinman, A. (1988). *The illness narratives*. New York, NY: Basic Books.

Ladwing, K. H., Muhlberger, N., Walter, H., Schumacher, K., Popp, K., Holl, R., et al. (2000). Gender differences in emotional disability and negative health perception in cardiac patients six months after stent implantation. *Journal of Psychosomatic Research, 48*, 501-508.

Levine, T. B., Levine, A. B., Raminski, P., & Stom, R. J. (2000). Reversal of heart failure remodeling in women. *Journal of Women's Health and Gender Based Medicine, 9*, 513-519

Lieberman, L., Mena, M., & Stewart, D. (1998). Cardiac rehabilitation: Gender differences in factors influencing participation. *Journal of Women's Health, 7*, 717-723.

Lincoln, Y., & Guba, E. (1985). *Naturalistic inquiry.* Beverly Hills, CA: Sage Publications.

Lorber, J. (1997). *Gender and the social construction of illness.* Thousand Oaks, CA: Sage Publications.

Lukkarinen, H., Hentinen, M. (1998). Asessment of quality of life with the Nottingham health profile among women with coronary artery disease. *Heart and Lung: Journal of Acute & Critical Care, 27*, 189-199.

Maclean, U., & Cockshutt, A. (1979). How women cope with their men-folk's heart attacks. *New Society, 26*, 183-185.

Mark, D. B. (2000). Sex bias in cardiovascular care: Should women be treated more like men? *Journal of the American Medical Association, 283*, 659-661.

McKinlay, J. B. (1996). Some contributions from the social system to gender inequalities in heart disease. *Journal of Health and Social Behavior, 37*(1), 1-26.

McSweeney, J. C., Cody, M., & Caren, P. B. (2001). Do you know them when you see them? Women's prodromal and acute symptoms of myocardial infraction. *Journal of Cardiovascular Nursing, 15*(3), 26-38.

Meischke, H., Larsen, M. P., & Eisenberg, M. S. (1998). Gender differences in reported symptoms for acute myocardial infarction: Impact on pre-hospital delay time interval. *American Journal of Emergency Medicine, 16*, 363-366.

Miles, A. (1991). *Women, health and medicine.* Great Britain: Open University Press.

Miller, C. L. (2002). A review of symptoms of coronary artery disease in women. *Journal of advanced Nursing, 39*(1), 17-23.

Norris, R. M. (1998). Fatality outside hospital from acute coronary events in three British heart districts, 1994-5. *British Medical Journal, 316*, 1065-1070.

Parson, T. (1951). *The social system.* London: Routledge & Kegan Paul.

Phillpott, S., Boynton, M. P., Feder, G., & Hemingway, H. (2001). Gender differences in descriptions of angina symptoms and health problems immediately prior to angiography: The ACRE study. *Social Science and Medicine, 52*, 1565-1575.

Pierret, J. (2001). Interviews and biographical time: The case of long- term HIV nonprogressor. *Sociology of Health & Illness, 23*, 159-179.

Poirier, S., & Lioness, A. (1997). Ending, secrets and silences: Overreading in narrative inqury. *Research in Nursing and Health, 20*, 551-557.

Remennick, L. I., & Raanan, O. (2000). Institutional and attitudinal factors involved in higher mortality of Israeli women after coronary bypass surgery: Another case of gender bias. *Health , 4*, 455-478.

Riessman, C. K. (1990). Strategic uses of narrative in the presentation of self and illness: A research note. *Social Science and Medicine, 30*, 1195-1200.

Robinson, C. A. (1993). Managing life with a chronic condition: The story of normalization. *Qualitative Health Research, 3*(1), 6-28.

Rose-Gail, L., Suls, J., Green, P., & Lounsbury, P. (1996). Comparison of adjustment, activity and tangible social support in men and women patients and their spouses during the six months post myocardial infarction. *Annals of Behavioral Medicine, 18*, 264-272.

Rosenfeld, J. A. (2000). Heart disease in women: Gender specific statistics and prevention strategies for a population at risk. *Postgraduate Medicine, 107*, 111-116.

Ruston, A., Clayton, J., & Calnan, M. (1998). Patient's action during their cardiac event: Qualitative study exploring differences and modifiable factors. *British Medical Journal, 316,* 1060-1064.

Sandelowski, M. (1991). Telling stories: Narrative approaches in qualitative research. *Image, 23,* 161-167.

Silverman, D. (1993). Theory and method in qualitative research (chapter 1). *Interpreting Qualitative Data: Methods for Analyzing Tallk, Text and Interaction.* Thousand Oaks, CA: Sage Publication.

Twaddle, A. C., & Hesslers, R. M. (1987). The sickness career. *A Sociology of Health.* (2nd Edition), (pp 143-161). New York, NY: Macmillan.

Uuskuela, M. (1996). Psychological differences between young male and female survivors of myocardial infarction. *Psychotherapy and Psychosomatics, 65*, 327-330.

Vakili, B.A ., Kaplan, R. C., & Brown, D. L. (2001). Sex-based differences in early mortality of patients undergoing primary angioplasty for first acute myocardial infarction. *Circulation, 104*(25), 3034-3038

Van Tiel, D., Van Vliet, K. P., & Moerman, C. J. (1998). Sex differences in illness beliefs and illness behaviour in patients with suspected coronary artery disease. *Patient Education & Counseling, 33*, 143-147.

Verbrugge, L. M. (1985). Gender and health: An update on hypotheses and evidence. *Journal of Health and Social Behavior, 26*, 156-182.

Verbrugge, L .M. (1986). From sneezes to adieux: Stages of health for American men and women. *Social Science and Medicine, 22*, 1195-1212.

Wenger, N. K. (1996). The high risk of CHD for women: Understanding why prevention is crucial. *Madscape Womens Health, 1*(11), 6.

Weidner, G. (2000). Why do men get more heart disease than women? An international perspective. *Journal of American College Health, 48,* 291-294.

Willis, E., Miller, R., & Wyn, J. (2001). Gendered embodiment and survival for young people with cystic fibrosis. *Social Science and Medicine, 53*, 1163-1174

In: Decision Making in Medicine and Health Care
Editor: P. C. Tolana, pp. 31-51
ISBN: 978-1-60021-870-5


*Chapter II*

# CARDIOLOGIST-PATIENT COMMUNICATION ABOUT HEART FAILURE

***Keri L. Rodriguez*[1,2,3,4,*]*, Phyllis N. Butow*[5] *and Robert M. Arnold*[2,3,4,6,7]**

[1]Center for Health Equity Research and Promotion, VA Pittsburgh Healthcare System, Pittsburgh, PA, USA;
[2]Division of General Internal Medicine, Department of Medicine, School of Medicine, University of Pittsburgh, Pittsburgh, PA, USA;
[3]Center for Bioethics and Health Law, University of Pittsburgh, Pittsburgh, Pennsylvania, USA;
[4]Institute for Doctor-Patient Communication, University of Pittsburgh, Pittsburgh, Pennsylvania, USA;
[5]Medical Psychology Research Unit, School of Psychology, University of Sydney, Sydney, New South Wales, Australia;
[6]Section of Palliative Care and Medical Ethics, University of Pittsburgh, USA;
[7]Institute to Enhance Palliative Care, University of Pittsburgh, USA.

## ABSTRACT

Studies suggest that effective doctor-patient communication is associated with higher levels of patient satisfaction, better treatment compliance, and better biomedical and psychosocial outcomes. Much of this research has been conducted in the field of oncology.

Given that effective doctor-patient communication has been linked to beneficial health-related outcomes, an examination of studies relevant to cardiologist-patient

* Correspondence concerning this article should be addressed to: Dr. Keri L. Rodriguez, PhD, Assistant Professor of Medicine, University of Pittsburgh, Research Health Scientist, Center for Health Equity Research and Promotion VA Pittsburgh Healthcare System, 7180 Highland Drive (151C-H), Pittsburgh, PA 15206 USA. Keri.Rodriguez@va.gov; Phone: 412-688-6000, ext. 81-5734; Fax: 412-688-6527.

communication appears warranted. As studies focusing on communication in heart failure patients are relatively sparse, this article provides a critical review of the larger literature within cancer on communication interventions and an exploration of lessons that can be learned.

Current empirical evidence suggests the importance of considering both the information needs of patients, as well as preferred decision-making processes. There are several types of methods and tools to promote patient understanding and to facilitate decision making, including patient information aids, techniques to reduce patient anxiety, patient decision aids, and communication training for patients and/or physicians.

While many of the findings in studies of oncologist-patient communication can be applied to the improvement of cardiologist-patient communication, further studies are needed to help cardiologists and other healthcare professionals meet the specific needs of patients with heart failure.

**Keywords:** Physician-patient communication; Patient-provider relationship; Decision making; Heart failure; Oncology

## 1. Introduction

The effective treatment of a patient with a life-threatening disease requires both biomedical and psychosocial care. Effective communication is critical for establishing a satisfactory doctor-patient relationship, maximizing information transfer and promoting good decision making. More recently, in Western countries, shared decision making [1] and informed choice [2] have become somewhat synonymous with effective communication. Effective communication in this sense refers to patient-centered behaviors by the physician and participatory behaviors by the patient.

During clinic interactions, physicians educate their patients about disease processes and treatment options, obtain informed consent for clinical procedures, and motivate patients to modify their lifestyle. Further, patient-centered behaviors include appropriate information-giving, partnership-building, and supportive talk. Despite the increasing use of nonphysician educators and decision aids, patients still rely primarily on their interactions with physicians to obtain medical information and make health-related decisions [3,4].

Studies of patients with chronic and life-threatening diseases have shown effective doctor-patient communication is correlated with a number of clinically important variables. For example, it has been shown to encourage patient treatment adherence [5-7], to help patients cope with the psychological ramifications of their illness and reduce anxiety and stress levels [5,6,8,9], and to result in better biomedical outcomes [5,6]. It has also been shown to increase patient satisfaction with care [10-14], reduce the likelihood of "doctor shopping" [8], and, in surgery, reduce the likelihood of filing malpractice suits [15].

Effective communication is particularly important in a progressive, chronic condition such as heart failure. Heart failure is a disabling chronic disease that remains a major cause of morbidity and mortality in the United States [16]. Like most life threatening illnesses, patients may feel affected not just physically, but also emotionally, socially, and financially. Although heart failure is a serious condition, much can be done to prevent it from developing and to manage its symptoms. Through frequent monitoring, detailed assessment, optimization of medications, and education, intensive management of heart failure patients has been shown to improve the quality of care, have a positive impact on quality of life, and reduce hospital readmissions [17,18]. Given that effective patient-physician communication has been linked to such beneficial health outcomes, an examination of studies specifically of cardiologist-patient communication appears warranted.

The purpose of this article is to provide some guidance to the cardiologist about what patients want from their physician, about the current state of knowledge concerning information transfer and decision making, and to offer some ways that cardiologists could improve their communication skills. Given that there is little research focusing specifically on cardiologist-patient communication in heart failure, we have also reviewed the literature in another life-limiting disease characterized by complex information and decision making: cancer. We describe oncologist-patient communication research, and the applicability of the findings to cardiologists.

# 2. Cardiologist-Patient Communication Studies

## 2.1. Information Needs of Heart Failure Patients

Patients with a life-limiting illness such as heart failure require information to facilitate decision-making involvement and to ensure treatment adherence. Yet a study comparing lung cancer and heart failure patients close to death showed that heart failure patients had less information about their illness and a poorer understanding of their prognosis [19]. Further, research shows that chronic heart failure patients often feel unable to ask their doctors questions about their illness and believe that doctors are reluctant to provide them with too much knowledge [20]. Not surprisingly, the available heart failure literature highlights specific informational deficits [21-25].

One contributing factor is a lack of information provision on the part of the doctor. For example, many patients are not receiving dietary restriction advice [26]. On the other hand, difficulties with information retention have been shown for chronic heart failure patients, due to such reasons as short term memory loss and confusion that can result from their condition [27,28]. Nonetheless, in general, researchers have found that many chronic heart failure patients lack a clear understanding of why they developed heart failure, what heart failure is, and what its presence implies [20,22,23]. Additionally, some patients have been found to believe that their heart failure symptoms are merely a result of "growing older" and that nothing medically can be done [20].

Recent studies confirm high symptom burden and communication needs, particularly in end-stage heart failure, that are not being met [20,29,30]. Study results have shown that, although some patients were unaware of their prognosis, most saw death as "inevitable" but felt that doctors were hesitant to talk about death [20]. Patients have confirmed that they would welcome timely and frank discussion about their prognosis to help them to prepare for the end of life [20]. A study of preferences of elderly patients hospitalized for heart failure found that advance planning of end-of-life procedures and doctor-patient communication regarding these issues remain poor and need improvement [31]. One study indicated information on medication, cardiovascular anatomy and physiology, and treatment were the most desired information items [32].

In the case of advanced heart failure, research shows that healthcare providers can meet patient information needs by offering honest explanations, focusing on enhancing quality of life, and outlining instructions for emergencies [25]. Symptomatically, higher fatigue has been correlated with wanting more information on aspects of care that need to be managed on a day-to-day basis, including diet, activity, and psychological and risk factors [32].

## 2.2. Decision-Making Processes Concerning Heart Failure

In the past, physicians tended to make decisions for patients, with little patient input. Currently, the legal and ethical consensus in Western countries recommends that important health related choices be made by a process called shared decision making. In this model, patients become involved in their healthcare decisions [1]. The treatment of heart failure involves many decisions, ranging from which medicines to try and when to initiate them, to the use of invasive technologies such as implantable defibrillators, home inotropes, and transplantation. Unfortunately, a study comparing lung cancer and heart failure patients close to death showed that heart failure patients had less involvement in making important palliative care decisions, such as decisions about initiating cardiopulmonary resuscitation, ventilator use, and tube feeding [19].

In general, optimizing disease management is particularly important and has been linked to improved outcomes in heart failure. For example, one study showed that, under the guidance of a cardiologist, closely monitoring heart failure patients with advanced-practice nurse care significantly improves heart failure management while reducing care costs [33]. Generally, positive health outcomes for heart failure patients have been shown to be dependent on patient participation in the selection and use of appropriately focused heart failure care [34]. Yet, for many heart failure patients, performing self-care is complicated by the complex medication regimen, symptom monitoring, and required decision making [35].

Literature suggests that effective everyday self-care decision making by patients can improve heart failure outcomes [36]. One study showed that self-monitoring by heart failure patients of worsening symptoms caused by fluid overload is a cornerstone of heart failure care and to improving outcomes [37]. Likewise, interventions combining patient education and post-discharge management have demonstrated benefits in patients with chronic heart failure [38]. Authors of a study of patients with a primary diagnosis of congestive heart failure, chronic obstructive pulmonary disease (COPD), or cancer further recommend a patient-centered approach to advance care planning needs - incorporating consideration of both treatment burdens and treatment outcomes (including the likelihood of these outcomes while recognizing that patients' valuations of these outcomes may change over time) [39].

# 3. Oncologist-Patient Communication Studies

Most doctor-patient communication research concerning life-limiting illnesses has been in the field of oncology [40,41]. Further, an increasing amount of research has been conducted to evaluate and improve the quality of communication and decision making between cancer patients and healthcare providers. Key cancer communication research findings and related intervention and educational efforts may provide specific, practical recommendations and tools for heart failure communication.

## 3.1. Information Needs

Like a cancer diagnosis, a heart failure diagnosis is a life-altering event, associated with multiple symptoms, diminished physiological and psychosocial functioning, and decreased quality of life [42,43]. Cancer and heart failure treatments are often complex and lengthy. Patients with either life-threatening disease are likely to experience high anxiety and depression levels, and expectations and preferences concerning the timing and extent of decision-making involvement are likely to vary between patients.

Giving bad news to patients and their loved ones is a common task facing physicians. In Western countries, the standard of practice is to tell patients the truth, and this is consistent with most patients' wishes. But it is important for clinicians to find out early on how much the patient understands about their illness. This will allow for correction of misconceptions, framing of treatment in terms of goals, and, when necessary, beginning preparation for unfavorable outcomes when the prognosis is poor. In short, "Hope for the best, prepare for the worst."

General skills that have been shown to facilitate communication include mutual respect, empathy, honesty, flexibility, humility, and exploration of patients' expectations [41]. In a study of female breast cancer patients, those who were unhappy with how their diagnosis was communicated predominantly noted a lack of empathy [44]. In contrast, patients to whom bad news was presented in an unhurried, honest, balanced and empathetic fashion, or who received more detailed information about their cancer diagnosis have been shown to report greater satisfaction with communication [45]. Even when cure or arrest of the disease is not a high probability, telling patients they will receive the best treatment available, explaining that clinical trials and experimental medicine advance every day, and letting patients know that other opinions may be considered, provide patients with important words of encouragement and can foster a sense of hope [46]. Further, developing and practicing a consistent approach can also help to relieve clinician stress associated with breaking bad news [46].

Important skills for building trust and rapport include taking an interest in patients' concerns, allowing patients to express their feelings, and listening and soliciting their opinions. Further, in a recent study in which cancer patients were asked about the most important aspects of receiving bad news, the following were in the top responses: having the doctor take time to answer all of my questions, having the doctor be honest about the severity of my condition, being given enough time to ask all of my questions, and having the doctor give me full attention [47]. In another study, cancer patients identified the following situations with their physicians as providing them with a hopeful outlook toward the treatment of their disease: the doctor offers to be a resource for all questions, the doctor assures me that he or she will not abandon me no matter what happens, and the doctor discusses all my treatment options [48]. Further, withholding information, telling the family, but not the patient, using euphemisms, and being overly optimistic can actually erode trust and hopefulness in patients [48].

The importance of empathy in doctor-patient communication was also highlighted in a randomized trial of a standard video with or without two additional segments in which the doctor showed support, sympathy, and compassion using words and touch [49]. Women viewing the video with the 40 seconds of compassion segments demonstrated significantly less anxiety than those watching the standard video, and assessed the doctor more favorably in attributes such as caring for the patient, acknowledging the patient's emotions, and encouraging the patient to ask questions and to take part in decision making.

Aspects of communication that are associated with patient dissatisfaction include excessive medical terminology, pessimistic information provision, inability to provide adequate medical information, and a cold or withdrawn informer attitude [50]. Literature suggests that it is preferable to use the word for the illness at hand (e.g., cancer), rather than euphemisms such as illness or tumor [51]. For example, in a study among women with newly diagnosed breast cancer, satisfaction with diagnosis information was greatest among those who were told that the diagnosis was "cancer" [51]. Use of the word cancer may raise short-term anxiety, but has not been shown to impact psychological adjustment to cancer [51] and using a euphemism may ultimately confuse and mislead patients [52].

Unfortunately, patients may not be able to absorb or understand all the information they are given at the time of diagnosis. For example, a survey of doctor-patient communication about lung cancer indicates that physicians are rarely aware that patients misunderstand the information they are given [53]. In this study, over 30% of patients believed that their treatment was curative rather than palliative, and over 36% misunderstood the extent of their cancer [53]. A follow-up appointment is a good way to assess a patient's emotional state and understanding of the situation, however, a number of studies have examined methods to facilitate and improve patient understanding of their cancer, including various information aids.

Question prompt sheets for patients provided before the oncologist consultation have been evaluated as a technique designed to promote active participation and asking questions during the visit. Providing patients with written information during pre-consultation, such as leaflets and prompt sheets listing potential questions, has been shown to result in more active participation and increased questioning [54-58]. For example, one study found that 35% of patients who received a question handout asked questions about prognosis compared to 16% of those solely receiving an information handout [59]. Doctors have been shown to be more satisfied with the consultation, and there is no evidence of increased demands, although there may be some increase in consultation duration [56,58].

Providing patients with an audiotape of their initial consultation after their visit with an oncologist also has been evaluated. The primary outcome variables have largely included information recall and patient satisfaction. Cancer patients and their kin have been shown to value the consultation audiotapes as an information aid and to assist in recall [50]. For example, one study found that using audiotapes improves newly diagnosed breast cancer patients' understanding of treatment side effects, but does not significantly influence patient satisfaction with communication, mood state, or quality of life [60]. In another study, 88% of patients indicated that an audiotape of the appointment helped to increase understanding of their diagnosis and treatment plan [61]. However, according to other empirical literature, the efficacy of providing patients with their cancer consultation recordings is unclear [62,63]. Overall, findings suggest that most patients benefit from receiving the audiotape, but its utility in improving patient-physician communication requires further examination.

### 3.2. Decision-Making Processes

Studies show that patients' communication styles influence the amount of information their physicians provide. Patients who ask more questions receive more details than patients who do not ask questions [64]. However, patients who are passive may be just as interested in getting the information as vocal patients, but may be too intimidated or reluctant to ask. By determining patients' information needs, physicians can ensure patients receive the amount of information they prefer and adhere to their treatment regimens. Well-informed patients who understand the importance and nature of their treatment and prognosis are more likely to abide by their treatment regimens and follow their physicians' instructions.

Yet research shows that oncology patients differ in the extent to which they wish to be involved in their care. In a survey of females with breast cancer, 22% preferred to take the lead in decision making, 34% preferred to delegate the responsibility to their doctor, and 44% wanted a collaborative model [65]. Another study found that only 42% of women had their decision-making preferences met and concluded that 9 out of 10 decisions made jointly by doctors and their patients in routine office visits were made on the basis of insufficient discussion to allow for informed treatment decisions [66].

Studies that have attempted to characterize why patients have different desires for decision making have shown that younger age (less than 50 years), higher education levels, and being married are related to a desire for active or collaborative roles [67]. Although ethnicity may influence oncologist-patient communication, to our knowledge this has not been explored to date.

Most physicians have multiple contacts with patients and caregivers. This is especially true in oncology. Cancer is considered to be a chronic disease, and oncologists often manage patient medical problems other than cancer. Because many patients see their physicians as an important source of support [3,4], they expect to be able to discuss issues not directly related to their disease, such as how to talk to the child of a newly diagnosed patient. Being receptive to these issues and exploring them further will allow clinicians to make an impact on their patients' quality of life; receptiveness can be accomplished by some simple listening techniques such as making eye contact, asking about concerns the patient may have, and using open-ended questions, such as, "Tell me more about it." [68].

Aside from their decision-making preferences, what patients understand, or misunderstand, about their disease-related prognosis can lead to varied disease management decisions. For example, a study of hospitalized patients with advanced non-small-cell lung or colon cancer found that while doctors were reasonably accurate in their prediction of patient life expectancy, 82% of patients overestimated their life expectancy, and 59% were significantly more optimistic about their life expectancy than their physician [69]. The perception patients had of their prognosis had a profound effect on their subsequent treatment decisions. Overly optimistic patients were nearly three times more likely to pursue aggressive therapy over supportive care, but their survival was no better than those who pursued supportive care alone.

Physicians also contribute to the increasingly aggressive management of cancer patients at the end of life, with as many as 18% of patients receiving chemotherapy within 14 days of death [54]. Clearly, physicians are obliged to determine what their patients wish to know, to provide information on prognosis, including life expectancy, the evidence-based impact of therapy on survival and quality of life, and to review all treatment options, including supportive care alone, in the setting of advanced cancer. Further, patients who understand their prognosis will be able to make informed care choices and participate in treatment decisions in accordance with their values [70].

A number of studies have examined methods to facilitate shared decision making, commonly focusing on decision aids for patients. Decision aids are defined as "interventions designed to help people make specific and difficult choices among options by providing information on the options and outcomes relevant to the person's health status" [55]. Decision aids have been developed to address issues of cancer screening, genetic testing, cancer prevention, and, less commonly, the management of advanced cancer. More than 50 studies of decision aids for cancer patients have been published, with most targeting patients considering primary or adjuvant treatment of early stage breast or prostate cancer. Many of these are developmental studies, but more randomized trials are testing decision aids.

A randomized trial in patients with node-negative breast cancer considering chemotherapy compared the effect of the standard medical consultation versus the consultation plus use of a validated decision board [58]. Patients randomly assigned to use of the decision board demonstrated a significant improvement in knowledge about disease and treatment, and greater satisfaction with decision making up to 12 months after the initial consultation; however the two arms exhibited no statistically significant difference in patient anxiety, consultation duration, or treatment choice, nor in physician satisfaction with decision making. Patients randomly assigned to use the decision board were more active participants in their medical decision making than those randomly assigned to the standard consultation.

Another randomized trial in patients with early-stage breast cancer used a computer program to assist patients and physicians with adjuvant systemic therapy decisions [57]. Patients randomly assigned to use the program were significantly more satisfied with the decision-making process and had a better understanding of adjuvant treatment. Patients randomly assigned to use the program were more likely to select either a chemotherapy-containing regimen or no systemic adjuvant therapy than those not randomly assigned to use the program.

These encouraging results in early-stage cancer patients do not necessarily predict the success of similar decision-support tools in advanced cancer. For patients with incurable cancer, the prognosis and treatment goals differ substantially from the goals of adjuvant therapy. The trade-off between benefits and toxicities of palliative therapy is more complex.

Advanced-stage cancer patients often have greater need for emotional support and symptom control, in addition to information and decision-involvement needs. Five studies have been published describing the development of decision aids for metastatic cancer patients, and one for locally advanced cancer [56,71-75]. However, none of these has been evaluated through a randomized trial.

In general, potential benefits of decision aids include enhanced patient understanding, reduced decisional conflict, enhanced harmonization between patient values and treatment decisions, and greater patient involvement and satisfaction with decision making. There are two systematic reviews of 18 randomized trials studying the effects of decision aids on early-stage cancer patients' decision making and outcomes [55,76]. These meta-analyses demonstrate that, compared with controls, most of the decision aids produced higher patient knowledge scores, lower decisional-conflict scores, and more active patient participation in decision making. Yet there were no reported differences in anxiety or satisfaction with decisions [55,76].

The effectiveness of these promising decision support tools for advanced-stage cancer patients and patients with other diseases (such as heart failure) and their role in current clinical practice have yet to be better defined through additional randomized trials. More specifically, decision aids and support tools may further improve the quality of decision making and overall care in heart failure patients grappling with their diagnosis through enhancing informed consent and decision satisfaction, better harmonizing of end-of-life treatment decisions with patient values, and improving patient well being.

### 3.3. Doctor-Patient Communication Training Interventions

In the field of oncology, patient advocate groups have called for further physician training in the management of psychosocial aspects of cancer care [77], and physicians have indicated an interest in participating if appropriate programs are available [78]. There are likely similar attitudes held by heart failure health professionals. To date, most applications of communication interventions have been directed toward improving physicians' skills, including communication skills training programs as well as consensus guidelines.

The use of intradisciplinary [79] and multidisciplinary [80] workshops has been advocated. Teaching models include didactic sessions and small group practice, having a learner-centered approach, and focusing on the physician's personal awareness of feelings and attitudes that can thwart communication [24,81,82]. For example, "Oncotalk" offers intensive communication skills training designed for medical oncology fellows; the focus is on communication skills for transitions from curative to palliative care—some of the most challenging situations faced by oncologists [83]. Generally, such programs aim to encourage clinicians to use more targeted consultation skills in patient assessments, to increase their confidence in communicating effectively, and to enhance their understanding of patients' psychosocial needs [21,24]. Such models have been found to be well-accepted by learners, but the optimal duration and content of such courses has not been determined [84-86]. While objective evidence of the value of intradisciplinary workshops is awaited, multidisciplinary workshops have proved successful in helping doctors and nurses acquire key communication skills [79].

Despite workshops being effective in changing communication behaviors, it is not certain how much of what is learned is applied to clinical practice; the effect of communication skills training programs for doctors on patient outcomes has not been studied extensively due to the complexity and size of the studies required. While the literature is comparatively small concerning the effectiveness of communication skills training programs, evidence suggests that such programs can make a difference to physician behavior and patient outcomes. Results of randomized controlled trials and meta-analyses have shown effectiveness in such interventions, particularly in improving cancer patients' emotional health and well-being and reducing their psychological distress [87-92]. For example, in one small U.S. study in which 18 oncologists were randomized to participate in a communication skills workshop and 18 oncologists served as controls, the patients of intervention group oncologists reported feeling less depressed and more in charge of their lives than did the patients of control group oncologists [25]. Another study reported that physicians in an intensive educational program to improve communication received higher scores (than non-participating physicians) from breast cancer patients in areas such as validating the patients' feelings and understanding the patients' need to feel in control [22,23].

Clinical practice guidelines are defined as "systematically developed statements to assist both practitioner and patient decisions about appropriate health care for specific clinical circumstances" [93,94]. To address reported problems in medical interactions where bad news is discussed, researchers have investigated the experiences and desires of health care providers, patients, and families in multiple medical settings and diagnosis, including cancer, and published recommendations [95,96]. On the basis of such results, others have developed guidelines. For example, in the U.S., guidelines for communicating bad news to patients and detecting distress have been published by the American Society of Clinical Oncology [97,98] and the National Comprehensive Cancer Network [99]. Further, the Australian National Health and Medical Research Council recently developed guidelines to help cancer treatment teams provide evidence-based supportive care to meet their patients' psychosocial needs [100]. Most of the consensus guidelines pertain to clinician-patient interactions, but advice is also given about appropriate referral circumstances for group support, counseling, psychiatric interventions, and other interventions.

Practice guidelines been developed regarding general clinician interactional skills, which include considering supportive communication, delivering medical information in plain English, strategies to aid recall and understanding, and ongoing support in any consultation [101]. Consensus guidelines outlining key components of disclosing a diagnosis such as cancer include exploring the patient's expectations, giving information at the patient's pace, allowing time for the patient to react, and eliciting patient's concerns [45]. Several general communication tenets emerge within guidelines for discussing disease progression and end-of-life care, including finding out what the patient understands; learning how much more or less information he or she wants to know; being sensitive to and empathic with whatever emotions the patient expresses; listening attentively and allowing tears and emotions to be expressed without signs of being rushed; and taking into account the family and its ethnic, cultural, and religious roots [102-105].

In addition, based on a literature review and recommendations of a consensus panel of doctors (with input from patients with cancer), Girgis and Sanson-Fisher published some useful guidelines on conveying information to patients about serious disease or death [106]. Their guidelines included a focus on ensuring privacy and allowing adequate time, assessing patients' understanding, giving information about diagnosis and prognosis simply and honestly, avoiding euphemisms, encouraging patients to express feelings, being empathic, giving a broad but realistic time-frame concerning prognosis, and arranging a review.

All of the aforementioned tenants may contribute to decisions about care [104,105]. Some versions of these guidelines also address ethical and cross-cultural concerns, such as whether to tell the truth and to whom to disclose the information [107-111]. In practice, these tenants should be applied with attention to the needs of traditionally medically underserved patients: those with little or no English proficiency, for whom care at the end of life is particularly difficult because communication is limited, and patients with chronic mental illness or limited education.

## 4. Are Lessons Learned from Oncology Relevant to Heart Failure?

Like most life-threatening illnesses, heart failure is characterized by decreased functioning, a waxing and waning course, and symptoms which are often diffuse and which come and go. The physical and psychological symptom burden common to most end-stage heart failure patients is similar to that in the dying cancer patient. More specifically, symptom data has focused on pain, dyspnea, depression, insomnia, anorexia, anxiety, constipation, nausea/vomiting, fatigue, difficulty ambulating, and edema [112].

Yet in patients with advanced heart failure, the 5-year survival rate is 25% for men and 38% for women, so the prognosis is worse than that associated with many common cancers [113,114]. With heart failure, active management to improve cardiac function is the mainstay of treatment throughout the illness, even in the very end stage. Improving quality of life remains a major goal in the treatment of heart failure [115]. But, although treatment can often slow the illness progression and substantially increase the patient's quality of life (e.g., symptom management), the disease cannot be cured [116,117].

Further, compared to cancer patients, heart failure patients have well-documented symptom control issues throughout their illness. The most commonly reported distressing symptoms are dyspnea, pain (often pain all over with non-specified cause), overwhelming tiredness, functional impairment (difficulty walking), depression, and anxiety. The high levels of depression found among people with chronic heart failure [118,119] may be partly related to a lack of open communication with their doctors.

Heart failure and cancer also differ in disease course and this may change some of the communication dynamics. Heart failure patients have a different illness trajectory from the more linear and predictable course of cancer patients. In cancer, the illness trajectory is relatively stable, often over several years. Patients with incurable cancer are most readily identified with having a terminal phase to their illness compared with end-stage heart failure. Hence, the vast majority of patients referred to palliative care services are cancer patients. In terms of treating the underlying condition, with cancer, palliation is often just that, symptom alleviation without being able to control the underlying cancer, especially in end-stage disease. Cancer patients, even those with advanced disease, generally retain a high degree of function until 3 to 6 months before death, at which time there is a predictable, relatively linear decrease in function. Although heart failure is a progressive, chronic disease with the potential for gradual deterioration, it follows a variable clinical course, and as many as one half of patients will die suddenly rather than dying of progressive heart failure [120].

People with advanced heart failure have episodes of serious illness, followed by periods of stability. There are acute exacerbations of illness from which the patient usually recovers (perhaps not to the same degree as they were before). The acute exacerbations are not as predictable as in cancer. Since death usually occurs during an acute illness, it will often be seen as "sudden." Other heart failure patients may seem to "recover" after such episodes, but they may not return to their previous level of functioning, and yet, at times, they may not seem to be very ill. For most, death seems sudden, even if the person has been ill for some time. But even taking into account activities of daily living, haemoglobin, sodium, creatinine, urea, urine output, and other factors in heart failure patients, it is still not possible to accurately predict time of death. Thus, in accordance with current prognostic tools, it is very difficult to make accurate predictions about illness outcomes and time of death for patients with chronic end-stage heart failure.

One of the greatest differences between cancer and heart failure is the lack of acknowledgement by patients, their kin, and healthcare professionals that heart failure is mostly a terminal disease. That being the case, this can lead to poor communication and loss of treatment choices for the patient, as they are not able to make informed healthcare decisions. Studies of cancer patients have highlighted the positive effect of open communication about likely prognosis [121]. Because heart failure has a worse prognosis than many cancers [113,114], effective prognosis discussion could have similar benefits to those shown for cancer patients. A study comparing dying with lung cancer or cardiac failure showed that heart failure patients had less information about their illness; a poorer understanding of illness and prognosis; less involvement in important decision making including cardiopulmonary resuscitation initiation, ventilation and tube feeding; frustration with progressive losses, social isolation, and the stress of complex medication regimen monitoring; fewer health services, social services, and financial benefits; less involvement with palliative care services; and poorly coordinated services [19]. Because it is more difficult to predict prognosis in chronic heart failure patients [122], the models of communication adopted in both cancer and palliative care may not be wholly appropriate for this group of patients.

## 5. Conclusion

In regards to the clinic visit, one author noted:

> A pair of kidneys or a heart will never come to the doctor for a diagnosis and treatment. They will be contained within an anxious, fearful, wondering person, who is

> asking puzzled questions about an obscure future weighed down by the responsibilities of a loved family, with a job to be held and with bills to be paid [123].

Central to ensuring quality of care is effective communication between the doctor, patient, and family [96,107]. Effective communication refers to patient-centered behaviors such as appropriate information-giving, partnership-building, and supportive talk, as well as participatory behaviors such as asking questions, expressing concerns, and being assertive.

Identification and management of physical and psychological symptoms hinge upon the clinic interaction. The patient-physician encounter involves several stages, including exchange of information between the doctor and the patient, deliberation, and decision making [124]. Many studies have emphasized the impact of doctor-patient communication in chronic illness care. In general, studies have shown that patients are more likely to be satisfied, adhere to treatment, report better quality of life, and have improvements in physical health [4,125] when physicians do the following: explore the disease and illness experience, understand the patient as a whole person, and find common ground in decision making [126-129]. Further, effective doctor-patient communication has been associated with better psychosocial and biomedical outcomes, such as reduced patient anxiety and increased treatment adherence [5-9].

In addition, an increasing amount of research has been conducted to develop and evaluate interventions for improving the quality of communication, particularly between cancer patients and healthcare providers. A variety of these descriptive and interventional studies, most conducted in the field of oncology, show that effective communication can be described and learned. Much of this research has produced several methods and tools aimed at promoting patient understanding and facilitating decision making. These include patient information aids, techniques to reduce patient anxiety, decision aids, and communication training for patients and/or physicians.

Replication studies and well-controlled experimental designs applied to a variety of healthcare providers in diverse settings are needed to confirm the validity of the empirical findings to date, and to facilitate further development of interventions aimed at enhancing patient-physician communication. While many of the oncologist-patient communication research findings may be applied to the improvement of cardiologist-patient communication, further studies are needed to help cardiologists and other healthcare professionals identify and meet the specific needs of heart failure patients.

## REFERENCES

[1] Braddock, CH 3rd; Edwards, KA; Hasenberg, NM; Laidley, TL; Levinson W. Informed decision making in outpatient practice: time to get back to basics. *JAMA* 1999;282:2313-2320.

[2] Gattellari, M; Butow, PN; Tattersall, MH; Dunn, SM; MacLeod, CA. Misunderstanding in cancer patients: why shoot the messenger? *Ann Oncol* 1999;10:39-46.

[3] Butow, PN; Kazemi, JN; Beeney, LJ; Griffin, AM; Dunn, SM; Tattersall, MH. When the diagnosis is cancer: patient communication experiences and preferences. *Cancer* 1996;77:2630-2637.

[4] Roter, DL. Patient participation in the patient-provider interaction: the effects of patient question asking on the quality of interaction, satisfaction and compliance. *Health Educ Monogr* 1977;5:281-315.

[5] Frederickson, LG. Exploring information-exchange in consultation: the patients' view of performance and outcomes. *Patient Educ Couns* 1995;25:237-246.

[6] Holman, H; Lorig, K. Patients as partners in managing chronic disease. Partnership is a prerequisite for effective and efficient health care. *BMJ* 2000;320:526-527.

[7] Stewart, MA. Effective physician-patient communication and health outcomes: a review. *CMAJ* 1995;152:1423-1433.

[8] Kasteler, J; Kane, RL; Olsen, DM; Thetford, C. Issues underlying prevalence of "doctor-shopping" behavior. *J Health Soc Behav* 1976;17:329-339.

[9] Molleman, E; Krabbendam, PJ; Annyas, AA; Koops, HS; Sleijfer, DT; Vermey, A. The significance of the doctor-patient relationship in coping with cancer. *Soc Sci Med* 1984;18:475-480.

[10] Carter, WB; Inui, TS; Kukull, WA; Haigh, VH. Outcome-based doctor-patient interaction analysis: II. Identifying effective provider and patient behavior. *Med Care* 1982;20:550-566.

[11] Cleary, PD; McNeil, BJ. Patient satisfaction as an indicator of quality of care. *Inquiry* 1988;25:25-36.

[12] Doering, ER. Factors influencing inpatient satisfaction with care. *Qual Rev Bull* 1983;9:291-299.

[13] Hall, JA; Roter, DL; Katz, NR. Meta-Analysis of correlates of provider behavior in medical encounters. *Med Care* 1988;26:657-675.

[14] Williams, SJ; Calnan, M. Key determinants of consumer satisfaction with general practice. *Fam Pract* 1991;8:237-242.

[15] Levinson, W; Roter, DL; Mullooly, JP; Dull, VT; Frankel, RM. Physician-patient communication. The relationship with malpractice claims among primary care physicians and surgeons. *JAMA* 1997;277:553-559.

[16] Rosamond, W; Flegal, K; Friday, G; Furie, K; Go, A; Greenlund, K; Haase, N; Ho, M; Howard, V; Kissela, B; Kittner, S; Lloyd-Jones, D; McDermott, M; Meigs, J; Moy, C; Nichol, G; O'Donnell, CJ; Roger, V; Rumsfeld, J; Sorlie, P; Steinberger, J; Thom, T; Wasserthiel-Smoller, S; Hong, Y; American Heart Association Statistics Committee and Stroke Statistics Subcommittee. Heart disease and stroke statistics--2007 update: a report from the American Heart Association Statistics Committee and Stroke Statistics Subcommittee. *Circulation* 2007;115:e69-171.

[17] Mcalister, FA; Lawson, FM; Teo, KK; Armstrong, PW. A systematic review of randomized trials of disease management programs in heart failure. *Am J Med* 2001;110:378-384.

[18] Rich, MW; Beckham, V; Wittenberg, C; Leven, CL; Freedland, KE; Carney, RM. A multidisciplinary intervention to prevent the readmission of elderly patients with congestive heart failure. *N Engl J Med* 1995;333:1190-1195.

[19] Murray, SA; Boyd, K; Kendall, M; Worth, A; Benton, TF; Clausen, H. Dying of lung cancer or cardiac failure: prospective qualitative interview study of patients and their carers in the community. *BMJ* 2002;325:929.

[20] Rogers, AE; Addington-Hall, JM; Abery, AJ; McCoy, AS; Bulpitt, C; Coats, AJ; Gibbs, JS. Knowledge and communication difficulties for patients with chronic heart failure: qualitative study. *BMJ* 2000;321:605-607.

[21] Baile, WF; Lenzi, R; Kudelka, AP; Maguire, P; Novack, D; Goldstein, M; Myers, EG; Bast, RC Jr. Improving physician-patient communication in cancer care: outcome of a workshop for oncologists. *J Cancer Educ* 1997;12:166-173.

[22] van den Brink, JL; Moorman, PW; de Boer, MF; van Bemmel, JH; Pruyn, JF; Verwoerd, CD. An information system to support the care for head and neck cancer patients. *Support Care Cancer* 2003;11:452-459.

[23] Burke, S; Kissane, DW. *Psychosocial support for breast cancer patients: a review of interventions by specialist providers: a summary of the literature 1976-1996*. Kings Cross, NSW: NHMRC National Breast Cancer Centre; 1998.

[24] Fallowfield, L; Jenkins, V; Farewell, V; Saul, J; Duffy, A; Eves, R. Efficacy of a Cancer Research UK communication skills training model for oncologists: a randomised controlled trial. *Lancet* 2002;359:650-656.

[25] Rutter DR; Iconomou G; Quine L. Doctor-patient communication and outcome in cancer patients: an intervention. *Psychology and Health* 1996;12:57-71.

[26] Morrow, DG; Weiner, M; Deer, MM; Young, JM; Dunn, S; McGuire, P; Murray, MD. Patient-centered instructions for medications prescribed for the treatment of heart failure. *Am J Geriatr Pharmacother* 2004;2:44-52.

[27] Dracup, K; Baker, DW; Dunbar, SB; Dacey, RA; Brooks, NH; Johnson, JC; Oken, C; Massie, BM. Management of heart failure. II. Counseling, education, and lifestyle modifications. *JAMA* 1994;272:1442-1446.

[28] Wehby, D; Brenner, PS. Perceived learning needs of patients with heart failure. *Heart Lung* 1997;28:31-40.

[29] McCarthy, M; Hall, JA; Ley, M. Communication and choice in dying from heart disease. *J R Soc Med* 1997;90:128-131.

[30] McCarthy, M; Lay, M; Addington-Hall, J. Dying from heart disease. *J R Coll Physicians Lond* 1996;30:325-328.

[31] Formiga, F; Chivite, D; Ortega, C; Casas, S; Ramón, JM; Pujol, R. End-of-life preferences in elderly patients admitted for heart failure. *QJM* 2004;97:803-808.

[32] Chan, AD; Reid, GJ; Farvolden, P; Deane, ML; Bisaillon, S. Learning needs of patients with congestive heart failure. *Can J Cardiol* 2003;19:413-417.

[33] Benatar, D; Bondmass, M; Ghitelman, J; Avitall, B. Outcomes of chronic heart failure. *Arch Intern Med* 2003;163:347-352.

[34] Artinian, NT; Magnan, M; Christian, W; Lange, MP. What do patients know about their heart failure? *Appl Nurs Res* 2002;15:200-208.

[35] Gary, R. Self-care practices in women with diastolic heart failure. *Heart Lung* 2006;35:9-19.

[36] Schnell, KN; Naimark, BJ; McClement, SE. Influential factors for self-care in ambulatory care heart failure patients: a qualitative perspective. *Can J Cardiovasc Nurs* 2006;16:13-19.

[37] Caldwell, MA; Peters, KJ; Dracup, KA. A simplified education program improves knowledge, self-care behavior, and disease severity in heart failure patients in rural settings. *Am Heart J* 2005;150:983.

[38] Koelling, TM; Johnson, ML; Cody, RJ; Aaronson, KD. Discharge education improves clinical outcomes in patients with chronic heart failure. *Circulation* 2005;111:179-185.

[39] Fried, TR; Bradley, EH. What matters to seriously ill older persons making end-of-life treatment decisions?: A qualitative study. *J Palliat Med* 2003;6:237-244.

[40] Ong, LM; de Haes, JC; Hoos, AM; Lammes, FB. Doctor-patient communication: a review of the literature. *Soc Sci Med* 1995;40:903-918.

[41] Tattersall, MH; Butow, PN; Clayton, JM. Insights from cancer patient communication research. *Hematol Oncol Clin North Am* 2002;16:731-743.

[42] Stevens, LM. Heart Failure. *JAMA* 2002;287:676.

[43] Zambroski, CH. Qualitative analysis of living with heart failure. *Heart Lung* 2003;32:32-40.

[44] Lee, SJ; Back, AL; Block, SD; Stewart, SK. Enhancing physician-patient communication. *Hematology Am Soc Hematol Educ Program* 2002;:464-83.

[45] Ellis, PM; Tattersall, MH. Consensus guidelines on disclosure of a cancer diagnosis may be helpful; "How should doctors communicate the diagnosis of cancer to patients?" *Ann Med* 1999;31:336-341.

[46] Hagerty, RG; Butow, PN; Ellis, PM; Lobb, EA; Pendlebury, SC; Leighl, N; MacLeod, C; Tattersall, MH. Communicating with realism and hope: incurable cancer patients' views on the disclosure of prognosis. *J Clin Oncol* 2005;3:1278-1288.

[47] Parker, P; Baile, W; de Moor, C; Lenzi, R; Kudelka, A; Cohen L. Breaking bad news about cancer: patients' preferences for communication. *J Clin Oncol* 2001;19:2049-2056.

[48] Sardell, S; Trieweiler, A. Disclosing the cancer diagnosis. Procedures that influence patient hopefulness. *Cancer* 1993;72:3355-3365.

[49] Fogarty, LA; Curbow, BA; Wingard, JR; McDonnell, K; Somerfield, MR. Can 40 seconds of compassion reduce patient anxiety? *J Clin Oncol* 1999;17:371-379.

[50] Tattersall, MH. Consultation audio-tapes: an information aid, and a quality assurance and research tool. *Support Care Cancer* 2002;10:217-221.

[51] Tayler, M; Ogden, J. Doctors' use of euphemisms and their impact on patients' beliefs about health: an experimental study of heart failure. *Patient Educ Couns* 2005;57:321-326.

[52] Dunn, S; Patterson, P; Butow, PN; Smartt, HH; McCarthy, WH; Tattersall, MH. Cancer by another name: a randomized trial of the effects of euphemism and uncertainty in communicating with cancer patients. *J Clin Oncol* 1993;11:989-996.

[53] Quirt, CF; MacKillop, WJ; Ginsburg, AD; Sheldon, L; Brundage, M; Dixon, P; Ginsburg, L. Do doctor's know when their patients don't? A survey of doctor-patient communication in lung cancer. *Lung Cancer* 1997;18:1-20.

[54] O'Connor, AM; Rostom, A; Fiset, V; Tetroe, J; Entwistle, V; Llewellyn-Thomas, H; Holmes-Rovner, M; Barry, M; Jones, J. Decision aids for patients facing health treatment or screening decisions: systematic review. *BMJ* 1999;319:731-734.

[55] Earle, CC; Neville, BA; Landrum, MB; Ayanian, JZ; Block, SD; Weeks, JC. Trends in the aggressiveness of cancer care near the end of life. *J Clin Oncol* 2004;22:315-321.

[56] Elit, LM; Levine, MN; Gafni, A; Whelan, TJ; Doig, G; Streiner, DL; Rosen, B. Patients' preferences for therapy in advanced epithelial ovarian cancer: development, testing, and application of a bedside decision instrument. *Gynecol Oncol* 1996;62:329-335.

[57] Ravdin, PM; Siminoff, LA; Davis, GJ; Mercer, MB; Hewlett, J; Gerson, N; Parker, HL. Computer program to assist in making decisions about adjuvant therapy for women with early breast cancer. *J Clin Oncol* 2001;19:980-991.

[58] Whelan, T; Sawka, C; Levine, M; Gafni, A; Reyno, L; Willan, A; Julian, J; Dent, S; Abu-Zahra, H; Chouinard, E; Tozer, R; Pritchard, K; Bodendorfer, I. Helping patients make informed choices: a randomized trial of a decision aid for adjuvant chemotherapy in lymph node-negative breast cancer. *J Natl Cancer Inst* 2003;95:581-587.

[59] Butow, PN; Dunn, SM; Tattersall, MH; Jones, QJ. Patient participation in the cancer consultation: evaluation of a question prompt sheet. *Ann Oncol* 1994;5:199-204.

[60] Hack, TF; Pickles, T; Bultz, BD; Ruether, JD; Weir, LM; Degner, LF; Mackey, JR. Impact of providing audiotapes of primary adjuvant treatment consultations to women with breast cancer: a multisite, randomized, controlled trial. *J Clin Oncol* 2003;21:4138-4144.

[61] Johnson, IA; Adelstein, DJ. The use of recorded interviews to enhance physician-patient communication. *J Cancer Educ* 1991;6:99-102.

[62] Dunn, SM; Butow, PN; Tattersall, MH; Jones, QJ; Sheldon, JS; Taylor, JJ; Sumich, MD. General information tapes inhibit recall of the cancer consultation. *J Clin Oncol* 1993;11:2279-2285.

[63] McClement, SE; Hack, TF. Audio-taping the oncology treatment consultation: a literature review. *Patient Educ Couns* 1999;36:229-238.

[64] Street, RL Jr; Gordon, HS; Ward, MM; Krupat, E; Kravitz, RL. Patient participation in medical consultations: why some patients are more involved than others. *Medical Care* 2005;43:960-969.

[65] Degner, LF; Sloan, JA. Decision making during serious illness: what role do patients really want to play? *J Clin Epidemiol* 1992;45:941-950.

[66] Degner, LF; Kristjanson, LJ; Bowman, D; Sloan, JA; Carriere, KC; O'Neil, J; Bilodeau, B; Watson, P; Mueller, B. Information needs and decisional preferences in women with breast cancer. *JAMA* 1997;277:1485-1492.

[67] Cassileth, BR; Zupkis, RV; Sutton-Smith, K; March, V. Information and participation preferences among cancer patients. *Ann Intern Med* 1980;92:832-836.

[68] Bensing, J. Doctor-patient communication and the quality of care. *Soc Sci Med* 1991;32:1301-1310.

[69] Weeks, JC; Cook, EF; O'Day, SJ; Peterson, LM; Wenger, N; Reding, D; Harrell, FE; Kussin, P; Dawson, NV; Connors, AF Jr; Lynn, J; Phillips, RS. Relationship between

cancer patients' predictions of prognosis and their treatment preferences. *JAMA* 1998;279:1709-1714.

[70] Hagerty, RG; Butow, PN; Ellis, PM; Dimitry, S; Tattersall, MH. Communicating prognosis in cancer care: a systematic review of the literature. *Ann Oncol* 2005;16:1005-1053.

[71] Fiset, V; O'Connor, AM; Evans, W; Graham, I; Degrasse, C; Logan, J. Development and evaluation of a decision aid for patients with stage IV non-small cell lung cancer. *Health Expect* 2000;3:125-136.

[72] Brundage, MD; Feldman-Stewart, D; Cosby, R; Gregg, R; Dixon, P; Youssef, Y; Mackillop, WJ. Cancer patients' attitudes toward treatment options for advanced non-small cell lung cancer: implications for patient education and decision support. *Patient Educ Couns* 2001;45:149-157.

[73] Brundage, MD; Feldman-Stewart, D; Cosby, R; Gregg, R; Dixon, P; Youssef, Y; Davies, D; Mackillop, WJ. Phase I study of a decision aid for patients with locally advanced non-small-cell lung cancer. *J Clin Oncol* 2001;19:1326-1335.

[74] Cassileth, BR; Soloway, MS; Vogelzang, NJ; Schellhammer, PS; Seidmon, EJ; Hait, HI; Kennealey, GT. Patients' choice of treatment in stage D prostate cancer. *Urology* 1989;33:57-62.

[75] Chadwick, DJ; Gillatt, DA; Gingell, JC. Medical or surgical orchidectomy: the patients' choice. *BMJ* 1991;302:572.

[76] Molenaar, S; Sprangers, MA; Postma-Schuit, FC; Rutgers, EJ; Noorlander, J; Hendriks, J; de Haes, HC. Feasibility and effects of decision aids. *Med Decis Making* 2000;20:112-127.

[77] Ramirez, AJ; Graham, J; Richards, MA; Cull, A; Gregory, WM. Mental health of hospital consultants: the effects of stress and satisfaction at work. *Lancet* 1996;347:724-728.

[78] Girgis, A; Sanson-Fisher, RW; McCarthy, WH. Communicating with patients: surgeons' perceptions of their skills and need for training. *Aust N Z J Surg* 1997;67:775-780.

[79] Fallowfield, L; Lipkin, M; Hall, A. Teaching senior oncologists communication skills: Results from phase 1 of a comprehensive longitudinal programme in the United Kingdom. *J Clin Oncol* 1998;16:1961-1968.

[80] Maguire, P; Booth, K; Elliott, C; Jones, B. Helping health professionals involved in cancer care acquire key skills -- the impact of workshops. *Eur J Cancer* 1996;32A:1486-1489.

[81] Association of American Medical Colleges. *Report III: Contemporary Issues in Medicine: Communication in Medicine*. Medical School Objectives Project. Washington, DC: Association of American Medical Colleges; 1999.

[82] Back, AL; Arnold, RM; Tulsky, JA; Baile, WF; Fryer-Edwards, KA. Teaching communication skills to medical oncology fellows. *J Clin Oncol* 2003;21:2433-2436.

[83] Back, AL; Arnold, RM; Baile, WF; Fryer-Edwards, KA; Alexander, SC; Barley, GE; Gooley, TA; Tulsky, JA. Efficacy of Communication Skills Training for Giving Bad News and Discussing Transitions to Palliative Care. *Arch Intern Med* 2007;167:453-460.

[84] Branch, WT; Arky, RA; Woo, B; Stoeckle, JD; Levy, DB; Taylor, WC. Teaching medicine as a human experience: a patient-doctor relationship course for faculty and first-year medical students. *Ann Intern Med* 1991;114:482-489.

[85] Kern, DE; Grayson, M; Barke, LR; Roca, RP; Cole, KA; Roter, D; Golden, AS. Residency training in interviewing skills and the psychosocial domain of medical practice. *J Gen Intern Med* 1989;4:421-431.

[86] Smith, RC; Lyles, JS; Mettler, J; Stoffelmayr, BE; Van Egeren, LF; Marshall, AA; Gardiner, JC; Maduschke, KM; Stanley, JM; Osborn, GG; Shebroe, V; Greenbaum, RB. The effectiveness of intensive training for residents in interviewing. A randomized, controlled study. *Ann Intern Med* 1998;128:118-126.

[87] Meyer, TJ; Mark, MM. Effects of psychosocial interventions with adult cancer patients: a meta-analysis of randomized experiments. *Health Psychol* 1995;14:101-108.

[88] Sheard, T; Maguire, P. The effect of psychological interventions on anxiety and depression in cancer patients: results of two meta-analyses. *Br J Cancer* 1999;80:1770-1780.

[89] Devine, D; Parker, PA; Fouladi, RT; Cohen, L. The association between social support, intrusive thoughts, avoidance, and adjustment following an experimental cancer treatment. *Psychooncology* 2003;12:453-462.

[90] Houtzager, BA; Grootenhuis, MA; Hoekstra-Weebers, JE; Caron, HN; Last, BF. Psychosocial functioning in siblings of paediatric cancer patients one to six months after diagnosis. *Eur J Cancer* 2003;39:1423-1432.

[91] Petruson, KM; Silander, EM; Hammerlid, EB. Effects of psychosocial intervention on quality of life in patients with head and neck cancer. *Head Neck* 2003;25:576-584.

[92] Pitceathly, C; Maguire, P. The psychological impact of cancer on patients' partners and other key relatives: a review. *Eur J Cancer* 2003;39:1517-1524.

[93] Institute of Medicine. *Clinical Practice Guidelines: Directions for a New Program*. Field, MJ; Lohr, KN (Eds). Washington, DC: National Academy Press; 1990.

[94] Institute of Medicine. *Guidelines for clinical practice: from development to use*. Field, MJ; Lohr ,KN (Eds). Washington, D.C: National Academy Press; 1992.

[95] Fallowfield, L; Jenkins, V: Communicating sad, bad, and difficult news in medicine. *Lancet* 2004;363:312-319.

[96] Ptacek JT; Eberhardt TL: Breaking bad news: A review of the literature. *JAMA* 1996;276:496-502.

[97] Von Roenn, JH. Are we the barrier? *J Clin Oncol* 2001;19:4273-4274.

[98] Eggly, E; Penner, L; Albrecht, TL; Cline, RJW; Foster, T; Naughton, M; Peterson, A; Ruckdeschel, JC. Discussing Bad News in the Outpatient Oncology Clinic: Rethinking Current Communication Guidelines. *J Clin Oncol* 2006;24:716-719.

[99] The National Comprehensive Cancer Network. NCCN Practice Guidelines for Distress Management; 2005. http://www.nccn.org. Accessed September 20, 2007.

[100] National Breast Cancer Centre, *National Cancer Control Initiative Clinical practice guidelines for the psychosocial care of adults with cancer*. Camperdown, NSW: National Breast Cancer Centre; 2003.

[101] National Breast Cancer Centre. *Psychosocial clinical practice guidelines: providing information, support and counseling for women with breast cancer*. Canberra: Commonwealth of Australia; 2000.

[102] Baile, WF; Kudelka, A P; Beale, EA; Glober, GA; Myers, EG; Greisinger, A J; Bast, RC; Goldstein, MG; Novack, D; Lenzi, R. Communication skills training in oncology. Description and preliminary outcomes of workshops on breaking bad news and managing patient reactions to illness. *Cancer* 1999;86:887-897.

[103] Baile, W F; Glober, G.A; Lenzi, R; Beale, EA; Kudelka, A P. Discussing disease progression and end-of-life decisions. *Oncology* 1999;13:1021-1031.

[104] Braun, KL; Pietsch, JH; Blanchette, PL. *Cultural issues in end of life decision making*. Thousand Oaks, CA: Sage Publications; 2000.

[105] The Hastings Center. *Guidelines on the Termination of Life-Sustaining Treatment and the Care of the Dying*. Briarcliff Manor, NY: Hastings Center; 1987.

[106] Girgis, A; Sanson-Fisher, RW: Breaking bad news: Consensus guidelines for medical practitioners. *J Clin Oncol* 1995;13:2449-2456.

[107] Mystakidou, K; Parpa, E; Tsilila, E; Katsouda, E; Vlahos, L. Cancer information disclosure in different cultural contexts. *Support Care Cancer* 2004;12:147-154.

[108] Kagawa-Singer, M; Blackhall, LJ. Negotiating cross-cultural issues at the end of life: "You got to go where he lives." *JAMA* 2001;286:2993-3001.

[109] Crawley, LM; Marshall, PA; Lo, B; Koenig, BA; End-of-Life Care Consensus Panel. Strategies for culturally effective end-of-life care. *Ann Intern Med* 2002;136:673-679.

[110] Elwyn, TS; Fetters, MD; Sasaki, H; Tsuda, T. Responsibility and cancer disclosure in Japan. *Soc Sci Med* 202;54:281-293.

[111] Lee, A; Wu, HY. Diagnosis disclosure in cancer patients: When the family says "no!" *Singapore Med J* 2002;43:533-538.

[112] Reisfield, GM; Wilson, GR. *Fast Facts and Concepts #144; Prognostication in Heart Failure*. October, 2005. End-of-Life Physician Education Resource Center www.eperc.mcw.edu. Accessed September 20, 2007.

[113] Ponikowski, P; Anker, SD; Chua, TP; Szelemej, R; Piepoli, M; Adamopoulos, S; Webb-Peploe, K; Harrington, D; Banasiak, W; Wrabec, K; Coats, AJ. Depressed heart rate variability as an independent predictor of death in chronic congestive heart failure secondary to ischemic or idiopathic dilated cardiomyopathy. *Am J Cardiol* 1997;79:1645-1650.

[114] Swan, JW; Anker, SD; Walton, C; Godsland, IF; Clark, AL; Leyva, F; Stevenson, JC; Coats, AJ. Insulin resistance in chronic heart failure: relation to severity and etiology of heart failure. *J Am Coll Cardiol* 1997;30:527-532.

[115] Liu, P; Arnold, JM; Belenkie, I; Demers, C; Dorian, P; Gianetti, N; Haddad, H; Howlett, J; Ignazewski, A; Jong, P; McKelvie, R; Mo,e G; Parker, JD; Rao, V; Rouleau, JL; Teo, K; Tsuyuki, R; White, M; Huckel, V; Issac, D; Johnstone, D; LeBlanc, H; Lee, H; Newton, G; Niznick, J; Ros,s H; Roth, S; Roy, D; Smith, S; Sussex, B; Yusuf, S; Canadian Cardiovascular Society. The 2002/3 Canadian Cardiovascular Society consensus guideline update for the diagnosis and management of heart failure. *Can J Cardiol* 2003;19:347-356.

[116] Hobbs, FD; Kenkre, JE; Roalfe, AK; Davis, RC; Hare, R; Davies, MK. Impact of heart failure and left ventricular systolic dysfunction on quality of life: a cross-sectional study comparing common chronic cardiac and medical disorders and a representative adult population. *Eur Heart J* 2002;23:1867-1876.

[117] Willenheimer, R; Rydberg, E; Cline, C; Broms, K; Hillberger, B; Oberg, L; Erhardt, L. Effects on quality of life, symptoms and daily activity 6 months after termination of an exercise training programme in heart failure patients. *Int J Cardiol* 2001;77:25-31.

[118] Freedland, KE; Carney, RM. Psychosocial considerations in elderly patients with heart failure. *Clin Geriatr Med* 2000;16:649-661.

[119] Koenig, HG. Depression in hospitalized older patients with congestive heart failure. *Gen Hosp Psychiatry* 1998;20:29-43.

[120] Cleland, JG; Massie, BM; Packer, M. Sudden death in heart failure: vascular or electrical? Eur *J Heart Fail* 1999;1:41-45.

[121] Meredith, C; Symonds, P; Webster, L; Lamont, D; Pyper, E; Gillis, CR; Fallowfield, L. Information needs of cancer patients in west Scotland: cross sectional survey of patients' views. *BMJ* 1996;313:724-726.

[122] Lynn, J; Harrell, F Jr; Cohn, F; Wagner, D; Connors, AF Jr. Prognoses of seriously ill hospitalized patients on the days before death: implications for patient care and public policy. *New Horiz* 1997;5:56-61.

[123] Tumulty, PA. *The effective clinician.* Philadelphia: W.B. Saunders; 1973.

[124] Charles, C; Whelan, T; Gafni, A. What do we mean by partnership in making decisions about treatment? *BMJ* 1999;319:780-782.

[125] Michie, S; Miles, J; Weinman, J. Patient-centredness in chronic illness: what is it and does it matter? *Patient Educ Couns* 2003;51:197-206.

[126] Brown, JB; Stewart, M; Ryan, BL. *Assessing Communication Between Patients and Physicians: The Measure of Patient-Centered Communication (MPCC).* 2nd Ed. Working Paper Series. London: Centre for Studies in Family Medicine; 2001.

[127] Cummins, R. *AARP North Carolina End of Life Care Survey: African American Members.* Washington, D.C.: AARP Knowledge Management; 2003.

[128] Street, RL Jr; Voigt, B; Geyer, C Jr; Manning, T; Swanson, GP. Increasing patient involvement in choosing treatment for early breast cancer. *Cancer* 1995;76:2275-2285.

[129] Takayama, T; Yamazaki, Y; Katsumata, N. Relationship between outpatients' perceptions of physicians' communications styles and patients' anxiety levels in a Japanese oncology setting. *Soc Sci Med* 2001;53:1335-1350.

whether patients are radically operated upon or just followed without special therapy over 6.2 yrs. (Holmberg et al. 2002 [4]) although cancer-related mortality was lower with prostatectomy with its risk of erectile incompetence. It is the patient's decision whether he wishes a statistically longer life with reduced quality or a potentially shortened but sexually happy life. Medically none of the decisions is superior. It is according to Wennberg (2004) a "preference-sensitive decision" (Mullhan 2004 [5]).

Unconsciously based upon the three suppositions in the paternalistic model, it is the cognitive-rational superiority in knowledge and experience of the doctor who dominates the patient and his or her non-sceptical confidence.

In the *"contract model"* patient and physician are legally and morally bound to an agreement which is based upon full reciprocal information in both directions as far as medical needs are concerned. The contract [6] includes (information about) diagnostic and therapeutic possibilities with their inherent risks and benefits and the alternatives. The patient has legal claims for best possible medical standards, for confidentiality, respect of his will and health needs. But he is also obliged to cooperative duties, e. g. the duty of consent, of compliance and the obligation to reveal medically relevant data (e.g. allergies, risk factors, actual medication etc.). Non-obedience to these obligations may reduce the legal claim for damage against the doctor. Clinical decision will be made on the basis of mutual information strictly within the frame of the contract.

There is a trend towards a *supplier-customer model* at least in Germany in which the doctor offers medical options and full information about pros and cons leaving the decision to the patient who may well get additional information from other people or from the internet or elsewhere. Since he has paid for full examination and treatment by insurance fees he is ready to claim for any medical measurement. Decisions are made by the patient. The main emphasis is put on his autonomy and his or her right of self-determination.

The model corresponds to the *expert-client model* and, as decision making is concerned, to the *informed patient model.* These models regard the cognitive and rational and psychological asymmetry in the patient-physician relationship as constitutive and they accept the patient's dependence upon the doctor's knowledge and experience. The illness and discomfort of the patient is reduced (!) to a definable disease with its medical problems. It is the expert's role and factual responsibility to decide about medical aspects whereas the patient denies any responsibility even to the point of regression in its psychoanalytical meaning.

The *physician-as-agent model* [7] stresses the informational, i.e. the cognitive asymmetry between the patient and the physician. Physicians are experts as far as medical, technical experiences are concerned. Patients, however, know better how the different medical measures accord to their health expectations, their health belief and lifestyle. Knowledge and existential preferences do not correspond to each other but are on different levels in the patient's desire. The patient therefore has to communicate his or her preferences to the doctor who now is the "decision-maker" and who assumes responsibility for the patient's best benefit and well-being.

With the *interpretive and deliberative model* the patient is given full information but with careful consideration and well weighed advice, taking into account psychological and social conditions as, e.g., fears, ignorance, personal preferences etc. Information will include the significance of the actual status and prognosis, possible means of diagnostics and treatment with risks and results to be expected. It also includes the information about uncertainties of any medical procedure.

In another model of patient-physician relationship according to the so-called *anthropologic medicine* (Viktor von Weizsäcker) the constitutive asymmetry is adequately taken into consideration. It stresses, however, the personal* and biographical dimension of an illness as potentially existential, life-shaking or -threatening, bringing men's fundamental contingency to consciousness. This is looked at as a general "condition humaine" underlying the intersubjective solidarity of patient and physician. Men's further constitutive features are also taken into account, e.g., his being a somatic and mental person, his temporality and biography, his sociality and the meaningfulness of his life even during his illness. This patient-centred model (Balint) [8] broadens the understanding of man and his affectability by illness, disease and death as a "bio-psycho-social" being (Engel [9]; Uexküll & Wesiack [10]; Weizsäcker [11]). Decision making in this model is aware of emotions, fears, self-interpretation, personal preferences, the effects of the "medical system" on daily life and future perspectives.

Considering the various models with regard to their influence on the mutual part patients and doctors play in clinical decision making one can confine them to three or four models [12,13]:

a) the paternalistic model,
b) the supplier-customer or informed patient or expert-client model
c) the deliberative or interpretive or shared decision model

**Table 1. Conceptual framework for clinical decision making**

| Analytical stages | Models | Paternalistic | Shared | Informed |
|---|---|---|---|---|
| Information | Flow<br>Direction<br>Type<br>Amount* | one way (mainly)<br>Physician > patient<br>Medical<br>Minimally legally required | two way<br>Physician ↔ patient<br>medical & personal<br>All relevant for decision-making | one way (mainly)<br>Physician > patient<br>Medical<br>All relevant for decision-making |
| Deliberation | | Physician alone or with other physicians | Physician and patient (plus potential others) | Patient (plus potential others) |
| Deciding on treatment to implement | | Physicians | Physician and patient | Patient |

*Minimum required

* „personal" in our context does not mean individual but personal as men's personhood and dignity is concerned.

Flow of medical information about medical management is predominantly one-way from physician to patient in the paternalistic model. In the informed patient model, corresponding to the supplier-customer or expert-client model, the transfer, again, is from the doctor to the patient. Deliberation processes can be supported by information from other doctors ("second opinion") or any other person. The final decision, however, is to be made by the patient with all the responsibilities.

Reducing the models to three according to Charles et al. (1999) [14] the main differences are summarized in Table 1.

The above-mentioned features of patient-physician relationship are not definitely restricted to the models named. They overlap and vary throughout the process of the mutual needs. They, however, characterize certain attitudes on both sides of the dyad.

## ASYMMETRY OF PATIENT-PHYSICIAN RELATIONSHIP

Whatever type of patient-physician relationship, there always remains an inevitable asymmetry of cognitive-rational and functional vs. an emotional, psychological and existential involvement in the situation of illness and disease, resp. This asymmetry is essential throughout the process from the first meeting to the end of treatment, although its grade or extent fluctuates. The doctor, of course, will have the responsibility for the appropriate diagnostic and therapeutic measures to be recommended and finally chosen. Rationality and objectivity are on his side. The patient is more or less emotionally concerned and may be struck in his existential self-confidence and faithfulness, realizing his contingency or affectability by disease and dying. This constitutive asymmetry burdens both partners of the dyad on the factual knowledge-related and the emotional level of being involved in the decision process with its often obscure perspective.

**Asymmetry of Patient-Physician-Relationship**

| Patient | Physician |
|---|---|
| Helplessness, perplexity | competence, routine |
| Need for help | matter-of-factness |
| Somatic, psychological, mental | impartiality |
| Social, existential involvement | objectivity |
| unforseeable duration of illness | momentary contact for help |
| "de-socialization" | pressure of expectations of the patient. |
| incapacitation | legal and moral obligation of decision |
| psychological regression refusal of responsibility | burden of responsibility |
| needs, demands and claims | confidentiality |
| Claim for information | obligation of information |
| Obligation of compliance and | acceptance of the patient's |
| Toleration | decision |

This asymmetry is like a red thread throughout the physician's acting for the patient. It has to be taken into consideration in clinical decision making, in particular in shared decision making. It brings about a bilateral burden – both for the patient and the physician. Regarding this, it seems obvious that the patient-physician relationship cannot renounce a "moderate paternalism", i.e. the patient needs counselling and advice above information and instruction. Decision making and performing depends on "informed consent".

## Shared Decision Making in the Context of Clinical Indication

It is within this interactive relationship that clinical indication has to be considered. This is a rather complex term which has to be thoroughly analysed although it is a widely, however, often inconsiderately or rashly used term which guides medical acting is one.

As a provisional definition, indication is the rational reasoning for any "clinical acting" for a person asking for medical help.

First of all, it has a pivotal function between all the steps of the process from the first encounter of the patient and the doctor to the very end of treatment and final epicritical judgment. It is the joint between perception, reasoning and acting – each in its broadest meaning. Indication should guide medical questioning while taking the patient's medical history and constructing the primary "picture of complaints" and trying to get on a diagnostic lane by differential-diagnostic exclusion and approximation towards a best possible, etiologically and pathogenetically plausible diagnosis and then to the appropriate therapy. Indication also has its pivotal function for the prognostic judgment which the patient is highly interested in.

Asked for the meaning of clinical indication, most medical students and even experienced clinicians would probably answer that it is the motivation and substantiation for his "acting" for the patient: "why shall I do this or that?" Asking "why...?" has two directions: backwards to preconditions and other factors determining the development of the actual illness or disease and its further course to be expected as well as the patient's coping attitudes and compliance with a view to the future. What is the goal of medical acting? What will be the prognosis of the disease once treatment is started? It is the Janus-faced clinical indication that shows the obvious interdependence of anamnesis and prognosis, the past and the future, both looked at as steps in the doctor's judging and acting.

Indication is at least two-dimensional: it is based upon factual, "objective" clinical reasons and individual, "subjective" and personal grounds. Within the clinical context one has to ask: what is "objectivity"? Viktor von Weizsäcker, one of the German inaugurators of psychosomatic medicine, differentiates between scientific and clinical objectivity which includes the patient's feelings, self-interpretation, the meaning of his illness in the biographical context, preferences for longer or better life (a qualitative and quantitative prognosis). In addition to the medical, scientific objectivity, it is this "clinical objectivity" that the physician caring for the patient has to take into account [16].

"Medical acting" does not only mean the performance of diagnostic or therapeutic procedures but also the overall interactive communication, the way of asking, arguing and examining the patient as well as medical reasoning and judging. These are bound to five modalities of human life: whether we must, we are ought to or allowed to or inclined to ... or, finally, whether we are able to do what we do as professionals. This is – according to Weizsäcker – the so-called pathic pentagram [17] which the doctor cannot escape from in clinical decision making. What the doctor *must do* is mainly determined by "objective data": the perhaps life-threatening findings, the patient's complaints and demands, the clinical picture or the diagnosis. Sometimes the social or scientific community dictate what the doctor has got to do. What he *ought to* do is in many instances more a moral decision, oriented by individual complaints, wishes or demands or by individual or social values including relief of pain and suffering, anxiety and other emotional stress. It is the moral codex of acting as a doctor. What he is *allowed to do*, again, is regulated by moral and legal rules (including "informed consent") and rights and individual and cultural barriers. What the doctor *wants to* do is determined by the patient's justifiable demands and by his own conviction and conscience. With his apparent spontaneity the doctor is influenced by the "objective" scientific and moral order – as far as the allowance and the capabilities are given. This, finally, is one of the prerequisites of medical acting: that the doctor is capable of performing what he decides to do. Although it seems self-evident, this prerequisite is sometimes violated.

Clinical indication and clinical decision making in particular takes place within this "pentagram". The strength of obligation of the five modalities as they determine medical acting varies dependent upon the clinical situation, the patient, the doctor, upon institutional and social circumstances. The changing superiority of one or the other of those determinants reflects the differences between objective and subjective aims.

Considering these five modalities of clinical acting, the question of clinical indication turns to the more complex question why and on what grounds the clinician has to decide on the "must, shall, allowance, wish and ability to do this or that for his patient?" And who is it who decides: the patient, the individual doctor, the team, the family or the social and scientific or the cultural community?

The core of this complex question is of course the factual medical situation and the possibility to influence it by medical means for the benefit of the patient. Treatment can be symptom-, etiology-, pathogenesis- or prognosis-centred with grades of urgency from so-called relative or prophylactic to "absolute" or vital indication. It is always an act of decision making, not an "objective" date or "fact". Making a decision considers this actual and individual and situational process.

This process has to regard the available methods of diagnostic and therapeutic procedures including their statistical relevance, reliability and effectiveness. It is an inevitable dilemma that clinical decision making which is obviously aimed at an individual patient, has to be based upon statistical, i.e. collective probabilities.

The personal part of clinical indication is still another dimension: the correspondence of patients' asking for help and the doctor giving help and care, the reciprocal confidence and responsibility. The personal dimension takes into account the personal bio-psycho-social situation of the patient in his illness. It makes a difference to see only the "objective" clinical situation or to be aware of the patient's endured complaints, his biography and existential ailment and his or her feeling of being life-threatened.

The social dimensions of clinical indication are its communicability and moral and legal justifiability. It is to be looked at in its social and economic framework and the socio-cultural values in which medicine is institutionalised.

Another aspect is the normative dimension of clinical indication: its orientation at scientific guidelines or recommendations or at evidence-based experience or ethical principles like the "Georgetown Mantra" of autonomy, beneficence, non-maleficence, justice and confidentiality [18]. The principle of "nil nocere" or – more appropriate – of "more benefit than harm" implies the anticipation of the outcome of medical acting including risks and benefits. Today, the patient's will ("voluntas ...") is often higher valued than his health ("salus aegroti suprema lex esto!") as the leading principle up to the self-determination to refuse or stop treatment in intensive care medicine which is legally protected. This obviously is one aspect of the change in patient-physician relationship outlined above.

Finally, there is the appellant aspect of indication, i.e. the doctor's obligation to follow strictly medical, moral and legal reasons for his judgment and acting "to the best of his knowledge and belief". This again points to the factual and the personal dimension of clinical indication.

Back to the fundamental question of clinical indication: what is the goal of acting as a clinician? Is it mending a defect, the cure and healing and rehabilitation of an acute or chronic disease, the re-institution of fitness for work in the meaning of life insurance, the complete physical, mental and social well-being (according to the WHO definition of health)? Is it palliation instead of cure, alleviation from suffering or is it enhancement of physical or mental capabilities (e.g. doping) or, finally, does treatment aim at overcoming a biographical, existential crisis? Those are but possible examples of reasons for therapeutic interventions. They again show the wide range of doctors' responsibilities in clinical indication. This has to consider the actual objective and subjective demands and the future consequences of any decision.

Once spelled out in its complexity, clinical indication is a multidimensional and perhaps one of the most difficult terms determining medical acting to be conscious of. It is within this framework that shared decision making is to be reflected.

## Shared Clinical Decision Making

The above-mentioned characteristics of clinical indication build up the fundament of shared clinical decision making (SDM): the differentiation of factual, medical reasons vs. personal constituents, the normative and the appellant aspects of clinical indication. SDM has also to regard men's psychosocial and cultural dimensions and his being a spiritual or religious creature. This becomes most obvious in his attitude towards end-of-life decisions, dying and death. Thus, these dimensions, although to be respected individually, are fundamental to human beings, anthropological constituents, as are men's temporality, subjectivity, rationality, sociality, the capability of being morally responsible.

With the following vignette of an everyday clinical situation we will now concentrate on SDM in particular.

Case 1

A 78 year old lady patient was admitted to our hospital because of shortness of breath, physical incapacitation and angina pectoris after recurrent episodes of left heart failure and one syncopal attack. Clinical findings of moderate to severe aortic valve stenosis was confirmed by cardiac catheterisation with a gradient of 85 mm Hg and an additional isolated stenosis of a small diagonal branch of the left anterior branch of left coronary artery. She was strictly advised by the catheter doctor to have an operation – a "clear-cut indication" for valve replacement. In a long conversation with the patient and her husband the physician caring for her explained the medical situation as a well-based justification for the advice: based upon the several episodes of left heart failure, the syncope and the angina pectoris which all would probably improve with valve replacement. The patient – surprised at the diagnosis and the doctors' recommendation – asked the doctor: "what would you do in my situation?" Asked for her hopes and for her life expectance she was even more surprised at framing the seemingly medical decision into the general perspective of her own responsibility.

## WHAT DOES SHARED DECISION MAKING MEAN?

The term "shared decision making" (SDM), in Germany called "partizipative Entscheidungsfindung" (in my opinion it would be better to call it "gemeinsam entscheiden"), is used with increasing frequency. It is fairly young [19] (according to Scheibler et al. it has been introduced by Maple in 1977 [20] and Cassileth et al. in 1980 [21]) and it is linked with the gradual shift in patient-physician relationship outlined above. It is a type of medical consultation where patients are actively involved in the process of clinical decision making by their physician. Both partners of the dyad are equal in their respective legal and moral rights. The flow of full decision-relevant information is "two-way". Patient and physician respect their criteria for the deliberative process and they both are responsible once the decision has been made. They both are involved in the control over the process that eventually aims at an "autonomous" decision by the patient.

This definition clearly shows serious implications:

- decision making as a cognitive and rational process;
- decision making has to regard personal preferences;
- it is a process of interactive communication;
- there are corresponding responsibilities on both sides;
- both, the patient and the physician take steps to actually participate in the process;
- best possible advice and honest compliance;
- the physician's final responsibility for adequate performance of the resolution.

As for the rationality or the cognitive level of medical decisions, it has to be considered that the patient has to accept the decision as a rational as well as an emotional and existential. For him it is a "pathic decision" which he cannot escape from – be it pro or contra a diagnostic or therapeutic step.

It is necessary for the physician to realize that the points of consideration are not only factual medical information but it needs psychological and social determinants and acceptance of the existential level of the patient's illness to be taken into account.

A deliberative communication style is necessary to convey this empathic understanding. Both partners are requested to open, honest conversation and mutual information as far as it is relevant to the decision at stake. The communication must not be directive in a paternalistic way. The patient should be given the opportunity to "control" the process of interaction in a corresponding way as much as the physician does; i.e. both parties take steps to actually participate in the decision process. Finally, patient and doctor are concerned at different levels. They both have to share this mutual responsibility for the decision and its consequences and sequels.

The purely legal concept of "informed consent" is a singular agreement for only one procedure at stake with the patient's power of veto. With the informed decision model, it is the patient who has the decisive vote after being fully informed about the intended management with its risks and alternatives. Shared decision making, however, involves both partners responsively in the decision process.

Several essential elements of SDM can be pinpointed [22]:

- The fundamental precondition is the respect for the autonomy and for the personality of the patient;
- An interactive, i.e. two-way communication with a careful assessment of the patient's understanding of the multidimensional facets of the decision to be made;
- A discussion of pros and cons of the options including alternatives with their respective benefits and risks;
- Although a meaningful dialogue should focus on virtually all health care decisions, it is increasingly important the more difficult and important the decision;
- Even the uncertainty of either way of decision has to be revealed;
- Furthermore, SDM needs eliciting patient's values and preferences and encouragement for claiming their personal wishes and rights and for actually participating in the process of decision.

The concept of equipoise as a prerequisite of SDM proposed by G. Elwyn [23] from the UK has to be looked at critically. Of course, the situation of equipoise with hardly any difference in the outcomes of two or more options is a fairly difficult problem where the patient is dependent upon the physician's counselling or even upon his advice. However, equipoise in the SDM model proposed is predominantly a medical, objective balance rather than a conflict between objective "facts" and the incommensurable personal reasons for or against the options. This conflict is the more important and often the more essential or existential one in comparison with the medical situation.

# DETERMINANTS OF SHARED DECISION MAKING

First of all, it is the patient's actual status of being ill and life-threatened and his concern about his condition, the need for help, the "diagnosis" or syndrome of complaints and findings with their prognosis "quoad vitae aut sanationem", i.e. with regard to the quantitative or qualitative expectance. It is not only the "objective" but also the individual "subjective" condition. Prognosis as a result of medical judgment and reasoning is based upon probabilities. It therefore subsumes the individual patient under collective experiences and applies general evidence to the singularity of the patient's situation. Prognostic judgment is bound to the scientific community and the society although it is always oriented at the best possible benefit of the ill person. It is the available spectrum of diagnostic and therapeutic options and facilities which determine decision making, including their feasibility, effectiveness and efficiency, their risks and success. The logistic, organisational and economic, the institutional conditions also have to be taken into account.

Given those "objective" determinants, there are also personal grounds of decision making: The feeling or fears of the patient for the presence as well as for the future; his bio-psycho-social situation which may more or less impede his ability for insight or cooperation, his willingness of risk, his compliance and skills, last not least the cognitive capability. It is the character of the doctor and the cooperating professionals, their knowledge, experience as well as the readiness for responsibility and for patient involvement which determines the physician's attitude towards SDM. And finally, it is the social network both partners of the dyad are bound to and supported by. Many of those determinants influence decision making more or less implicitly, however often rather efficaciously.

**Determinants of shared decision making**

- Medically objective factors:
  1. Dignity of the patient's clinical status and the underlying disease (e.g. minimally influenced or life threatened);
  2. diagnostic efficacy of the procedure thought of;
  3. therapeutic success to be expected;
  4. prognostic relevance of either of the procedures and of clinical signs and symptoms.
- Personal subjective factors:
  1. the patient's reasonable wishes, values and preferences;
  2. thorough, however appropriate information according to the patient's rationality and capability of understanding and reasoning (mental state);
  3. the patient's values and preferences as for his or her health and quality and life expectancy;
  4. the patient's "psychology".

## Medical Facets of Shared Decision Making

Once again, SDM is a process of judgment based upon "objective" findings and the estimation of their diagnostic and even more their prognostic dignity. According to the two categorically different (although inseparable) levels of personal and factual patient-physician relationship, clinical decision making has to take into account these two levels of reasoning.

The hitherto discussed situation is valid for the usual adult patient, mentally alert and not in any way incapacitated. Difficulties may arise in this group of patients whenever the well informed, rationally capable and ready-to-decide patient decides against the physician's advice. In this case the doctor has to accept the self-determined person. He is not allowed to do anything against the patient's will even if he is convinced that the decision will have serious, even deadly consequences, e.g. refusal of operation with the foreseeable need for blood supplementation in Jehovah's Witnesses

## Decision Aids

Given the many difficulties in any model of patient-physician relationship, it is necessary to think about possibilities to facilitate and to encourage patients' involvement in DM. Both, patients and doctors have to be regarded. Several studies have focused on patient-physician communication with regard to patients' involvement in the process [24]. They clearly demonstrate that patients do feel best the better the communication on the side of the physician. Gravel et al. (2006) [25] reported about three main facilitators for implementing SDM into practice: the provider's motivation, the positive impact on the clinical process and the positive impact on patients' outcome. Patients will be better motivated to share the decision process when they are asked for their own expectances and their thoughts about their illness and its explanation. Patients have to be encouraged to ask questions. Information sheets or formulas or brochures are only a surrogate for verbal, personal information and explanation. Better training of medical students and doctors for more adequate communication and developing a non-paternalistic attitude towards the patient is needed. Physicians can and should train at risk communication as well as exploring patients' preferences and their will. Various types of respective courses have been inaugurated: Audio-video-tapes of office consultations with analyses of the physicians' skills and attitudes [26], risk communication tools [27], questionnaires of self-assessment of physicians and patients, group discussions about the rationale of SD and the "informed shared decision model" [28] and problem-specific questionnaires, e.g. for antihypertensive treatment [29], anticoagulants in atrial fibrillation, statines in hypercholesterolemia etc. Training programs in self-help associations can also promote SDM.

As shown by Edwards and Elwyn [30], in a study with eight female and twelve male General Practitioners, female doctors indicated greater support for patient involvement than their male colleagues after teaching intervention courses independent of whether a first course focused at communication skills or SDM and the second course at the other part of the program. The female doctors included in the study rated patient involvement as more important, they felt patients more likely to respond positively to involvement and they felt more competent in SDM after the second training intervention.

Although but a small study, it clearly demonstrates improvement in medical skills and SDM. As the authors comment, similar studies should be performed with larger and more widely representative samples of professionals and more preference-centred decision conflicts.

The physician should gain a flexible communication style to be able to adjust to the individual patient in his or her actual situation. He should learn to interactively communicate the necessity of shared decision on the medical and the personal level of decision (as e.g. in our vignette lady patient). He should also learn to empower the patient's arguments. This needs empathic conversation and communication and a dynamic view of decision making in general. Flexibility in response to the patient's actual needs seems most important.

The OPTION scale with its 12 items developed by Elwyn et al (2005) is but one instrument to measure patient-physician communication and the patient's contentment. The catalogue of questions serves as a means to assess to what degree clinicians involve their patients in decision making although it concentrates on the actual decision (regardless earlier episodes of illness or medical procedures and the way how the patient managed the problems then).

Summarizing the results, Barry [31] concludes that in many patients decision aids improve information for really "informed choice"; there was a trend to more conservative treatment choices (for coronary revascularization, prostatectomy and mastectomy) by patients after decision aids were offered. Heterogeneity of the results may be due to the setting and the kind of the aids including physicians' engagement, the decision to be made and its consequences.

Further investigation in this field has to consider the change in patient-physician relationship and its effect on patient-involvement. Van den Brinck-Muinen et al. [32] have shown an increase in patient-involvement, especially in younger age groups of patients, by professionals who participated in SDM and risk communication training courses. Since the articles reviewed go back to the early 90ies, comparable investigation will have to focus on more recent cohorts of patients confronted with more favourable treatment options (as for early breast cancer and prostate hypertrophy and non-surgical treatment for ischemic heart disease) and enlarged information about prognosis [33].

## Do Patients Wish and What do they Wish with Shared Decision Making?

Several surveys in Europe and in the USA show sociological differences as to the demand for SDM among (potential) patients. A questionnaire-based investigation by Böcken et al. (2004) [34] found a 60 – 83 % and 50 – 75% range of supporters in Germany and in Europe, resp., with a social gradient of 46 to 62 % in elderly people (over 65 yrs. of age) and (younger) upper class people. Similar results were found by Rosen et al. (2001) [35]. One has to differentiate between the patient's wish to be sufficiently informed and to be involved with his or her preferences and participate in the definite decision ("Informations- vs. Partizipationspräferenz" [36]).

Surveys of that kind, however, have to take into account the patient-physician relationship, the communication style of the doctor, the medical problem at hand, the management options and other co-factors of the decision process. At any rate, the clinician should ask for and support the patient's involvement.

Patients ask for more comprehensive information about their illness and disease, the diagnostic and therapeutic possibilities. They ask for the necessity of treatment, risk and benefit of various options of therapy and its influence on physical and mental life including sexuality and the rehabilitation and thus the final outcome or prognosis. Thus it needs empirical data about life expectance and quality with any type of medical treatment with its inherent probabilities of risk and benefit. These have to be adjusted to the patient's actual situation.

Achieving these goals improves coping, compliance and physical outcome of medical treatment (DiBlasi et al. 2001) [37]. As is to be expected, it is the doctor's way of allowance and attendance to the patient and of the patience and adequacy of explaining the medical part of the decision to be made still regarding personal problems, fears, values which promote patients' involvement. Finally, it is often the physician who has to point to the different dimensions of medical vs. personal decision.

## A Physician's Feeling about Shared Decision Making

Despite of the increasing experience with SDM (mainly in Great Britain) and the almost exploding literature, there is – with some delay – some empirical research going on in Germany. Preliminary results reveal a certain reluctance of physicians in accepting and implementing SDM into daily office or clinical practice. They point to the factual and psychological need for medical counselling and final decision by the doctor in charge. They also point to the patient's emotional instead of rational reasoning, to the time-consuming and costly process of deliberating the disease and the procedures at hand for the patient.

It obviously needs a deeper change in patient-physician relationship towards a partner-like communication style. A few studies of physicians' self-assessment as for their actually involving their patients give the impression that doctors often feel themselves practicing SDM although videotaped office encounters or patients' contentment questionnaires did show marked discrepancies between self-esteem and reality.

There are some subtle conflicts to be thoroughly considered:

- the inevitable, constitutive asymmetry mentioned above with its mutual burdens and the (unconscious) temptation of paternalistic communication and deciding style seemingly justified by the ignorance and the reluctance in resolution of the patient;
- the patient's tendency to leave the treatment decision to the clinician (a tendency to regression) and the physician's transfer of the decision to the patient: thus, it seems a reciprocal delegation of responsibilities.

Pertinent studies show the shortness of time for adequate conversation as one of the important impediments for SDM. Furthermore, many physicians are not able to elicit their patients' preferences and values and they are unable to appropriately communicate risk and uncertainty as for treatment options and alternatives with their respective outcomes. They often do not know the rationale and the elements of SDM and they often have a mental reservation toward the patient's rationality. Last not least, there is the concern about legal consequences.

It is, however, to be expected that along with the change in the mutual attitude of patients and physicians towards each other and with increasing skills on both sides there will be a gradually positive practice of SDM with less paternalistic interaction style.

## How Does Shared Decision Making Affect the Outcome of MEdical Procedures?

SDM is conceptualized with the aim to improve patient- and outcome-related orientation, i.e. the contentment of patients and the results of medical procedures. It is to be expected that SDM is most important in preference-sensitive decisions where no clear-cut "best" choices between two or more options exist. In these situations it is weighing the preference of the patient: whether he feels better, e.g., with operative removal of prostate hypertrophy or of a lump in her breast to reduce the uncertainty of later risk of cancer or whether both are happier with their actual quality of life including sexuality.

The outcome of SDM should not only be judged from the economical view with regard to shorter and less frequent hospital-admissions but also with regard to the personal well-being and contentment and the greater respect of personality.

## Legal Aspects of Shared Decision Making

Medical acting takes place within legal orders. So does SDM. Regardless the type of patient-physician relationship, "informed consent" is a basic prerequisite of any medical management for the patient. He or she has to be adequately informed about the disease and the indication for diagnostic and therapeutic procedures with their inherent risks. Communication should avoid harm and embarrassment for the patient.

In case of incapacitated patients or with children a well-informed and legalized surrogate person is asked to understand and accept the physician's established recommendation. In any case, seeking consent needs a process of empathic communication. Legally the patient must also be capable and entitled to consent.

The informed consent must be signed by the patient or his or her represent or proxy. The process of obtaining informed consent can become a ritualised formality which has little to do with either effective communication or even the confirmation of real choices when consent forms are signed. This is valid for SDM also.

It is within the right of self-determination that the patient has the right to refuse both information and SDM and leave the entire process to the doctor. Juridical consequences of responsibility are, in case, based on the written consent. This holds true for health insurance and for civil right. The physician is accountable for his acting for the patient because he is the expert.

**Legal aspects of shared decision making**

- "informed consent" as inevitable prerequisite for the physician's medical acting for the patient;
- the physician's obligation for sufficient and appropriate information comprehensible for the patient or his surrogate;
- accountability for the performance of the patient's consented will;
- the patient's right to refuse both information and shared decision making.

## Ethical Aspects of Shared Decision Making

Legalisation of "informed consent" as well as patients' rights is but a formal, although inevitable regulation of medical acting. The underlying principle is the patient's autonomy. This is not the same as capability or any other functional characteristic of a person, be it cognitive or emotional. Autonomy is an invulnerable constituent of mankind irrespective of the person's actual alertness or consciousness, his or her mental ability from birth to death. The person's ability can be permanently or transiently impaired so that he or she cannot claim their wills, their consent or dissent to medical treatment. In that case a relative or proxy pleads for his or her moral rights. His personality, however, is untouched. Autonomy, in addition, does not mean accountability or identification with a person's action.

Autonomy is often thought of as self-determination or independence. It is questionable whether this is applicable to the ill person who is dependent upon medical help. Is he or she really free? It is at least a rather ambivalent freedom for a choice since the patient needs information and advice and, eventually, medical acting. Therefore it is a concerted process even in the case of a well-informed, "autonomous" patient. He or she is to be respected even if they decide against the doctors' best convincement. This may raise the conflict of a possible discrepancy between the patient's self-determination and the physician's obligation for care for the patient. The patient's (presumable) will or decision is superior to the physician's advice or his values. This may include the priority of the patient's emotional or existential values to the cognitive-rational medical criteria of decision making. The right to refuse the medical information and advice is not just a legal but a personal, a moral right.

Another ethical aspect is the problem of justifiable management, e.g. the handling with resources (including time) in case of expensive procedures and to do the patient justice. Again, this is not only a legal or even an economical question but a moral duty of righteousness towards the ill person.

The conflicts given are suspended in the mutual responsibility and confidence for adequate information and conscientious cooperation and communication. This interpersonal, social process should not be thought of as purely rational and individual consideration the factual medical problem in which patient and physician are involved. Both the partners should aim at mutual understanding on the different levels of being inflicted by the disease and the decision to be made [38].

The physician's ethical obligation is to present the relevant medical facts accurately to the patient or the person responsible for him or her and to recommend management in accordance to good medical practice. The information has to be accurate, comprehensible, honest, but not in all cases complete and it has to avoid upsetting the patient. The physician has to be aware of the patient's emotional instability and of his potential tendency to regression in its psychoanalytic meaning.

This leads to the fundamental ambivalence of shared decision making: the danger of reciprocal delegation of responsibility to the respective partner, i.e. the physician or the patient or his or her surrogate.

Informed consent is a basic social policy for which exceptions are permitted: (1) where the patient is unconscious or otherwise incapable of consenting and harm from failure to treat is imminent; or (2) when risk-disclosure poses such a serious psychological threat or detrimental to the patient as to be medically contra-indicated. Social policy does not accept the paternalistic view that the physician may remain silent because divulgence might prompt the patient to forgo needed therapy (Council on Ethical and Judicial Affairs of the AMA [39]).

Along with this obligation the physician has to judge the patient's capability to reliably comprehend and to decide on the matter at stake. When others must decide for the incapacitated ill, the principles of beneficence and non-maleficence should prevail, i.e. avoiding any harm and provide best possible benefit.

### Ethical aspects of shared decision making

- autonomy and non-availability of personality;
- personal justice and adequacy to the patient;
- truth telling and risk communication without psychological harm to the patient;
- responsibility for best possible management regarding priority of patient's (presumable) will and preferences;
- incommensurability of rational (medical) and personal, existential decision for the presence and the future;
- correspondence of confidence and responsibility;
- honest, adequate communication;
- over-estimation of cognitive-rational (medical) criteria;
- patient's right to refuse information and shared decision making;
- physician's obligation to best possible care vs. patient's right of self-determination and self-responsibility;
- patient's sovereignty makes the physician more accountable for the overall management;
- fundamental ambivalence of reciprocal delegating responsibility to the partner in the dyad.

## Summary

Shared decision making (SDM) with regard to medical management has to be looked at in the framework of accountable clinical indication (CI). Both, SDM and CI, are preserved within and determined by the patient-physician relationship. Although there is a change of this relationship, there remains an inevitable and constitutive asymmetry of rational and existential concern by the patient's illness and disease. Nevertheless, it is a dyad of two morally and legally equal partners. They accept their respective values, preferences and criteria for the decision.

It is the physician's responsibility to appropriately inform the patient about prerequisites and consequences of the decision and, eventually, to perform the final resolution. The physician's interactive communication skills are necessary including weighing risks and benefits of the options, his empathetic attendance to the patient. The patient is asked for and should be encouraged in his or her readiness of being appropriately informed and to actually participate in the process of the DM. In case of incapacity a surrogate decision maker must be involved.

Patient decision aids should be offered as adjuncts to counselling (not replacements) to promote SDM as an act of self-determination.

Legal problems include those of (documented) "informed consent" as a fundamental requirement and the final responsibility. A non-directive sufficient information about options and consequences avoiding harm or embarrassment of the patient and respect for the priority of the patient's decision are legal demands.

Finally, the ethical basis of SDM is the respect for the patient's autonomy. It is the patient with his or her values and preferences who has the last word to say even if the decision will be against medical advice. The physician has to be most sensitive to the patient's tendency to regression. On the other hand, he must be aware of his own seemingly justified paternalistic way of communication and deciding. SDM is based on a fundamental correspondence of reciprocal responsibility and confidence.

Not addressed in this article are special problems of SDM in preventive, in reproductive medicine, in obstetrics and neonatology, in intensive care, in psychiatric medicine.

## References

[1] Wieland W. (1986): *Strukturwandel der Medizin und ärztliche Ethik*. Heidelberg: Universitätsverlag Carl Winter.

[2] Weizsäcker V. v. (1949): Psychosomatische Medizin. In: Achilles P, Janz D, Schrenk M, Weizsäcker C.F. v. (edit.): *Viktor von Weizsäcker Gesammelte Schriften*. Frankfurt/M.: Suhrkamp, vol. 6, pp 451 - 464.

[3] Emanuel E.J. & Emanuel L.L. (1992): Four models of the physician-patient relationship. J Amer Med Ass 267: 2221-2226; Charles C., Gafni A. & Whelan T. (1999): Decision-making in the physician-patient encounter: revisiting the shared treatment decision-making model. *Social Science & Medicine 49*: 51-661.

[4] Holmberg L, Bill-Axelson A, Helgesen F et al. (2002): A randomized trial comparing radical prostatectomy with watchful waiting in early prostate cancer. *New Engl J Med 347*: 781 – 789.

[5] Mullhan F (2004): Wrestling with Variation: An interview with Jack Wennberg. Health Affairs; Web Exclusive: Oct 7th 2004; cited in Klemperer D (2005): Shared decision making und Patientenzentrierung – vom Paternalismus zur Partnerschaft in der Medizin. Teil 1: Modelle der Arzt-Patient-Beziehung. *Balint 6*: 71 – 79.

[6] In *German Civil Right § 611 regulates the employment contract; violations of it may be persued through § 242.*

[7] Charles C., Gafni A. & Whelan T. (1999): Decision-making in the physician-patient encounter: revisiting the shared treatment decision-making model. *Social Science & Medicine 49*: 651 – 661.

[8] Balint M. (1965): *Der Arzt, sein Patient und die Krankheit*. Stuttgart: Ernst Klett.

[9] Engel G.L. (1980): The clinical application of the biopsychosocial model. *Amer J Psychiat. 137*: 535 – 544.

[10] Uexküll Th. V. & Wesiack W. (¹1988, ³1998): *Theorie der Humanmedizin*. München – Wien – Baltimore: Urban & Schwarzenberg.

[11] Weizsäcker V. v. (1948): Grundfragen anthropologischer Medizin. In: Achilles P., Janz D., Schrenk M., Weizsäcker C.F. v. (Edit.): Viktor von Weizsäcker – *Gesammelte Schriften (GS)*. Frankfurt / M. (1987): Suhrkamp. Vol. 7, pp 255 – 282. Weizsäcker V. v. (1951): Der kranke Mensch – Eine Einführung in die Medizinische Anthropologie. *GS vol. 9*, pp 311 – 641.

[12] Emanuel E.J. & Emanuel L.L. (1992): Four models of the physician-patient relationship. *J Am Med Ass 267*: 2221 – 2226.

[13] Charles C, Gafni A & Whelan T (1999): Decision-making in the physician-patient encounter: revisiting the shared treatment decision-making model. *Social Science & Medicine 49*: 651 - 661.

[14] Ibid.

[15] Ibid. Cf. Scheibler F., Janssen Ch. & Pfaff H. (2003): Shared decision making: ein Überblicksartikel über die internationale Forschungsliteratur. *Soz.-Präventivmed 48*: 11 – 24.

[16] Weizsäcker V. v. (1926): Psychotherapie und Klinik. *GS vol. 5*, pp 161-176.

[17] Weizsäcker V. v. (1956): Pathosophie. *GS vol. 10.*

[18] Beauchamp T.L. & Childress J.F. (1994): *Principles of Biomedical Ethics*. New York: Oxford University Press.

[19] Elwyn G. (2001): *Shared decision making – Patient involvement in clinical practice.* Nijmegen: Ponsen & Looijen B.V. pp 9 – 24.

[20] Maple F. F. (1977): *Shared decision making*. Beverly Hills; London: Sage (cit. in Scheibler et al. 2003).

[21] Cassileth B. R., Zupkis R.V., Sutton-Smith K. & March V. (1980): Information and participation preferences among cancer patients. *Ann Intern Med 92*: 832 – 836.

[22] Braddock C.H., Fihn St.D., Levinson W., Jonsen A.R. & Pearlman R.A. (1997): How doctors and patients discuss routine clinical decisions. Informed decision making in the outpatient setting. *J Gen Intern Med 12*: 339 – 345.

[23] Elwyn G., Edwards A., Kinnersley P. & Grol R. (2000): Shared decision making and the concept of equipoise: the competences of involving patients in healthcare choices. *Brit J Gen Pract 50*: 892 – 899 (in: Elwyn G. (2001): *Shared decision making –Patient involvement in clinical practice*. Nijmegen: Posen & Looijsen B.V., Wageningen. – This thesis is the most comprehensive and pacemaking research about SDM.

[24] Elwyn G., Hutchings H., Edwards A., Rapport F., Wensing M., Cheung W.-Y. & Grol R. (2005): The OPTION scale: Measuring the extent that clinicians involve patients in decision-making tasks. *Health Expectations 8*: 34-42. Charles C., Gafni A. & Whelan T. (1999): Decision-making in the physician-patient encounter: Revisiting the shared treatment decision-making model. *Social Science & Medicine 49*: 651-661.

[25] Gravel K., Legare F. & Graham I.D. (2006): Barriers and facilitators to implementing shared decision-making in clinical practice: a systematic review of health professionals' perceptions. *Implement Sci. Aug 9*; 1:16.

[26] Towle A., Godolphin W., Grams G. & LaMarre A. (2006): Putting informed and shared decision making into practice. *Health Expectations 9*: 321-332. Towle A. & Godolphin W. (2001): Education and training of health care professionals. In: *Evidence-based patient choice – inevitable or impossible?* (Edited by Edwards A. & Elwyn G.) Oxford: Oxford University Press 2001: 245-269. O'Connor A.M., Stacey V., Entwistle H, Llewellyn-Thomas D. et al. Decision aids for people facing health treatment or screening decisions. *The Cochrane Database of Systemic Reviews* 2003, Issue 1.

[27] Elwyn G., Edwards A., Wensing M., Hood K., Robling M., Atwell C. & Grol R. (2001): Shared decision making in primary care: a cluster randomised trial of practitioner skill development. In: Elwyn G. (2001): *Shared decision making – Patient involvement in clinical practice*. Nijmegen: Ponsen & Looijen B. V., pp 149 – 164.

[28] Charles C., Whelan T., Gafni A., Willan A, & Farrell S. (2003): Shared treatment decision making: What does it mean to physicians? *J Clin Oncol 21*: 932 – 936.

[29] Steel N. (2000): Threshold for taking antihypertensive drugs in different professional and lay groups: questionnaire survey. *Brit Med J 320*: 1446 – 1447.

[30] Edwards A. & Elwyn G. (2004): Involving patients in decision making an communicating risks: a longitudinal evaluation of doctors's attitudes and confidence during a randomized trial. *J Evaluation in Clinical Practice 10*: 431 – 437.

[31] Barry M.J. (2002): Health decision aids to facilitate shared decision making in office practice. *Ann Intern Med. 136*: 127- 135.

[32] Van den Brinck-Muinen A., van Dulmen S.M., de Haes H.C.J.M., Visser A.Ph., Schellevis F.G. & Bensing J.M. (2006): Has patients' involvement in the decision-making process changed over time? *Health Expectations 9*: 333 -342.

[33] *For the almost exploding literature about the development of shared decision making ("Partizipative Entscheidungsfindung") in Germany*, see Abstracts 4th Deutscher Kongress zum Thema Shared Decision Making. Heidelberg 30.3. – 1. 4. 2006.

[34] Böcken J., Braun B. & Schnee M. (Edit.): *Gesundheitsmonitor 2004. Die ambulante Versorgung aus Sicht von Bevölkerung und Ärzteschaft*. Verlag Bertelsmann Stiftung: Gütersloh 2004.

[35] Rosen A., Anell A. & Hjortsberg C. (2001): Patient views on choice and participation in health care. *Health Policy 55*: 1212 – 128.

[36] Cf. Scheibler F., Janssen & Ch. Pfaff H. (2003): Shared decision making: Ein Überblicksartikel über die internationale Forschungsliteratur. *Soz.- Präventivmed. 48*: 11 -24.

[37] DiBlasi Z., Harkness E., Ernst E., Georgiou A. & Kleijnen J. (2001): Influence of context effects on health outcomes: A systematic review. *Lancet 357*: 757-762.

[38] Stiggelbout A. M., Molewijk A. C., Otten W., Timmerman s D. R. M., van Bockel J. H. & Kievit J. (2003): Ideals of patient autonomy in clinical decision making: a study on the development of a scale to assess patients' and physicians' views. *J Med Ethics 30*: 268 – 274.

[39] American Medical Association, Council on Ethical and Judicial Affairs, „Confidential Care of Minors" in *Code of Medical Ethics: Current Opinion with Annotations*. Chicago: AMA 1997, 5.055, 86-87.

In: Decision Making in Medicine and Health Care
Editor: P. C. Tolana, pp. 77-95
ISBN: 978-1-60021-870-5


*Chapter IV*

# Making Decisions about Managing Medications in Hospital

***Elizabeth Manias****

School of Nursing, The University of Melbourne, Australia.

## Abstract

The purpose of this chapter is to examine the extent to which patients are involved in making decisions about their medications in hospital. Traditionally, decision-making about medications has involved patients taking a passive and receptive role without active participation. In contemporary health care, there is a focus on self care, shorter hospital stays, treatment of individuals with an increasing severity of illness, and positive benefits of patient involvement in improving health outcomes. Furthermore, patients have complex medication regimens that they are expected to manage when they are discharged home from hospital. It is therefore timely to consider how patients contribute to medication decisions. For this study, a descriptive prospective qualitative design was used, incorporating observations with health professionals and patients. Data collection was undertaken in a metropolitan university teaching hospital in Australia, using a stratified random sampling to recruit patients from 12 ward settings. This sampling method ensured that a broad cross-section of patients with different health problems was involved in the study. A medication decision making model was used as a framework to analyze the data according to four principles: identifying treatment goals, selecting different medication options, determining medication monitoring and evaluation, and identifying patient self care. Data findings demonstrated that patients continued to play a passive role in making decisions about their medications in hospital. On the other hand, there were instances where health professionals assisted patients to decide their own course of action about managing medications. In such situations patients were adequately

* Correspondence concerning this article should be addressed to: Associate Professor Elizabeth Manias RN MPharm, PhD School of Nursing, The University of Melbourne, Level 1, 723 Swanston Street Carlton Victoria 3053. Telephone: +61 3 8344 0778; Fax: +61 3 9347 4172; Email: emanias@unimelb.edu.au.

prepared for their transition from hospital to home. This chapter examines the implications of findings for practice and health care policy.

## INTRODUCTION

This chapter examines the extent to which patients are engaged in making decisions about their medications in hospital. Traditionally, decision making about medications has involved patients taking a passive and receptive role without active participation. In contemporary health practice, there is a focus on self care, shorter hospital stays, an increasing severity of illness sustained by individuals living in the community, and positive benefits of patient involvement in improving health outcomes. Furthermore, patients have complex medication regimens that they are expected to manage when they are discharged home. It is therefore timely to consider how patients contribute to medication decisions in the hospital setting.

The framework adopted for this chapter is an adaptation of a medication decision making model for examining patients' involvement in medication management (Chewning & Sleath, 1996). In this model, patients interact with health professionals through four major dimensions: identifying treatment goals, choosing from different treatment options, monitoring symptoms and evaluating regimens, and integrating self care into communication processes. The process of health professional-patient decision making comprises the adoption of a patient-centered approach, where patients' views are collaboratively incorporated into decisions or a medical approach where patients are passive, receptive and compliant and where health professionals control the decisions made. In reality, health professional-patient decision making lies along a continuum of these two approaches. However, in order to examine distinctions and analyze the extent of patient participation, it is useful to consider decision making in terms of these two approaches. Defining the regimen goals involves ensuring that the patient's desired outcomes are acknowledged (Chewning & Sleath, 1996). From a medical approach for this dimension, it is assumed that the health professional's expertise about clinical symptoms and outcomes are the most important determinants of treatment decisions. Regimen selection involves the need to uniquely tailor the patient's personality, lifestyle and health care priorities into judgments made about choosing medication therapies (Chewning & Sleath, 1996). From a medical approach, treatment selection is a unidirectional decision made by the prescriber who considers that patients fit into a standardized treatment program. The dimension of medication monitoring and evaluation involves using the patient as an active problem solver whose experiences and perceptions are accepted openly by health professionals (Chewning & Sleath, 1996). According to a medical approach for this dimension, health professionals evaluate clinical outcomes without incorporating the patient's viewpoint. The self care dimension involves the range of behaviors undertaken by patients to promote or improve their health. From a patient-centered approach self care involves health professionals including the patient's specific needs into decision making (Chewning & Sleath, 1996). Particular emphasis is placed on how patients continue their medication regimen when they are discharged home. On the other hand, a medical approach for self care is associated with regimented control by health professionals involving the communication of set instructions about medication use without considering individualized needs.

According to the traditional view, medications are prescribed by a doctor, supplied by a pharmacist, and administered by a nurse (Bullock *et al.*, 2007). In hospitals, this traditional view has become somewhat indistinct in recent times since health professionals have a number of medication-related functions. Nurses, pharmacists and doctors educate patients and other health professionals about medication use. Due to the greater specialization of medical roles in hospitals, doctors are often responsible for patient care in several settings. Therefore, doctors may not be present in any one particular setting for long periods. Multiple doctors may also be responsible for managing the same patient (Charles *et al.*, 1999; Manias *et al.*, 2005). Research on how decision making occurs with medication management has largely focused on two parties – the patient and the doctor in the community setting (Cox *et al.*, 2004; Ong *et al.*, 1995). There has been very little consideration of how decision making occurs in hospitals where health care needs of patients are very complex and patients feel vulnerable about their treatment, diagnosis, clinical outcomes and wellbeing. Another complexity not considered in past work is that patients do not only interact with their doctors about medication issues. Patients may have discussions with family, nurses, pharmacists, and other doctors before making medication decisions.

The aims of this chapter are two-fold: to examine the extent of patient involvement in medication decisions in the hospital setting, and to explore how patients and health professionals make decisions about medications in the hospital setting.

## METHOD

A descriptive prospective design was used (Schneider *et al.,* 2003), incorporating naturalistic observations of medication management activities. Medication management activities were defined as any interaction between a health professional and a patient about situations that involved medications. They included: patient assessment prior to giving medications, planning patients' medication care, administering medications and evaluating patient outcomes after medication administration. The study was conducted in a metropolitan university teaching hospital in Australia. Data collection occurred between January and December 2005 and the hospital and university ethics committees gave approval to conduct the study.

### Participants

A stratified random sampling method was used to recruit 10 patients each from 12 ward settings. The 12 ward settings involved were: colorectal surgery, cardiology, vascular surgery, plastic surgery, neuroscience, general medicine, respiratory medicine, emergency short stay, oncology, cardiothoracic care, orthopedics and rehabilitation. This sampling method ensured that a broad representation of patients with different health problems was involved. Recruitment of patients was undertaken at the patients' bedside, when the investigator spoke about the study and invited participation. Inclusion criteria for patients were: those aged at least 18 years, the ability to understand and communicate in English, and competency to consent participation. Exclusion criteria included: patients with a medical condition that required emergency care, and those suffering from a debilitating condition that prevented them from expressing themselves clearly. Verbal and written information was provided also to doctors, nurses and pharmacists to inform them about the study.

## Procedure

Thirty observations were undertaken of four hours duration between the hours of 0600 and 2200. For each ward setting between two to three observations were carried out. Observations were randomly selected at times that corresponded to when medication management activities occurred. Medication management activities occurred around five main time periods: early morning, late morning to midday, mid-afternoon, early evening and late evening. All observations were audio-taped using a Sony TCM-45V cassette recorder with an attached microphone, to allow for fast and accurate description of medication management activities.

## Analysis

Observations were audiotaped and transcribed verbatim. Transcripts were analyzed using the "framework" approach, as delineated by Ritchie and Spencer (1994). This approach comprised five stages: familiarization, identifying a theoretical framework, indexing, charting, and mapping and interpreting. Familiarization required gaining an overview of the data by reading transcripts over many times. The next stage involved developing a thematic framework, which included the four dimensions that mapped onto the medication decision making model (Chewning & Sleath, 1996): identifying treatment goals, selecting different medication options, determining medication monitoring and evaluation, and identifying patient self care. For each dimension, data were examined to determine whether a medical approach was followed, or a patient-centered approach was maintained. It was perceived a medical approach was used if health professionals: emphasized the clinical status of patients; defined the regimen selection; monitored and evaluated clinical outcomes with little collaboration from patients; and imposed self care options with negligible involvement from patients. A patient-centered approach was perceived to occur if: patients' priorities for quality of life and clinical status were emphasized for defining goals; patients were involved in selecting medication options; patients' perceptions were included in managing and monitoring the treatment regimen; and patients' views were considered in determining self care needs. The thematic framework stage also involved the derivation of sub-themes from the four dimensions of the medication decision making model. Indexing involved labeling data into manageable units for subsequent retrieval and exploration. Charting required a process of abstraction and synthesis whereby transcripts were annotated with particular sub-themes associated with the four dimensions of the framework. The mapping and interpreting stage involved comparing and contrasting participants' experiences and searching for patterns from the dataset as a whole.

Strategies to ensure rigor included prolonged field engagement by an experienced observer to minimize distortion caused by her presence. The investigator independently conducted data analysis with another colleague who was not associated with the study to identify emerging sub-themes, and 100% agreement was obtained. Data analysis was essentially qualitative; however, in determining whether a medical approach or a patient-centered collaborative approach was used, frequency counts were employed to judge the extent of patient involvement.

# RESULTS

## Medication Management Activities During Observations

In total, 422 medication management activities were identified during observations. Of these activities, 56 followed a patient-centered collaborative approach and 366 medication activities involved a medical approach. Table 1 indicates the breakdown of how decisions were made for the four dimensions of the framework. Table 2 shows the dimensions and sub-themes relating to how decisions were made about managing medication regimens in hospital: identifying treatment goals, selecting different medication options, determining medication monitoring and evaluation, and identifying patient self care. Excerpts from the data are used to illustrate how decisions were made. For data excerpts from the 30 observations, a code number has been assigned together with the abbreviation 'obs' to identify the particular observation under consideration.

**Table 1. Types of Decisions Made in Relation to a Medical Approach and a Patient-Centered Approach (N = 422 Medication Management Activities)**

| Dimension | Medical approach n (% of total) | Patient-centered collaborative approach n (% of total) |
|---|---|---|
| Identifying treatment goals | 34 (8%) | 5 (1%) |
| Selecting different medication options | 132 (31%) | 15 (4%) |
| Managing medication monitoring and regimen evaluation | 185 (44%) | 26 (6%) |
| Identifying patient self care | 15 (4%) | 10 (2%) |

## Identifying Treatment Goals

The identification of treatment goals involved two sub-themes, recognizing physiological outcomes and detecting psychosocial dimensions of medication therapy. The findings showed tensions between concern for patient priorities and health professionals' aims of the medication regimen. Health professionals were bound by institutional policies and protocols, and were observed to follow documented orders and expected norms of behavior. Their practice of adhering to documented medication orders and expected norms sometimes meant that patients' views were not always considered in identifying treatment goals.

**Table 2. Themes and Sub-themes of the Study (N = 422 Medication Management Activities)**

| Themes | Sub-themes |
|---|---|
| Identifying treatment goals | Physiological outcomes of medication therapy<br>Psychosocial dimensions of medication therapy |
| Selecting different medication options | Health professionals deciding on treatment options<br>Health professionals collaborating with patients in determining the medication prescription |
| Managing medication monitoring and regimen evaluation | Association of medication monitoring with other clinical activities<br>Use of simple questioning for determining effects of medications<br>Differential involvement of patients |
| Identifying patient self care | Structured directions provided by health professionals<br>Active involvement by patients and their families |

In the following observation excerpt, a 63-year-old woman with end-stage respiratory disease had experienced difficulties with sleeping due to a chronic infection. While the nurse sought information from the patient about her sleep, there was no further discussion about the difficulties she had with sleeping and the ways in which these difficulties could have been alleviated. The patient's priority was to overcome her feelings of tiredness and lethargy, which she attributed to lack of sleep. On the other hand, the nurse was concerned about the patient's breathlessness and oxygen level.

> The patient has just come back from her shower. Trailing behind her is a long piece of plastic tubing connected to an oxygen cylinder, which she wheels beside her. The nurse asks, 'How did you sleep?' Breathless from her shower, the patient says, 'I had little sleep last night. I spent most of the time sitting up and coughing. I was also having Ventolin [medication to dilate the airways] every two hours so that also kept me up. It would be nice to have something to help me to sleep. Apart from that, I'm alright.' The nurse bustles around the patient, takes her blood pressure…'147/97 mmHg, that's okay,' she says. The oxygen saturation machine is next to the patient's bed and the nurse measures the proportion of oxygen in her blood, '96% is your saturation level – it just shows how much you need your oxygen and Ventolin,' she says. 'I have no oxygen in my blood,' the patient agrees. 'The physiotherapist will be coming up to see you soon. She will be able to help with your breathing. I'll put your Ventolin nebuliser [medication administered by a misting device to dilate respiratory airways] on and that should also help,' explains the nurse. 'Oh, I couldn't see the physiotherapist today. I feel too unwell from being up all night,' the patient replies. 'Fair enough, but it would really help with your breathlessness. Just think about it a little more, says the nurse. (obs4)

The nurse was concerned about the patient's breathing, as shown by her attempts to convince the patient of the need to see the physiotherapist and to receive nebuliser therapy. While the patient agreed that her breathing was not optimal, she was more worried about her lack of sleep. This excerpt demonstrates a situation where the patient and health professional had different goals of medication management. The patient had hoped to receive sleeping medication; however, the nurse's priority was to address the breathing problems.

The following excerpt involved a 24-year-old female patient who had a laproscopic cholecystectomy two days previously for treatment of cholelithiasis. The patient was looking forward to going home, but was concerned about how her pain after surgery would be managed when she went home:

> The gastrointestinal team comes to the patient's bed, including the attending physician, resident and pharmacist. The physician asks the patient, 'How are you feeling?' The patient replies, 'My stomach feels very sore, that's all. I feel good in my spirit, but I'm just very, very sore.' The physician answers, 'You'll probably be sore for a while with this type of surgery, but you've been taking something here for that, haven't you?' The patient says, 'Only Panadol [acetaminophen], and I am not sure if it is helping that much' The physician comments, 'You can have some Panadol at home, if you need to. That's what is normally given' 'Sure,' replies the patient. 'We'll let you go home this morning, and we'll get you back to the clinic, probably Monday week' adds the physician. 'Great,' says the patient. 'Okay?' queries the physician. 'Thank you,' replies the patient. The physician confirms, 'You don't need any other medication.' (obs15)

While the physician acknowledged that pain was an issue, only a particular intensity of pain was attributed to the type of surgery performed. Subsequently, the patient was only prescribed an analgesic used for the treatment of mild pain. While both the patient and surgeon had pain relief as a common goal, the way in which to obtain this relief was perceived to be different. The patient revealed that her medication regimen was not relieving her pain adequately enough but she conceded to persist taking this form of analgesic because it was recommended by her doctor.

In the following observation excerpt, an 81-year-old woman was diagnosed with obstructive jaundice, which needed hospital admission for surgical insertion of a biliary stent. The biliary stent was inserted to facilitate the flow of bile from the liver to the bile duct. Unfortunately, soon after surgery the patient developed a bacterial blood infection, which required a prolonged hospital stay for five months. During this time she was administered long-term intravenous antibiotic therapy:

> The surgical physician and registrar stop by the patient's bedside. They looked at their notes before speaking with the patient. 'Because of this infection in your gut, we want you to stay in hospital a bit longer. Possibly in the next two or three days you can go home,' says the surgical physician. 'Well, I'd rather be home than here. I have been here for so long. It would be good if someone could visit me to give me the antibiotics at home,' says the patient. 'Yes, I know, but it would be better for you to be here. We put a bit of plastic inside you and we don't want the bugs to hang around on the plastic. As soon as we stop your antibiotics, if we haven't cleared the blood completely, then the bugs will be back again. You'll end up back in here for longer. Is that alright?' comments the surgical physician. 'Yes,' answers the patient. (obs14).

The patient had initially been admitted to hospital for a procedure that would normally require about a two-week stay in hospital. While the patient acknowledged the importance of clearing the blood infection associated with the biliary stent, she did offer a potential solution that would enable her to go home. The physician perceived that the goal could be better achieved in hospital rather than at home, but he did not offer a reason to the patient.

In some situations, health professionals and patients communicated with each other to achieve a collaborative goal relating to medication use. For instance, in the following situation, an 84-year-old male patient was admitted with blood in the stools for investigation. He had a past history of hypertension and ischemic heart disease. There were several medications that had to be administered in the morning and one of the key goals of responsibility for the nurse was to ensure that the patient had received his medications on time. However, he was nauseated and unable to take his medications. According to the observation excerpt:

> The patient says he is feeling sick. He is starting to shake a bit as the nurse looks at the medication chart. The nurse checks the medication order chart and decides to give him a dose of Maxolon [anti-nausea tablet]...The nurse goes out of the room to get a Maxolon tablet...she comes back and gives him the tablet with some water. 'Can you just swallow this little white tablet Harry? It will stop you from feeling sick.' She adds, 'You have nine tablets here that are ordered for 8 o'clock,' she says to the patient. 'But I really don't think you are in a state to have your medicines since you feel so sick. None of them need to be given right now – we can wait half-an-hour and see how you feel then.' The patient nods in agreement as he puts the small white tablet in his mouth and lies down. (obs24)

## Selecting Different Medication Options

The dimension involving the selection of different medication options was associated with two sub-themes. These were: health professionals deciding on treatment options with patients maintaining a passive role, and health professionals collaborating with patients in determining medication prescription. When patients maintained a passive role in the selection process it was difficult to identify their perspective on a particular situation. Sometimes, undesirable outcomes were achieved when medications were administered in situations where patients demonstrated a passive stance.

The following situation involved a 47-year-old man who had drainage of an abscess located in his left buttock and insertion of a plastic tube under general anesthetic. These procedures were necessary to facilitate drainage from the abscess and prevent further infection. He had a past history of Crohn's disease, which caused skin excoriation and eventual skin breakdown:

> The patient's wound dressing needs to get done. The nurse informs the patient that the doctors want him to stop having the fentanyl [strong analgesic for pain relief] injection and to try other pain relievers that are not as strong and can be taken by mouth. Climbing into bed, the patient nods in agreement and the nurse goes off to set up the dressing. The nurse returns with an analgesic [acetaminophen and codeine combination

> tablet] and gives it to the patient. [Fifteen minutes later] the nurse starts the dressing...The patient is in excruciating pain during the dressing procedure. He groans as he tightens his eyes and tears roll down his face. Using a torch, the nurse examines the abscesses on the perianal area, which are very deep. The nurse tries to be very gentle as he cleans the wound site with antiseptic and applies the dressing…Following the procedure, he turns to the patient and says, 'That was not a pleasant experience for you. Obviously you are not yet ready to be taken off the fentanyl. I will make sure the order is changed back so that you can have it next time.' (obs13)

In this situation, the patient passively agreed with the change in medication for managing his wound pain. Despite his passive acceptance for a weak analgesic agent, the patient openly expressed his dissatisfaction with the change during the dressing procedure. Nevertheless, the nurse continued with the procedure even though it was obvious that the analgesic administered was inadequate. It was not until the procedure was completed that the nurse acknowledged the problem and sought to alter the medication order.

In other situations while physicians made decisions to alter medications without consulting with patients or family members, patients attempted to resist the change by expressing their dissatisfaction at the time when medications were administered. The following observation excerpt involved a 90-year-old Greek lady who was admitted with ongoing chest pain that was unrelieved by her prescribed heart medications. The cardiac physician examined her medications and made some changes based on the patient's continued unresolved chest pain. While the patient was able to understand English, she preferred to communicate in Greek through her daughter who often visited. The patient also had limited vision in her right eye, and was blind in her left eye.

> The patient sits out of bed with her daughter beside her while the nurse checks her medication drawer and pulls out a couple of Augmentin Forte [antibiotic] tablets. The lady groans when she sees them and starts to talk in Greek to her daughter. 'Isn't there anything else she can have? She says these tablets are too big for her to swallow,' says the daughter. 'I might be able to get it in a syrup form. Could she take it as a syrup?' asks the nurse. The patient shrugs her shoulders as the nurse checks off the other medications on her chart. 'Just try and get her to take it for now,' the nurse adds as she leaves the room. The patient scowls as she puts the two tablets in her mouth. She begins to crush them with her teeth while drinking copious amounts of water. [Half-an-hour later] the patient has just vomited and the nurse begins to clean up the bed area. (obs28)

Less commonly, health professionals attempted to involve patients when decisions were made about changing medications. Incorporating patient views in decisions meant their individual needs could be considered, which often led to improved quality of care. The following observation excerpt involved a 66-year-old lady admitted after having a stroke. Following her stroke she required rehabilitation for dysphasia, verbal dyspraxia and limb weakness on one side of her body:

> The rehabilitation team stops by the patient's bed. The medical consultant says, 'We are planning to have you go home in another two weeks. We want to keep you here for that time so you can build some strength in your legs. I can see that you are having quite a lot of medicines [looking at the medication order chart]' The patient replies slowly,

> 'Since coming to hospital I have started on so many more tablets than what I had at home. I seem to be taking medicines all the time. I don't know how I will cope when I go home. Can something be done about it?' 'Well, how long have you been on captopril [tablet for high blood pressure]?' asks the consultant. 'Many years,' replies the patient. 'There's a medication that you will only need to take once a day that is very similar. Would you like to change? It's up to you. We can stick with this one that you take twice a day. You have probably got heaps of it at home. And then there's this one called perindopril [alternative tablet for high blood pressure] that you only take once a day. And it is practically the same.' 'Yes, thank you – that would help,' the patient replies. (obs30)

In this situation the patient was very concerned that she had to consume many tablets when she went home. The medical consultant was able to address her concerns by prescribing a medication for lowering her blood pressure that only had to be taken once instead of twice daily.

## Managing Medication Monitoring and Regimen Evaluation

The dimension of medication monitoring and evaluation involved the process of assessing the effects of individual preparations before they were administered and examining their benefits and side effects after they were administered. Three sub-themes were associated with this dimension: association of medication monitoring with other clinical activities (e.g. medication rounds), the use of simple questioning for determining effects of medications, and differential involvement of patients. In the hospital setting, this monitoring role was generally undertaken by nurses due to their ongoing presence at the patient's bedside.

Common monitoring activities included: completion of a standard set of vital sign observations such as blood pressure, breathing rate, pulse rate and temperature. Nurses were especially concerned about medications that affected the heart, blood pressure and breathing. Most nurses organized their work so that assessment of patients' vital signs occurred during the time that medication rounds were conducted. Patients were regularly involved in discussions about vital sign findings before they received their medications and nurses also interpreted these findings to patients. As medications were given to patients at specified time points, for example, 8 a.m. for once daily medications, and 8 a.m., 2 p.m. and 6 p.m. for medications administered three times daily, these time points also became the instances when vital signs were performed. Therefore, nurses did not gather information about the immediate beneficial or adverse effects of medications after administration, which could then be relayed to patients.

The presence of specific symptoms, such as pain, nausea and constipation, was also monitored by nurses to evaluate the effectiveness of analgesics, anti-emetics and laxatives respectively. Similar to the monitoring of vital signs, nurses' assessment of specific symptoms tended to be undertaken at the time of the medication rounds just before medications were given rather immediately following their administration. Simple closed questions tended to be used by health professionals in determining whether a particular symptom occurred. The following are examples of simple questions asked by doctors or nurses and the patient responses:

The nurse asks the patient, 'Do you have any chest pain at the moment?' And the patient says, 'No, it's okay.' (obs6)

The doctor says, 'Is the pain from your leg okay?' The patient replies, 'Yeah, it's fine. Just a bit tender when I move.' (obs9)

'Do you still feel sick from the anesthetic?' asks the nurse. 'No, not really. If I keep still, it's not too bad,' replies the patient. (obs10)

As indicated, simple questioning by health professionals usually obtained a brief response from patients. Aside from what appeared to be straight forward answers health professionals only occasionally followed up on the additional information given by patients. For example, the symptoms of pain and nausea were often aggravated by movement; yet, health professionals often accepted the 'no' component of the patients' response and did not seek out further clarification about the situations that may trigger a particular symptom. Health professionals were also observed to ask patients questions that made judgments about their symptoms, for example, 'Now that walk wasn't too painful, was it?' (obs8) or, 'You think back to a week ago and the nausea you had then.' (obs17)

Pathology tests were actively monitored by nurses for certain medications, depending on whether it was perceived to be a small margin between a safe and toxic dose. The results of pathology tests were discussed at ward rounds and during informal discussions away from the bedside. Usually, patients were not involved in these discussions. Sometimes patients offered information about pathology tests that assisted health professionals to make decisions about their care. The following example indicates how a patient with diabetes showed initiative in seeking information about his blood glucose levels and the way in which the nurse used the patient's blood glucose levels to make proactive decisions about his insulin requirements. The patient involved was a 73-year-old man admitted with ongoing abdominal pain for investigation repair. At home, he routinely had insulin two times each day before eating his meals for the management of diabetes:

The patient rings his bed bell and asks the nurse about his blood sugar level. He says to the nurse, 'I have had my morning dose of insulin and now the doctors are fasting me for my CAT scan.' The nurse looks the patient's blood sugar level by taking a finger prick of blood... 'It is 5.6 mmol/L – this is still okay. You don't need to worry about your blood sugar,' she says. (obs3)

A patient's ability to swallow was also considered to be important by some health professionals in monitoring the use of medications. This ability was particularly a problem for elderly patients who were on several medications, mainly of which were quite large. To address this issue, nurses sought information from pharmacists to identify if particular medications could be crushed before giving them to patients. Usually, nurses did not consider administering different forms of medication such as a liquid or a lozenge preparation or spacing out the medications during the day. In the following observation excerpt, an 85-year-old lady admitted with collapse for investigation. Following hospital admission, the patient had gastrointestinal surgery where part of her bowel was removed as she was found to have a large carcinoma:

> The nurse is popping the medications in the medicine cup – in all there are 12 medications in the cup. The patient sits up in her bed, with her son next to her. They are big tablets and the lady breaks them in half before putting them in her mouth. She is crushing them in her mouth and says to her son, 'It's a bit difficult. There are just too many tablets to swallow.' 'Are these different to the types of medicines she takes at home?' asks the nurse. The son replies, 'No, but she usually spreads them out during the day. She doesn't take them all at the same time of day at home.' The nurse encourages the patient to take sips of water to get the tablets to go down. It continues to be a struggle. (obs27)

## Identifying Patient Self Care

Self care related to preparing patients for the transition from hospital to home by examining the behaviors undertaken by patients in promoting or restoring their health. There were two sub-themes associated with this dimension: structured direction provided by health professionals and active involvement by patients and their families. When structured direction was provided by health professionals, this form of information giving tended to occur during formalized discussion forums such as ward rounds. Ward rounds involved large numbers of health professionals and the sessions were led by a medical consultant. As individuals who attended ward rounds were required to review several patients in different areas of the hospital, time spent with each patient was often quite limited. In addition, due to the presence of many health professionals at ward rounds, patients were sometimes reluctant to speak about their self care needs.

Active involvement of self care needs was largely influenced by patients' familiarity with patterns of previous management. If patients were aware of and participated in their medication regimen at home, they were more likely to ask questions about their medications in hospital, especially if any changes were involved. Conversely, patient education about medications tended not to be offered by health professionals on a routine basis. As a result, patients who were committed in seeking out information from health professionals did receive medication education. In the following observation excerpt, a 47-year-old man returned from the operating room after a ureteroscopy procedure and lithotomy of ureteric stones. He had a previous hospital admission about a year ago for the same problem. The patient was well informed about the circumstances surrounding his medical condition and about taking preventative measures to stop the ureteric stones from reoccurring:

> The patient asks if he would be given any medication to prevent the stones from forming again or if it is just drinking lots of water, which he has been doing since his last admission for the same thing. The nurse tells him he will need to keep on using the urinal when he needs to pass water so that they can collect the stones, send them to the laboratory and find out what they are made of and then the most appropriate treatment would be discussed with him. He says that he has already been through this discussion with his own doctor and that they were 75% calcium oxalate. The nurse says that she will let the doctors know but they would still want to send samples of the stones that had formed this time and they would be the most important people with whom to discuss this issue. He says that his groin is still sore and that 'it hurts to pass water. It would be good to have something to stop the problem happening again.' (obs18)

Family members who were well-informed about their relatives' circumstances also attempted to influence and clarify patients' self care needs. The following observation excerpt involved an 86-year-old man for removal of a recurrent bladder tumour. Four years ago he had a stroke caused by clots in his brain, which were subsequently treated with warfarin:

> The oncology team arrives at the bedside when the patient comes back from his shower. His wife is sitting next to the patient's bed... 'And doctor, what about the warfarin?' she asks. 'We have spoken to the neurology doctors at the hospital and he doesn't need it,' replies one doctor. [The patient has been receiving care from a neurologist relating to a stroke the patient had four years ago.] 'But he has taken those tablets for over four years,' says his wife. 'Yes, but when they put him on it, they said they only wanted him to have it for six months and then stop,' replies the doctor. 'But he has always had symptoms like stroke. It starts on the left side [pointing to her chest] and goes up here [pointing to her head] and he gets dizzy and lightheaded,' comments his wife. The doctor says, 'When was the last time he had that?' 'The last time would have been only four weeks ago,' she says. 'That's right, we did the test [CAT scan of the head] but that was normal. Nothing there,' the doctor recalls. His wife shrugs her shoulders, 'Even so, he has had the problems.' 'He really does not need it. Don't worry about it. We'll keep monitoring him though and see how it goes,' replies the doctor as he begins to walk away. (obs16)

During the ward round discussion occurred about the patient's warfarin regimen before he came to hospital. While the doctors accepted the information offered by the patient's wife relating to his use of warfarin for the last four years, they did not agree that he had to continue taking this medication. Evidence for this view was based on the CAT scan result obtained on the patient. On the other hand, information provided by the patient's wife in relation to symptoms of stroke was not acknowledged by the doctors in making their decision about whether to continue administering warfarin. The doctor's response, 'He really does not need it. Don't worry about it...' effectively terminated the discussion and discouraged the patient's wife from pursing her concerns further.

Some patients were also seen to express concerns about how changes in a medication regimen in the clinical setting would be perceived by their local doctor outside of the hospital. The following observation excerpt involved a 76-year-old man admitted for insertion of a permanent pacemaker for ongoing heart rhythm problems. On a previous hospital admission he had part of his right lung removed because of cancer. In this example, the doctors sought patient involvement in his self care before making decisions about the medication regimen. However, the patient was still concerned about how the planned management was different to what he experienced before his hospital admission and the relationship with his own local doctor:

> 'Were you on any blood pressure tablets before your operation [pacemaker insertion]?' asks the doctor. 'No, nothing,' replies the patient. 'Well, your blood pressure is a bit up and you have problems with your heart rhythm, which is not very good and that's already because the blood pressure is not being controlled. We'll start you on blood pressure tablets before you go home,' answers the doctor. 'I've got my own doctor and I look after myself but no one has ever told me about that,' explains the patient.

> 'We're going to start you on blood pressure tablets and you might need to be on them for quite some time. We'll let your doctor know,' says the doctor. 'Will that medication stop me drinking?' asks the patient. 'One or two beers a day is okay but not more than two,' suggests the doctor. (obs25)

Interactions between patients and nurses during medication administration times also brought about opportunities for decision making in self care. In the following observation excerpt, a 63-year-old lady was admitted to hospital following a severe asthma attack. She was receiving 17 different medications during the day for several medical problems, including osteoporosis, diabetes, severe vitamin deficiency, and gout:

> The nurse notices prednisolone [steroid agent that decreases inflammation of respiratory airways] is prescribed on the medication order chart, which the patient is receiving for increasing severity of asthma symptoms since her admission to hospital. The patient is on a gradually decreasing dose over time and the nurse asks her about the prednisolone. 'Have you been taking it at home?' she asks. 'Yes, but at a lower dose. The dose has been gradually going up since I have come to hospital and now it is gradually going down,' the patient replies. 'Has it been playing up with all your sugars [blood glucose levels for diabetes]?' the nurse asks. 'The patient replies, 'No, the sugars have been fine.' (obs29)

In most observed situations, nurses placed all medications to be administered to a particular patient at a specified time in a small container called a 'medicine cup'. The contents of the medicine cup were then given to each patient, usually without any education about the medications prescribed. Less commonly, medication administration times also enabled nurses to identify how the medications patients were taking in hospital compared with what they had to take at home. The following observation excerpt involves a 78-year-old man admitted with severe pneumonia. He also had chronic obstructive pulmonary disease, hypertension and right heart failure, which required administration of 15 different medications during the day:

> The nurse is checking the medications and the packets against the medication orders and distributing them into the medicine cups. She signs the chart and asks the patient questions as she goes through the chart. 'Are they the ones you usually take at home?' she asks the patient, looking at the tablets. She adds, 'This big round one is the potassium, which helps to increase the amount of potassium you get from your diet. That's aspirin, which stops clots forming in your body. And this little one here is a blood pressure tablet,' informs the nurse. 'Oh, I don't take that one at home', says the patient pointing to the blood pressure tablet, perindopril. 'You just need to remember to take it once a day – a lot of people need to take care in getting up from a lying to a sitting position because it can make them dizzy if they move around too quickly,' says the nurse. (obs26)

The following observation excerpt involved a 68-year-old Maltese lady admitted with a severe respiratory infection and exacerbation of asthma. Before her admission, she had enormous problems trying to get her breath following a small exertion of energy and right pleuritic pain. Her husband, who spoke better English than she did, often sought out clarification about her management while in hospital. The example demonstrates how nurses could address patients' medication concerns in great detail to the point where problems were resolved by the time the doctors came to the bedside:

> The patient's husband is sitting next to the patient, a lady who has been having some breathing problems. The husband is asking the nurse why his wife has been having aspirin. The nurse says, 'She was having some chest pain the other night and because of that she's been put on aspirin.' He adds, 'Will she need to stay on aspirin when she goes home?' 'She probably will,' responds the nurse... The doctors arrive for the ward round. 'Everything is going well and you should be able to go home tomorrow morning, if everything checks out okay with the blood tests she had earlier today,' says the consultant. 'That's great, and her tablets? Will she keep taking everything she is having in hospital?' asks the husband. 'Yes, we'll just keep everything going,' replies the consultant. The doctors say goodbye to the husband and patient and they move to the next bed. (obs26)

## Discussion

This chapter provides valuable information on how decisions are made about managing patients' medication regimens in hospital and most importantly, the extent of patient involvement in such decisions. Three key characteristics differentiate this work from previous studies. First, an observational technique was used, which enabled identification of how the complexities of care affected the ways in which decisions were made. Second, the clinical activities of various health professionals were considered including nurses, doctors and pharmacists. The perspectives of all these professional players must be considered because they each make an enormous contribution in managing patients' medications in hospital. Third, patients were recruited from a variety of hospital settings who were at different stages of recovery during their hospital stay. Fourth, data were examined in terms of various dimensions of medication decision making to identify the extent of patient involvement.

The findings showed that patients were not usually incorporated into decisions about how their medications were managed in hospital. For all dimensions, patient-centered participation was less commonly encountered compared to the medical approach where decisions were directed by health professionals. Patient participation ranged from 6% in terms of monitoring the effectiveness of medications to only 1% in relation to identifying treatment goals of care. Regardless of whether patients were central to collaborative efforts, the majority of decisions encountered in clinical practice surrounded selection of the medication regimen, and monitoring and evaluating the effectiveness of therapy. On the other hand, decisions rarely involved identification of treatment goals or patient self care.

With respect to defining regimen goals, a patient-centered approach comprised 5% of all medication management activities compared with 8% where health professionals directed the decisions. For this dimension of decision making, goals of therapy focused mainly on physiological outcomes of care rather than on psychosocial aspects of medication therapy. Health professionals largely emphasized goals that relied on signs and symptoms of clinical significance, such as maintaining normal levels of blood pressure, breathing and heart rate.

Subsequently, there was the possibility that health professionals did not adequately consider patients' concerns unless they were of a physiological nature. Liaschenko and Fisher (1999) suggested that goals associated with physiological outcomes are easier for health professionals to interpret because they trigger expectations about what objective procedures should be followed.

Patient participation for regimen selection comprised 4% of all medication management activities compared with 31% in which health professionals made the decisions. Usually, health professionals decided on treatment options rather than collaborating with patients in determining which medications to prescribe. Health professionals also did not usually seek patients' opinions about changes made to a medication regimen. It was found that patients' opinions sometimes differed from that of the doctor, nurse or pharmacist. There was little evidence of exploring or sharing of views and to determine the ways in which health professionals' views about medication selection differed from patients.

In past work involving communication between physicians and patients in community settings, physicians were asked if they were aware of patients' views on which medications should be prescribed for them. In 19 out of 55 situations, physicians indicated that they had no idea about their patient's view about medications selected for a particular treatment regimen, and in six situations physicians decided on what medications to prescribe based on guesses about a patient's view. In the other 30 situations, physicians used general impressions of the patient, knowledge about the patient's previous medication-taking behavior and the patient's family background to determine medication selection (Stevenson *et al.*, 2000). While in community settings it appears as though patients' views are only sometimes considered in relation to medication selection, obstacles that are specific to hospital settings may stand in the way of patient participation in medication selection. The hospital setting is characterized as an acute care environment where health professionals are required to make fast and critical decisions (Degner & Sloane, 1992). With patients being confronted with unfamiliar demands and expectations in regard to diagnosis, treatment and recuperation, it is not surprising that they may defer to health professionals to find out about treatment choices. Interactions involving treatment options may become asymmetrical since a collaborative response to decision making may be abandoned if patients are viewed to be too ill to make judgments about their care. As a result, patients can experience a sense of helplessness while in hospital, which can also increase their hesitation in communicating their health needs (Pierce & Hicks, 2001). Health professionals need to understand this sense of helplessness and to develop proactive communication strategies to encourage involvement and allay fear (Manias *et al.*, 2006). Nevertheless, in the current study, there were examples of patients and family members who actively attempted to guide prescribing practices of doctors and they were met with resistance. If health professionals fail to acknowledge the patient's view in treatment selection, it is possible that patient adherence to a treatment regimen following hospital discharge may not be high.

In relation to monitoring and evaluating medication regimens, patient participation involved 6% of all medication management activities, while health professionals directed 44% of all decisions with respect to this dimension. Nurses tended to complete medication monitoring activities with other specified tasks that were conducted at particular times, including ward rounds, wound dressings, and medication administration rounds. As nurses often used simple questioning to determine the effects of medications, patients' interpretation of their experiences may not have been fully gauged. A patient's hospital stay provides an opportune time for training patients to monitor their own regimen with specific diaries and observation sheets (Chewning & Sleath, 1996). Examples of situations where patients can monitor benefits and side effects is by involving them in recording blood glucose levels following insulin therapy and interpreting changing intensities of pain following anti-arthritic therapy. Siegal *et al.* (1999) identified patients as being 'naïve scientists' in their homes (p. 247) since they develop hypotheses about their medications, and then test these hypotheses by changing doses, switching between medications or stopping them altogether to monitor effects produced. In view of this tendency, when patients leave hospital they should be encouraged to actively monitor their own symptoms, and given information not only about the anticipated benefits of a particular medication but also about any risks or unwanted effects, and any uncertainty of treatment effectiveness (Bugge *et al.*, 2006).

In terms of self care management, a patient-centered approach involved 2% of medication management activities while a medical approach comprised 4% of these activities. There were few situations where patients' self care needs were addressed, either through structured instructions provided by health professionals or by active involvement of patients and their families. Health professionals face a dilemma between a conviction that they have expert knowledge about therapeutic regimens to treat various medical conditions and a concern about the impact that full knowledge about a medication's actions could have on patients' motivation to participate in treatment. Nevertheless, it has been demonstrated that patients receiving inadequate counseling about their medications may be less likely to adhere to their prescribed regimen because they do not fully understand how to take the medications and the rationale for their use (Stevenson *et al*, 2000; Tarn *et al.*, 2006; Vermeire *et al.*, 2001).

## Conclusion

Despite the current emphasis in health care about the importance of patient involvement and participation, this study showed that patient-centered decision making occurred in only 13% of all observed medication management activities. This finding has important implications for clinical practice. Health professionals need to be more active in assisting patients to select treatment regimens and in explaining the beneficial and unwanted effects of these regimens. Encouraging patients to talk with others who are receiving similar regimens may help some individuals and family members to anticipate their own adaptation to taking certain medications. Health professionals can support patients by presenting medication options clearly, and in ways that encourage active involvement. In recent times there has been endorsement from health professional societies and patient safety organizations about the need for effective communication and patient involvement (Institute of Safe Medication Practices, 2007; Society of Hospital Pharmacists of Australia, 2007). The foundation has therefore been laid for informed patient-health professional partnerships in medication management. The challenge now remains for doctors, nurses and pharmacists to work collectively to facilitate patient and family involvement in the hospital setting. Creating an atmosphere that generates trust and confidence is crucial for encouraging patients to become effective and active participants in managing their medications.

## REFERENCES

Bugge, C., Entwistle, V.A., & Watt, I.S. (2006). The significance for decision-making of information that is not exchanged by patients and health professionals during consultations. *Social Science & Medicine, 63*, 2065-2078.

Bullock, S., Manias, E., & Galbraith, A. (2007). *Fundamentals of pharmacology: A text for nurses and allied health professionals* (5th ed.). Melbourne, Australia: Pearson Education Australia.

Charles, C., Gafni, A., & Whelan, T. (1999). Decision-making in the physician-patient encounter: Revisiting the shared treatment decision-making model. *Social Science & Medicine, 49*, 651-661.

Chewning, B., & Sleath B. (1996). Medication decision-making and management: A client-centered model. *Social Science & Medicine, 42*, 389-398.

Cox K, Stevenson F, Britten, N., & Dundar, Y. (2004). *A systematic review of communication between patients and health care professionals about medicine-taking and prescribing.* London: Medicines Partnership

Degner, L.F., & Sloane, J.A. (1992). Decision making during serious illness: What role do patients really want to play? *Journal of Clinical Epidemiology, 45,* 941-950.

Institute of Safe Medication Practices (ISMP) (2007). *ISMP mission statement.* Retrieved April 28, 2007, from http://www.ismp.org/about/mission.asp

Liaschenko, J., & Fisher, A. (1999). Theorizing the knowledge that nurses use in the conduct of their work. *Scholarly Inquiry for Nursing Practice: An International Journal, 13*, 29-41.

Manias, E., Aitken, R., & Dunning, T. (2005). Graduate nurses' communication with health professionals when managing patients' medications. *Journal of Clinical Nursing, 14,* 354-362.

Manias, E., Botti, M., & Bucknall, T. (2006). Patients' decision-making strategies for managing pain in the postoperative context. *The Journal of Pain, 7*, 428-437.

Ong, L.M.L., de Haes, J.C., Hoos, A.M., & Lammes, F.B. (1995). Doctor-patient communication: a review of the literature. *Social Science & Medicine, 40*, 903-918.

Pierce, P.F., & Hicks, F.D. (2001). Patient decision-making behaviour. *Nursing Research, 50,* 267-274.

Ritchie, J., & Spencer, L. (1994). Qualitative data analysis for applied policy research. In A. Bryman, & R.G. Burgess R.G. (Eds.), *Analyzing qualitative data* (pp. 173-194). London: Routledge.

Schneider, Z., Elliott, D., LoBiondo-Wood, G., & Haber, J. (2003). *Nursing research: Methods, critical appraisal and utilization* (2nd ed.). Marrickville, Australia: Mosby.

Siegal, K., Schrimshaw, E.W., & Dean, L. (1999). Symptom interpretation and medicine adherence among late middle age and older HIV infected adults. *Journal of Health Psychology, 4*, 247-257.

Society of Hospital Pharmacists of Australia (SHPA) (2007). *SHPA vision and mission.* Retrieved April 28, 2007, from http://www.shpa.org.au/

Stevenson, F.A, Barry, C.A., Britten, N., Barber, N., & Bradley, C.P. (2000). Doctor-patient communication about drugs: The evidence for shared decision making. *Social Science & Medicine, 50*, 829-840.

Tarn, D.M., Heritage, J., Paterniti, D.A., Hays, R.D., Kravitz, R.L., & Wenger, N.S. (2006). Physician communication when prescribing new medications. *Archives of Internal Medicine*, *166*, 1855-1862.

Vermeire, E., Hearnshaw, H., Van Royen, P., Denekens, J. (2001). Patient adherence to treatment: three decades of research. A comprehensive review. *Journal of Clinical Pharmacology and Therapeutics*, *26*, 331-342.

In: Decision Making in Medicine and Health Care
Editor: P. C. Tolana, pp. 97-114
ISBN: 978-1-60021-870-5


Chapter V

# DECISION-MAKING IN PEDIATRIC CARE

***Inger Hallström****
Division of Nursing, Dept of Health Sciences/the Vårdal Institute, The Swedish Institute for Health Sciences, Lund University, Lund, Sweden.

## ABSTRACT

The UN Conventions on the Right of the Child was adopted in 1989, and efforts have been made to implement the intentions of the Convention. When decisions are to be made in pediatric care, comprehensive collaborative work is involved and multiple confounding factors are included. The area comprises several concepts that may be interpreted in various ways. The results from a systematic literature review including concepts like consent, competence, the child's best interest, knowledge, values and attitudes, roles and partnership, power, and economy are discussed. Furthermore, research projects concerning children's and parents' needs and participation in decision-making are described. To identify everyday situations in medical and nursing situations we followed twenty-four children during the course of events during their hospital stay. The aim of the study was to identify needs and various levels of participation, actual and optimal, and to describe the way in which children, parents and staff interact during the decision-making process. The results were analyzed according to the Scale of Degree of Self-Determination, which divides participation into decision-making into five levels. In the article the results are discussed from both a theoretical and a clinical perspective.

## INTRODUCTION

When decisions are to be made in pediatric care, three parties are involved, the child, the child's legal guardian (usually the parents) and various staff members. Professionals often, but not always, have the same opinion. Parents are often, but not always, united in their decision. Parents' and professionals' opinions may differ from that of the child. In an ideal situation, after receiving information and communicating with one another, all concerned will reach a common decision influenced by the various parties (Hallström, Runesson, Elander, 2002b, Runesson et al., 2002b, Hallström & Elander, 2004). The future of children and young people in need of care are dependent on the legal system as well as on social welfare and their parents and family. Communication between the persons involved and the systems is therefore vital for the child (Winn Oakley, 2002).

Historically, professionals have been the major decision-makers in pediatric care, and it is still a common thought that they know how children think and feel about treatment and care (Beauchamp & Childress, 2001). However, reasons for involving children and adolescents in decisions regarding their care and treatment are several. Ethical principles of autonomy, integrity, and the right to self-determination apply to children as well as adults. If children are encouraged to take an active part in decisions, the communication between professionals, parents, and children are improved, which sometimes directly facilitates not only the child's co-operation but also his/her care and treatment. Furthermore, when children are involved in decisions they get information that may make them feel they are in control, which may in turn enhance a positive adjustment (King & Cross, 1996, Bijstervelt, 2000). Involving children in a decision-making process demonstrates respect for them and may provide opportunities for their further development and decision-making capabilities (Anderson et al., 2002).

The UN Convention on the Rights of the Child (1989) formulates the needs of children and young people in terms of human rights and point out that children should be recognized as a group to whom human rights legislation applies. The Convention can be summarized as: children are to be respected, and parents and professionals working with children have a responsibility to ensure that the structures, systems and programs that are enacted enable children to claim their rights.

## Levels of Decision

To legally give one's consent, in Sweden one must be 18 years of age or older, but many younger children are competent to give their consent. Children are usually considered to understand the implications of the process of informed consent at the age of 12 (Manley & Smye, 2001). Compared to adults children's perceptions of benefits and risks differ; they are less resistant to social influence and more affected by the opinions of parents, family members and hospital staff which makes consent for children difficult (Brody et al., 2001). With increasing age and maturity, children are able to participate to an increased extent in decisions about their care.

Three levels of participation in decision-making is discussed, consent being the highest (Walker & Doyon, 2001). Consent means that children are mature enough to receive and

* Correspondence concerning this article should be addressed to: Professor Inger Hallström, Division of Nursing, Dept of Health Sciences, Lund University, Lund, Sweden, Box 157, S-221 00 Lund, Sweden. tel: +46 46 222 18

understand information and to give voluntary consent to the treatment or procedure proposed. Seeking and obtaining consent is a process rather than simply agreement about a certain act. The decision must be based on knowledge about the proposed decision as well as the consequences, and must be voluntary, volitional and rational. Assent is a lower level of consent and often used to involve minors in decision making. The child's agreement to participate is a commonly accepted definition of assent (Kuther, 2003). Children are considered to assent when they have sufficient competence to have some appreciation of the procedure, but not enough competence to give full consent. When children agree with a decision this gives them some control regarding choices, and the child does not need to require full knowledge and understanding to make the final decision (Lind, Anderson & Oberle 2003). If a decision already has been made, there is no point in seeking the child's assent; the child's view must not be sought if there is no intention to weigh that view seriously (Kuther, 2003).

Dissent involves a difference of opinion and a lack of agreement between the child and the other parties. This requires a certain understanding of the proposed action and its effects. If there is evidence that the child understands and has sufficient knowledge about the issue, the child's dissent ought to be taken seriously (Walker & Doyon, 2001). Sometimes a child is considered competent to consent but not to refuse. In other words the child's competence is not questioned and the child is allowed to make a decision as long as it is in accord with the parent's and staff's views, but not if it's not. We are many who argue that there should be no difference in the requirement for competence for consent and for refusal, since the right to give consent is worthless if there is no right to refuse.

Hermerén (1986) describes one way to differentiate participation in decision-making by using a scale of five levels:

1. "A (where A is a member of the staff and B is the child or the parent) does not listen to B's opinions, wishes, and valuations.
2. A listens but refuses to discuss the opinions with B; no consultation, no two-way communication exists.
3. A communicates with B but does not care about B´s answer; B's opinions, wishes and valuations do not influence A's actions.
4. A cares about what B says but acts only partly in accordance with B's opinions, wishes and valuations.
5. A acts in accordance with B's opinions, wishes and valuations (Hermeren, 1986 p 456):" When used in clinical research the scale was found to well differentiate between children's (Runeson et al., 2000, Runeson et al., 2002b) and parents' (Hallström, Runeson & Elander, 2002b) participation in decision-making during hospitalization.

96; fax: +46 46 222 19 35; Email: Inger.Hallstrom@med.lu.se.

## Literature Review

A literature review for articles during the years 1994 to 2004 (Hallström & Elander, 2005) identified the concepts of competence, the child's best interests, knowledge, values and attitudes, roles and partnership, power and economy to be of importance when discussing decision-making in pediatric care.

To be able to participate in decision-making a child must be competent. If an adult is regarded as being incompetent, this has to be proved, whereas children are presumed to be incompetent (Walker & Doyon 2001). Mouradian (1999 p 300) states that "A child's competence is a function of age, cognitive abilities and personal experiences". Assessing a child's competence is however, difficult. A child can have a general competence, which can be established by a test, and still be incompetent to make a decision regarding health care issues (Schuman 2000). Children who have experienced prior hospitalizations are probably more competent to decide about issues that are new to less experienced children, even if the children are of the same age and maturity. A child who has been used to participating in discussions at home, and whose views have been appreciated, is probably better equipped to engage in decision-making when the child is hospitalized.

The situation and their own security influence the competence of the parents. When a child is hospitalized parents attain security in different ways, e.g. from trusting that the professionals know how to take care of the child, from having control over what is happening to the child, and from being the one who knows the child best (Kristensson-Hallström, Elander 1997, Kristensson-Hallström 1999).

Everyone involved in decisions concerning a hospitalized child would agree that the decision should be made based on the child's best interests. However, opinions may differ about what that means. Perhaps, what is said to be in the child's best interests is in reality in the best interests of the family (Clayton 2000). When the child is not judged to be competent or to have legal right to make a decision the parents are most often obligated to act as proxy decision-makers. According to Beauchamp & Childress (2001, p 102,) "A surrogate - or proxy decision maker, must determine the highest net benefit among available options assigning different weights to interests the patient has in each option". Beauchamp and Childress (2001, p 154) suggest that the following qualifications are needed for a person to be able to make decisions for incompetent patients (including new-borns): "(1) ability to make reasoned judgements (competence), (2) adequate knowledge and information, (3) emotional stability, and (4) a commitment to the incompetent patient's interest that is free of conflicts of interest and free of controlling influence by others who may not act in the patient's best interest".

If the child, its parents and the professionals disagree on a treatment, or on what is seen by adults as something in the child's "best interests", then children's roles in decision-making must be mitigated by giving parents the moral and legal space to make decisions which will facilitate the child's long-term autonomy. Capron (1982) talks about "identity-of-interest doctrine" which means that proxies are allowed to decide for an incompetent person because *"the interest of the third party and those of the incompetent are so close that in choosing his or her own interests the third party will choose very much as the incompetent would"*. The legal concept of the "best interests of the child" is seen as a standard of reasonableness in law and is thought to be most applicable when used in conjunction with the parents' right to consent for their child (Stokes & Drake-Lee 1998). However, some feel it is vague, unknowable, individualistic and open to abuse (Kopelman 1997).

The concept of information and its value is commonly used in situations where decisions about the child's care have to be made. However, information is usually one sided, the professionals inform the parents and the child about important matters concerning the hospital admission and the parents inform them of the child's illness. There must be communication in order to emphasize the importance of the participation of everybody involved in the necessary decisions. The parents and the child have to inform staff members about the child's condition and, when staff members explain about procedures, they have to confirm that the family members have understood. It should be emphasized that children and adults vary in their need for information, (Mc Cabe 1996) and that this should not be forced upon patients or their relatives.

Receiving understandable information is crucial for making decisions. Hinds et al., (1997) mean that the information children and parents receive from healthcare professionals are most important for their decision making. Consequently, the communication must not be hurried when a decision is to be made. The more important the decision, the more time it should be allowed to take. If parents do not receive sufficient information from professionals, or if they do not comprehend what has been said to them, they may turn to other parents who have had similar experiences. This communication process will be especially important if they have not received sufficient support and advice from healthcare providers, (Yeh et al., 1999) possibly because they are in the same situation and at the same level regarding knowledge and understanding. However, information from other parents may give rise to a misunderstanding and result in wrong decisions.

During hospitalization parents are often encouraged to ask questions, but to do that they have to know which questions to ask. When people do not know what they are missing, they cannot ask for it. This might be reason why parents often claim that they have not received enough information (Guerriere et al., 2003) or optimal information, or that they have not understood the information they have been given. When asked, parents may not wish to make a final decision but they most often want to participate in the decision process (Hallström, Runeson, Elander, 2002b).

The values of an individual often determine how that individual acts in different situations and towards other persons. They also influence a person's decisions, and it is important to consider values when different treatments are discussed because conflicts may otherwise arise. Sometimes the medical facts and individual values differ in terms of importance, which influences how discussions are conducted. Professionals may believe that family members have the same values as they themselves have because they all belong to a supposedly similar culture. In dealing with families from obviously different cultural backgrounds, staff members tend to be more sensitive about possible differences in values. These are easier to accept when staff members know that the family originates from another country or has a different religion (Truog 1999). The more similar the families are to oneself, the stronger is the assumption that values are shared.

The attitudes of staff members are of utmost importance regarding children's participation in decision-making. If professionals value a child as a person with the right to an opinion, they listen to the child and try to satisfy the child's wishes as far as possible. In one study it was found that children who wanted to take part in decision-making were given information until they understood and were satisfied. In other cases, the children's wishes were ignored or sometimes not even sought (Runeson et al., 2002b). How sprofessionals behave, both verbally and physically, also affects parents with respect to how much they dare to assert their opinions and support the child's wishes.

In recent decades parents have became increasingly involved in the care of their hospitalized child. Consequently, they participate more in decisions regarding the child. If a child refuses a treatment, the parents can either support the child or take the staff member's side. The role of staff members in acting in the child's best interest is similar to that of the parents, but opinions of professionals have greater weight. Runeson et al., (2001) found that an action rarely took place if not supported by the responsible nurse. It is important that parents and professionals discuss the role that parents are supposed to have. Parents have different expectations; some want to participate in care actions that are impossible for other parents to deal with (Kristensson-Hallström & Elander 1997). Nurses and parents have shown to have different perceptions of their individual roles (Kawik, 1996). Parents want to participate according to their own choosing (Neill, 1996 a,b) and some want a collaborative role instead of being active in decision-making (Pyke-Grimm, Degner & Small, 1999). Through guidance, support and negotiations between parents and nurses it should be possible for parents to participate according to their own wishes (Blower & Morgan, 2000, Tait 2001, Brinchmann, Förde & Nortvedt 2002). The participant's role in decision-making varies with the context of the person and the situation. The patient's role expectations, attitudes and knowledge regarding the facts involved in the decision that has to be made should determine the patient's role (Dalton 2003).

There is supposed to be a difference between just participating in the child's care and being part of a partnership. Sometimes participating in a partnership means that everyone is participating on equal terms, whereas in other cases this could involve just doing what others tell one to do. Working as partners is viewed as an ideal situation when children are hospitalized. However, parents need to have a say about whether they want to be part of a partnership or if they want to leave all decisions to professionals, or something in between. The responsibility of each member of the partnership must be established. Who should decide about the responsibility of each member? The professionals are in charge of deciding about partnership and nurses may feel that, since the parents are seeking help for their child, they are less able to participate in the child's care (Lee 1999). Families who are frequently in hospitals are more accustomed to negotiating, and they propably have an easier time achieving the role they want. More experienced nurses who feel secure in their profession are more able and willing to negotiate than less experienced nurses (Kristensson-Hallström & Elander 1994). Parents are expected to participate in their child's care. Sometimes they may not be asked to do so, but their roles are implicit in their being there. When the child is discharged from hospital, the parents are expected to take responsibility for ongoing care at home. If they do not agree to do that, the child may have to stay in hospital. Thus, since alternatives are lacking, there may be no real possibility for the parents to refuse to take on this responsibility or to negotiate in terms of roles (Kirk 2001).

All patients are dependent on those in charge of their health care. Some individuals are able to handle the situation better than others, depending on their strength, verbal capacity, social circumstances and network. Parents of a sick child are in the same dependent situation they would be in if they were patients themselves. Power in healthcare is exercised in various ways. Those in charge of health care resources and facilities have the power to decide which care to give to a certain patient. This power is expressed in the concept "owning the patient"( Shields et al., 2003 p 213), and it has been suggested that "the doctor owns each patient who is admitted under their responsibility, and it may be equally true that nurses in charge of the co-ordination of the care feel the same way". If a staff member has the feeling that he or she owns the child, a conflict might arise regarding the child's best interests.

Another important part of power is knowledge. A patient can easily be encouraged to accept a decision by the use of knowledge that the patient does not have. When parents are reacting emotionally, the way a choice is presented to them may have an influence on their decision (Higgins, Kayser-Jones, Savedra, 1996). Being very positive about one treatment and emphasizing its advantages may induce the person to choose that treatment. In building a relationship with the parents, the parents want to do the right thing, which may be a kind of masked power relation that minimizes the potential for resistance (Wilson, 2001).

Research and development in health care have made many new treatments possible. People in general are aware of this and may demand such treatments, which may increase costs. Resources do play a role when decisions in healthcare are made, although this should not be the case. When deciding about spending a large amount of money on one patient, there is naturally a conflict between the benefit to the population and the needs of an individual. The costs may have to be related to the outcome of a treatment (Ham, 1999). Parents' participation in the child's care is not always simply for the benefit of the child; the aim may also be to lower costs (Lee, 1999). By being with the child, parents learn about the child's illness and its treatment, which means that the child can be discharged earlier. Staff members can be reassigned to other patients and productivity may be increased. Although more time has to be spent on instructing parents when they, instead of hospital staff, care for a child, the hospital costs are decreased (Kristensson-Hallström, Norlund, Malmfors 1999).

The articles in the literature review were almost exclusively from Scandinavia, the USA and northern Europe. Only two English language articles were found from Asia and Africa and none from South America. There may be more research on the topic written in native languages but the uneven global distribution of publications may reflect that other issues of healthcare are of greater importance in parts of the world e.g provision of basic and medical care.

## Research

In several of our studies we have seen that parents play a large role in their child's nursing and medical treatment and also that they want to have increased input into their child's care. But are parents participating in decisions concerning their child's care and do they want to be involved? And perhaps more important are children participating in their care and do the want to? In one of our research projects the aim was to illuminate children

(Runeson et al., 2002a), and parents' needs (Hallström, Runesson & Elander, 2002a) and their participating in care and treatment during the child's hospitalization (Hallström, Runesson, & Elander, 2002b, Runeson et al., 2002b).

During a nine-week period, 24 children and their parents were followed during the course of events during hospitalization at a university hospital in the south of Sweden. The observers were available on specific days, when children were chosen with respect to gender, age, diagnosis, and type of admission. No children with life-threatening diagnoses were included. However, if the child needed intensive care during the hospital stay it was observed there as well. Children were between five months and 18 years and were hospitalised at seven different units: the emergency department, and in infectious diseases, neurology, endocrinology, cardiology, and surgery units. Eight of the children sought care at the emergency department. The others were planned admissions. Observations were made during both day care (15 children) and longer hospital stays (nine children). In total we made observations for 135 h. Non-participant observations provided an opportunity to observe parents, their child and health care professionals in different situations during the hospitalisation.

The observers (two pediatric nurses both trained in performing observations and research) recorded field notes immediately after each period of observation. Field notes were systematic notations and records of events, behaviours, words and sentences written as detailed, non-judgmental and concrete descriptions of what was observed. The observers had no personal involvement with the patients or the care, and tried not to influence any events in the care. Field notes were analysed by manifest and latent coding in different steps by three researchers, first independently and then jointly.

In step one children's (Runesson et al., 2002a) and parent's needs (Hallström Runesson & Elander, 2002a) during the hospital stay were identified and analysed. Needs were assigned to broad areas such us, for example, what children and parents needed, wanted, looked for, longed for, or missed. In the words of Georg Henrik von Wright (1982), needs were what was bad for them to be without. The coded incidents were categorised and divided into themes.

## Children's Needs During Hospitalization

Needs emerged that could be grouped into ten categories (Runesson et al., 2002a). All needs were found during almost the whole observation time, but at different intensities. Six categories clearly emerged when the child was not exposed to threatening, unpleasant or painful occasions such as when the child was at play therapy, in the hospital corridor or in his or her own room with one or both parents. On other occasions, in threatening, unpleasant or painful situations, other needs were more important.

During situations the child found non-threatening, the following needs were expressed:

A need for activity - as soon as the children's physical condition permitted them to move about freely, they gave vent to their need to move around. They joked and were rowdy when they had the chance. The children had a need for new experiences and for information. By posing questions to the staff and their parents, the children obtained information about hospital routines and also what was planned for them. Children showed a strong need participate in care and in decisions concerning themselves. They wanted to be involved in discussing issues concerning their care and they wanted to make decisions. These discussions often took place with their parents and mainly concerned issues regarding daily life, food, clothes, and activity. But the staff was also challenged concerning treatment and care. They had a need for praise and recognition when they managed a task successfully. Physiological needs such as hunger or thirst children most often asked their parents for. Other needs, such as the need for rest, could be demonstrated very plainly by the child but were not always detected by the staff. It could be said that these needs are a child's normal needs, even when not in the hospital.

In situations that the child found threatening, other needs were of greater importance. Children showed a need to have control over the situation in which they found themselves. If the parent or staff showed that they had control over the course of events, this made things easier for the child, who then had only to concentrate on having control over his or her own behaviour. They had a need to have their parents nearby. This was not important in non-threatening situations, but when the situation became threatening to the child it became more and more important. A need for what was familiar. Many children said they wanted to go home and they wanted to be surrounded by familiar things, like a toy, their own pram and so on. Children showed a need for integrity. There were situations when the child asked their parents and the staff to leave them alone. Some children became hesitant when unfamiliar persons got too close or wanted to touch them. They did not want to be questioned too much about their friends, school, or other interests and they certainly did not want to be laughed at.

And who does?

## Parental Needs During a Child's Hospitalization

The identified parental needs were categorised and compiled into nine themes (Hallström Runesson & Elander, 2002a). The most prominent parental need was the need for security. The need for parental security was demonstrated in the expressed need for competent caregivers. Competent caregivers included many factors such as professionals with good education, experienced staff members, the right medical and nursing treatment, the parents being treated with respect, and the child being treated in an individualised way and as a special person. But security also involved how the competence was manifested, for example in a work organisation with continuity so that children and parents were cared for by the same staff, and in good planning, a quiet environment, short waiting periods, and that parents felt they were expected and that preparations for the child's care had been made when they arrived at the hospital. And perhaps most of all, parents had a need to be close to their child.

The need for mediating security to the child was manifested both by being close to the child and by doing things that felt natural and familiar. Parents thought they were able to recognise the child's needs, and they expressed those needs and comforted, encouraged, and diverted the child to satisfy the child's needs. Parents served as a link between the child and the staff in order to get the child's needs satisfied. Parents tried to protect the child in different ways, sometimes by trying to maintain a quiet environment by following the child's normal routines, and sometimes by questioning procedures.

The need for communication involves a reciprocal exchange of information between parents and staff. Parents wanted information from the staff, verbal, written, repeated and appropriate information. Parents also wanted to share their knowledge about the child with the staff. They wanted to be treated as partners in the care and they wanted to be involved in decisions before they were made.

Parents expressed a strong wish to be in control of what was happening during the hospitalisation. They checked their child's condition, the treatment, and the competence of caregivers in different ways. Some parents defined themselves as the overseers of their child's care.

Parental competence was demanded by the parents themselves and also by the child and the staff. This can be illustrated in the following situation.

> A boy at the day care unit looks at the bandage around his intravenous cannula and asks,
>
> What's this? Well, I don't know, answers his mother,
>
> What is it? he asks again. Well, I'm not very good at these things, answers the mother. The nurse tells them that it's an intravenous cannula. And the mother repeats this to the boy.
>
> Why do I have it? asks the boy. Well, you're going to have it for a while and then the nurse will remove it.
>
> Why? Asks the boy. Well, I don't know answers the mother.
>
> The father who is also in the room says, You're his mother, you have to know.

Many of the parents had a strong need to fit in. Parents hid their feelings and did not want to say or do anything that might be interpreted as criticism of the staff. And this of course influenced how the parents got their needs satisfied.

Parents and their children were seen as parts of the family. Parents were in contact with other family members and relatives during the hospitalisation, and they did not want to stay at the hospital longer than they had to.

Parents thought that staying at the hospital was quite demanding. They had to be alert all the time, and their need for relief became successively greater the longer or more demanding the hospital stay became.

> One parent reported, "Sometimes you can't leave the room for days and weeks. Our son is vomiting and has to go to the toilet, and has to spit, and so on, you're busy all the time. When you get out of there once in a while you start talking with other parents. And we laugh. We nearly die laughing. Sometimes we say that the way we're behaving, it's hard to believe that our children have cancer. But that's exactly what we need.

Parents had some basic needs that had to be satisfied such as eating and sleeping. Those needs did not predominate, however, and parents thought their own needs were of secondary importance while their child was hospitalised.

## Parental Satisfaction of Needs

Parents were also interviewed at the end of the hospital stay (Hallström, Runeson & Elander, 2002a). One question focused on what the parents did to satisfy their needs during their child's hospital stay. Five different strategies were identified concerning the way parents' needs were met. One group of parents was afraid of being a bother, they were quiet, waited, and did nothing at all, but trusted and hoped that the staff would do what they were supposed to do. One strategy parents used was to try to be nice and positive towards the staff. Parents did not complain, and while they might ask questions, they waited for the right moment to ask. Another strategy was to discuss things with their partner, ask each other questions, complain, verbalise and take care of the situation themselves. Preparing themselves for the hospitalisation was a strategy one group of parents used. They sought information from libraries, the Internet, and other professionals. They did not feel that they needed so much attention from the staff as they were well prepared when they came to the hospital. Another strategy was to inform the staff about how they wanted things to be. Those parents related that they knew how they wanted things, and they actually made sure that things were the way they wanted them.

## Children's and Parents' Participation in Decision-Making

In a second step in the analysis of field notes decision-makings or, parts of it were identified when a child (Hallström, Runeson & Elander 2002b) or a parent (Runeson, et al., 2002b) were involved. We agreed on 137 situations including a decision process where children were involved and 119 situations where parents were involved. Each situation was graded according to the Scale of participation in decision-making (Hermerén, 1986). The scale contains five different levels and was used to assess the child's and the parent's actual participation and thereby the respect shown for their integrity.

A one-way communication where professionals followed a decision they had already made themselves characterised situations assessed as grade 1. The child or the parent did not question the decision made in front of the professional. Ten situations graded as grade 1 where children were involved and 32 situations where parents were involved were found. Those situations could be illustrated by the following situation.

> "A girl and her mother are visiting the emergency ward. The paediatrician has examined the girl, she has had local anaesthetic cream applied, and they are waiting for her to receive an intravenous cannula. A nurse comes into the room and introduces herself. She says the nurse who took care of them in the morning has gone off duty and that she is in charge of them now.
>
> The nurse asks, "Do you know you are going to be admitted to the ward. No said the mother and the girl look surprised."

Eleven situations where children were involved and five when parents were involved were graded as grade 2. At grade 2, children and parents were informed about a decision that had been made but the child's or the parent's opinion was not asked for in any way.

At grade 3 the child or the parent was involved in the decision-making process but their views were ignored. Fifty-one situations when a child was involved and 21 situations when a parent was involved were graded as grade 3.

> "A mother and a dietician are discussing the child's nutritional status. The dietician starts to talk about extra nutritional supplements; she is worried that the boy does not eat enough. The mother says that she is well aware of this, but says that the boy refuses to drink them.
>
> The mother says "I don't want to force him as that will only make him angry, and then I get angry and unhappy, and that's not good for either of us. I just won't do it". The dietician gives the mother packages of different kinds of nutritional drinks saying, "You might try to give him some of those." (P17 p8)

Seventeen situations were assessed as grade 4 when a child was involved and 14 situations when a parent was involved. Children and parents gave voice to their views; staff listened and acted partly in accordance with their wishes. The example is from the day care surgery unit.

> "A boy is scheduled for minor surgery and the nurse has told him and his parents that he should change into a white gown, but the boy refuses. Both the nurse and the mother try to convince the boy to change clothes at many times, but the boy refuses. The father says, can't we wait a little? Maybe he'll be more co-operative after the sedative." The nurse agrees.

The father gave voice to his opinion, the nurse listened and acted partly in accordance with his wish but she did not change the decision, the child still had to change into a white gown.

When the child came to the operation theatre the father asked the anaesthesia staff if the child was supposed to change into a white gown but the staff said that is was not necessary.

Situations graded as grade 5 were characterised by a mutual communication; children's or parental wishes and opinions were asked for and treated with respect. 48 situations when a child was involved and 47 situations when a parent was involved were graded as grade 5.

In the next step in the analysis 218 situations including a decision-making process involving children and/or parents were scrutinised with respect to 1) who was present, 2) what decision was made, 3) who made the decision, 4) reaction of the decision, and 5) if the decision was reconsidered (Hallström & Elander, 2004). In most situations one or both parents, children and professionals were present. The situations involved 130 decisions concerning medical care and 88 decisions about nursing care. Most of the situations including decisions about medical care were decisions about what was to be done. Situations concerning nursing care described mostly decisions of how things were to be done.

In three of the situations the child made the decision alone. In ten situations the parent made the decision expressing that they knew what was best for their child. Parents clearly stated their opinion and made sure that their decision was followed. Professionals alone made the decision in 106 situations. In many of those situations parents did not give voice to their wishes and professionals followed hospital routines and guidelines. Decisions were made in mutual agreement with those affected by the decision in 99 of the situations. This means that opinions and views were asked for and discussed before the decision was made. In those situations the initiative sometimes came from the child, sometimes from the parent and sometimes from the staff. In seven of these situations the parent and the child were of different opinions.

In 83 situations one or more persons protested against the decision that was made. However, the decision was reconsidered only in 12 of the situations, most commonly because of the child's protest.

In a further analysis, two of the researchers, working independently of one another, formulated a normative judgement of each reported situation a child was involved in, being aware of the substance and the decision to be made, and the availability alternatives to planned procedure (Runeson et al., 2002b). It was found (see table 1) that the children's participation was not considered as optimal in any of the 21 situations classified as grades 1 and 2. In 43 of the 68 situations judged as belonging to grade 3 and 4, the children's participation was considered as optimal: they received information, took part in the decision making process, and in some cases compromises were made and appropriate alternatives to what had originally been planned were suggested. In no case it was thought that the child took part in decisions that were too difficult for them

Two factors seemed to influence the level of parental participation in this study; 1) how explicitly parents explained their needs; and 2) how sensitive the staff were in identifying the parent's needs. In situations assessed as grade 1 parents did not express any need or any wish to be involved in the decision. Nor did the staff make any effort to invite parents to take part in the decision making. Instead staff told them what was going to happen when the decision had already been made. In situation assessed as grade 5, the parents explicitly expressed their own or their child's needs, sometimes after the staff showed that they wanted the parents to be involved in the decision.

**Table.1. Numbers of optimal and not optimal participation situations at each level**

| Level | Optimal | Not optimal | Total (n= 137) |
|---|---|---|---|
| 1 | 0 | 10 | 10 |
| 2 | 0 | 11 | 11 |
| 3 | 32 | 19 | 51 |
| 4 | 11 | 6 | 17 |
| 5 | 48 | 0 | 48 |

## Increased Parental Participation

Increasing child's and parental involvement in the care can be don in different ways. I will shortly describe one of the changes we did at one children's day care surgery unit at a university children's hospital in the south of Sweden (Kristensson-Hallström, Elander & Malmfors, 1998). By giving parents information and education about postoperative care, and inviting them to participate in care and decisions concerning care, the goal was to facilitate the child's recovery and minimise family disruption. The surgeon had previously seen children who were admitted to the day care unit. A booklet is mailed to them describing the course of events at the hospital, and the parents and child together should read this. On admission, the child is weighed, measured, and examined by the surgeon. Every child receives EMLA cream (a local anaesthetic). A preparatory booklet with photographs describing the course of events is shown to the parents and child. About 15 minutes prior to induction the child is offered premedication to minimise anxiety and is taken to the operating room by a nurse and a parent. Parents are allowed to remain until the child is fully asleep.

In the intervention, parents received extra preparation and supportive care in three different ways, including information and education about the child's post-operative behaviour.

First, each parent received individualised verbal information about the child's postoperative behaviour, including information about drinking, eating, analgesics, and coping styles.

In addition, information was given about how the parent could participate in the child's care, and the parental role in the unit was discussed and agreed upon. Secondly, parents received written information about the post-operative course and treatment, including information about drinking, eating, voiding, bandages, caudal block, and analgesics. Third, a nurse telephoned the parents during the evening of the day of surgery in order to check on the child's condition.

The results showed that parents were well prepared to assume a greater part of the care of their children. With the new routines, children started to drink earlier, were mobilised earlier, had less pain, and fewer children vomited postoperatively. No complications were found.

In addition, the new routines led to a decrease in the time spent at hospital for both children and parents, and also to a decrease in the number of staff involved in the care.

## Conclusion

Successful patient or parent- nurse partnerships do not just happens. Routines and planned ways of working are required so that child and parental concerns are dealt with even though they are not expressed explicitly. This is not only because professionals are in a much stronger position than patients and their relatives. It is also because of the fact that for different reasons, such as the fear of being bothersome or not knowing whom to turn to, they do not always express their concerns.

It can be argued that the medical profession should make medical and nursing decisions. But this is not always true. Professionals have superior medical knowledge, but children themselves and their parents have superior knowledge about the child's preferences and best interests, which are based on the personal values of the family. It is not only in major, life changing decisions that children and parents have a right to contribute. Children are not always mature enough to choose therefore they cannot always make decisions for example about medical interventions. But in order to satisfy their needs, they can almost always participate in one way or another when decisions are being made.

Is it important for children to participate in decision-making? Children are probably like adults, so some want to be involved whereas others do not (Enskär, von Essen 2000). The

Commission for Health Improve concluded after having taken in 59 separate reports from voluntary bodies and statutory organisations (Boylan 2004) that children and teenagers felt that they had the right to participate in decisions about their treatment when hospitalized in Great Britain. However, they were unhappy about the lack of communication and they did not think that they were sufficiently involved in decision-making.

Illness reduces a person's capacity for autonomy. The same can be said for parents with an ill child. Health professionals need to support children and parents when ethical issues such as autonomy in relation to consent to treatment for the child are raised. Children are a vulnerable group, and it is important to recognise the influence and significance of the socio-cultural context in the implementation of informed consent. Professionals working with children play a key part in promoting children's right to participate in decisions and to include this into the ward's philosophy and values. Children's nurses work in close relation with children and their family and have important roles as informant, and communicators. The advocacy role involves protecting the child's right to self-determination, enabling them to participate in decisions, and have their wishes, goals and views considered in relation to individual children and for sick children as a group. Having a voice in decision-making helps the child to develop a sense of himself as a person and gives the parents a feeling that they are part of a team giving their child optimal care during hospitalisation.

## Acknowledgements

Parts of this paper have been published previously in *Journal of Pediatric Nursing* 2002a;Apr7(2):140-8, *International Journal of Nursing Practice.* 2002a; 3(3): 156-162, *Journal of Clinical Nursing* 1997;**6:**297-302, *Journal of Clinical Nursing* 2004;13:367-75, *Nursing Ethics* 2002b; Mar 9(2): 202-14, *Nursing Ethics* 2002b;9(6):583-98, *Nursing Ethics*, 2005;12(3):223-238.

## References

Anderson ES, Jackson A, Wailoo MP, Petersen SA. Child care decisions: parental choice or chance. *Child: Care Health and Development* 2002;28(5):391-401.

Beauchamp T, Childress J. *Principles of Biomedical Ethics*. 5th Ed ed. New York: Oxford University Press; 2001.

Bijstervelt P. Competent to refuse? *Paediatric Nursing* 2000(12):33-35.

Blower K, Morgan E. Great expectations? Parental participation in care. *Journal of Child Health Care* 2000;4(2):60-65.

Boylan P. Children's voices project. Feedback from children and young people about their experience and expectations of health care. In: www.chi.nhs.uk/childrens _voices/index.shtml. London; 2004. Retrieved 19 November 2004

Brody JL, Scherer DG, Annett RD, Pearson-Bish M. Voluntary Assent in Biomedical Research with Adolescents: A comparison of Parent and Adolescent Views. *Ethics & Behaviour* 2003;13(1):79-95.

Brinchmann BS, Förde R, Nortvedt P. What matters to the parents? A qualitative study of parents´experinces with life-and-death decisions concerning their premature infants. *Nursing Ethics* 2002;9(4):388-404.

Capron A. (1982) The authority of others to decide about biomedical interventions with incompetents. In W Gaylin, R Macklin (eds). *Who speaks for the child?* New York: The Hastings Center: 115-152.

Clayton M. Consent in children: legal and ethical issues. *Journal of Child Health Care* 2000;4(2):78-81.

Dalton JM. Development and testing of the theory of collaborative decision-making in nursing practice for triads. *Journal of Advanced Nursing* 2003;41(1):22-33.

Enskär K, von Essen L. Important Aspects of Care and Assistance for Children with Cancer. *Journal of Pediatric Oncology Nursing* 2000;17(4):239-249.

Friedman Ross L. Children, families and health-care dicision-making. *Journal of Medical Ethics* 2000;26(4):1-3.

Guerriere DN, McKeever P, Llewellyn-Thomas H, Berall G. Mother´s decisions about gastrostomy tube insertion in children: factors to contributing to uncertainty. *Developmental Medicine and Child Neurology* 2003(45):470-476.

Hallström I, Runeson, I & Elander G. Observed parental needs during their child's hospitalization. *J of Pediatric Nursing* 2002a;Apr;7(2):140-8.

Hallström, I, Runesson, I & Elander, G. An observational study of the level at which parents participate in decisions during their child's hospitalization. *Nursing Ethics* 2002b Mar; 9(2): 202-14.

Hallström I, Elander G. Decision-making during hospitalisation: parents´and children´s involvement. *Journal of Clinical Nursing* 2004;13:367-75.

Hallström, I. & Elander, G. Decision-making in paediatric care – an overview with reference to nursing care. *Nursing Ethics*, 2005;12(3):223-238.

Ham C. Tragic choices in health care: lessons from the child B case. *British Medical Journal* 1999;319(7219):1258-1262.

Harrison C, Kenny N, P., Sidarous M, Rowell M. Bioethics for Clinicians, 9. Involving Children in Medical Decisions. *Canadian Medical Association Journal* 1997;156(6):825-829.

Hermerén G. *Kunskapens pris* (The price of knowledge). 2nd edition ed. Stockholm: Humanistisk-samhällsvetenskapliga forskningsrådets förlagstjänst; 1996.(In Swedish)

Higgins SS, Kayser-Jones J, Savedra M. Parental Understanding of Consequences of Pediatric Cardiac Transplantation. *Progress in Cardiovascular Nursing* 1996;11(3):10-16.

Hinds PS, Oakes L, Furman W, Foppiano P, Olson M, Quargnenti A, et al. Decision Making by Parents and Healthcare Professionals when Considering Continued Care for Pediatric Patients with Cancer. *Oncology Nursing Forum* 1997;24(9):1523-1528.

Kawik L. Nurses´and parents´perceptions of participation and partnership in caring for a hospitalised child. *British Journal of Nursing* 1996;5(7):430-437.

King N, Cross A. Children as decision makers: guidelines for pediatricians. *The Journal of Pediatrics* 1996(115):10-16.

Kirk S. Negotiating lay and professional roles in the care of children with complex health care needs. *Journal of Advanced Nursing* 2001;34(5):593-602.

Kopelman L.M. (1997) The best-interests standard threshold, ideal, and standard of reasonableness. *Journal of Medicine & Philosophy* **22** (3), 271-89.

Kristensson-Hallström I, Elander G. Parental participation in the Care of Hospitalised Children. *Scandinavian Journal of Caring Sciences* 1994(8):149-154.

Kristensson-Hallström I. Strategies for feeling secure influence parents' participation in care. *Journal of Clinical Nursing* 1999(8):586-92.

Kristensson-Hallström I, Elander G. Parents´ Experiences of Hospitalization - Different Strategies for Feeling Secure. *Pediatric Nursing* 1997;July-August 23(4):361-367.

Kristensson-Hallström, I., Elander, G. & Malmfors, G. Increased parental participation in a paediatric surgical day-care unit. *Journal of Clinical Nursing* 1997;**6:**297-302.

Kristensson-Hallström I, Norlund A, Malmfors G. Paediatric day care surgery - increased parental participation reduces costs. *European Journal of Public Health* 1999;8(3):247-249.

Kuther TL. Medical decision-making and minors: Issues of consent and decent. *Adolescence* 2003;38(150):343-58.

Lee P. Partnership in care: a critical exploration of how this may be applied to children attending the Accident and Emergency department. *Accident in Emergency Nursing* 1999(7):119-123.

Lind C, Anderson B, Oberle K. Ethical Issues in Adolescent Consent for Research. *Nursing Ethics* 2003;10(5):504-511.

Manley RS, Smye V, S. S. Addressing Complex Ethical Issues in the Treatment of Children and Adolescents with Eating Disorders: Application of a Framework for Ethical Decision-Making. *European Eating Disorders Review* 2001(9):144-66.

Mc Cabe MA. Involving Children and Adolescents in Medical Decision Making: Developmental and Clinical Considerations. *Journal of Pediatric Psychology* 1996;21(4):505-16.

Mouradian WE. Making decisions for children. The Angle Orthodontist 1999;69(4):300-05.

Neill S. Parent participation 1: literature review and methodology. *British Journal of Nursing* 1996a;5(1):34-40.

Neill S. Parent participation 2: findings and their implications for practice. *British Journal of Nursing* 1996b;5(2):110-117.

Pyke-Grimm KA, Degner L, Small A, B. M. Preferences for participating in treatment decision making and information needs of parents of children with cancer: a pilot study. *Journal of Pediatric Oncology Nursing* 1999;16(1):13-24.

Runeson I, Enskär K, Elander G, Hermerén G. Professionals´perception of children´s participation in decision making in healthcare. *Journal of Clinical Nursing* 2001(10):70-78.

Runeson I, Hermerén G, Elander G, Kristensson-Hallström I. Children´s consent to treatment: Using a scale to assess degree of self-determination. *Pediatric Nursing* 2000;26(5):455-459.

Runeson, I., Hallström, I., Elander, G. & Hermerén, G. Children's needs during hospitalisation. An observational study of hospitalised boys. *International Journal of Nursing Practice.* 2002a; 3(3): 156-162.

Runeson I, Hallström I, Elander G, Hermeren G. Children's participation in the decision-making process during hospitalisation. An observation study. *Nursing Ethics* 2002b;9(6):583-98.

Schuman A. Parental and Institutional Decision Making about Children's Healthy Development: Conflicts and Interests across Cultures. *Journal of Immigrant Health* 2000;2(1):43-51.

Sheilds, L. A review of the literature from developed and developing countries relating to the effects of hospitalization on children and parents. *International Nursing Review* 2001;48: 29-37.

Shields L, Kristensson-Hallström I, Kristiansdottir G, Hunter J. Who owns the child in hospital? A preliminary discussion. *Journal of Advanced Nursing* 2003;41(3):213-222.

Stokes MA., Drake-Lee AB. (1998) Children who withdraw consent for elective surgery. *Paediatric Anaesthesia* 8(2), 113-5.

Truog RD. "Doctor, if this were your child, what would you do?" *Pediatrics* 1999;103(1):153-155.

UN. *Convention on the Rights of the Child.* New York: United Nations; 1989.

von Wright, H. Om behov. (About needs) *Filosofisk tidsskrift.* 1982; 3: 1-12. (in Swedish)

Walker NE, Doyon T. Fairness and Reasonableness of the child's decision:" A proposed legal Sandard for Children's Participation in Medical Decision Making. *Behavioral Sciences and the Law* 2001;19:611-636.

Wilson HV. Power and partnership: a critical analysis of the surveillance discourses of child health nurses. *Journal of Advanced Nursing* 2001;36(2):294-301.

Winn Oakley M, Ed IRcspasdI. Children and young people and care proceedings. In: Lewis A, Lindsay G, editors. *Researching children's perspectives.* 2nd ed. Buckingham: Open University Press; 2002.

Yeh C-H, Linnn C-F, Tsai J-L, Lai Y-M, Ku H-C. Determinants of parental decisions on "drop out" from cancer treatment for childhood cancer patients. *Journal of Advanced Nursing* 1999;30(1):193-199.

In: Decision Making in Medicine and Health Care
Editor: P. C. Tolana, pp. 115-131
ISBN: 978-1-60021-870-5


*Chapter VI*

# Pathways Into Substitute Health Care Labor

***Sally Lindsay****
Institute for Social, Cultural and Policy Research,
University of Salford, United Kingdom.

## Abstract

Despite the increased use of substitute health care providers in an effort to save money and fill gaps in physicians shortages, little is known about why people decide to enter such work. Gaining further insight into decisions to enter these occupations may help with recruitment and retention strategies, which is critical at a time when health workforces are facing severe shortages. Most research on the employment of substitute health care providers focuses on career choice among various specialties within an occupation while there has been little exploration of why men and women enter these occupations in the first place. Most of what is known about career pathways for substitute providers focuses on job satisfaction and experiences once in the profession but not why people entered the occupation. This chapter examines three health care professions: physician assistants, nurse practitioners and nurse anesthetists. These domains of health care were chosen because they are among the largest substitute providers in the U.S. This chapter draws on normative decision theory to frame an analysis of how people decided to enter these occupations. This project drew on 53 in-depth interviews with substitute health care providers to gain insight into why men and women enter such areas of work. Findings suggest that for this sample, choosing these occupations was the best decision amongst the alternatives because it offered the most desirable consequences with the minimum loss. Both men and women claimed that role models and exposure to the profession influenced their decision to enter. Many women chose their career because they were in the caring field for a long time and this offered

* Correspondence concerning this article should be addressed to: Dr. Sally Lindsay, Institute for Social, Cultural and Policy Research, 4th Floor Humphrey Booth House, University of Salford, Salford, United Kingdom M5 4QA. Phone: +011 44 161 295 5029; Email: s.lindsay@salford.ac.uk.

them a challenge. Men, on the other hand, often entered their job as a second career choice as an opportunity to expand their skills and increase their autonomy. Male nurse practitioners often came from diverse backgrounds while many physician assistants and nurse anesthetists had military backgrounds. Men and women both claimed that these occupations offered a comparable alternative to the time consuming and expensive training required to become a physician.

# Introduction

Despite the increased use of substitute health care providers in an effort to save money and fill gaps in physicians shortages, little is known about why people decide to enter such work. The health care industry is labor intensive and comprises a large proportion of health care expenditures. Consequently, governments are keen to find opportunities to reduce health care spending (Deuben 1998). One common cost saving measure is the substitution of less expensive workers for more costly physician providers (Auerbach 2000; Deuben 1998). Health economists estimate that up to $8.75 billion could be saved annually if nurse practitioners were used more extensively since their salary is about three and a half times less than physicians' (Calpin-Davies and Akehurst 1999). Physician assistants are also proposed as a cost-effective solution to America's health care crisis in that they can free doctors' time to treat more complicated patients (AAPA 2003). There are also significant cost savings in using nurse anesthetists, who make on average $84,000, compared to anaesthesiologists who make an average of $244,000 per year (AANA 2003). Examining such 'substitute' health care providers is salient because they comprise an increasing proportion of the labour force where their numbers are expected to increase by 150% in the U.S. over the next decade (Bureau of Health Professions 2000; Cooper et al. 1998). The use of substitute providers also offers an effective solution to physician shortages and increasing access to rural and underserved areas (Fallacaro et al. 1996). Although there has been an increased use of substitute health care providers, relatively little is known about why men and women enter these health care occupations. Gaining further insight into decisions to enter such occupations may help with recruitment and retention strategies, which is critical at a time when health workforces are facing severe shortages.

## Who are Substitute Providers?

Substitute providers, also commonly known as 'mid-level' or 'non-physician clinicians' are increasingly offering health care that has traditionally been provided by physicians. Substitute providers can perform up to eighty percent of the same tasks as physicians for a fraction of the cost (AANA 2003). Nurse practitioners are registered nurses who have additional training in either primary or acute care. They work with clients, physicians and other professionals to assess, manage and diagnose common illnesses (AANP 2003). Physician assistants are health professionals who are licensed to practice medicine under physician supervision. Nevertheless, in many states supervision is loosely defined, whereby physicians need only be available somewhere in the hospital, or even simply by phone

(AAPA 2003). Physician assistants make clinical decisions and provide a broad range of diagnostic, therapeutic, preventive and health maintenance services (AAPA 2003). Finally, nurse anesthetists are nurses with additional training in anesthesia who work either independently or as part of an anesthesia team (AANA 2003; Miller 1996). These occupations provide examples of efforts to reduce costs by breaking down skilled jobs into smaller components and by substituting less skilled workers for skilled workers.

Most research on the employment of substitute providers focuses on career choice among various specialties within an occupation (e.g., why physician assistants enter certain specialties or why nurse practitioners choose collaborative versus independent practice) (Amundsen and Corey 2000; Singer and Hooker 1996). Most of what is known about career pathways for substitute providers focuses on job satisfaction and experiences once in the profession. There has been little exploration of why men and women enter these occupations in the first place.

Three domains of health care were chosen (physician assistants, nurse-practitioners and nurse anesthetists) because they comprise the largest physician-substitute providers in the U.S. and represent a range in variability in substitute providers (Bureau of Health Professions 2000). In Canada, nurse practitioners are a key substitute provider for family physicians. Moreover, anesthesia arguably provides 'an excellent laboratory' for studying workforce substitutions because nurse anesthetists offer a cost-effective alternative to physician anesthesiologists (AANA 2003; Miller 1996).

Previous research examining substitute health care labour tends to focus on its cost-effectiveness, reimbursement, and differences in the scope of practice and quality of care given by substitute providers (Calpin-Davies and Akehurst 1999; Deuben 1998; Kernick 2002; Richards et al. 2000). Such studies tend to be from a health economics or health policy perspective while there is only a modest literature from a psychological perspective. Despite the increased use of substitute health care providers, little is known about why people enter these occupations.

## The Health Care Division of Labor

The health care workforce has undergone great change over the past decade—especially with the transformation of existing professions and the introduction of new workers. Although medicine has typically dominated the health care division of labour, its dominant position is being increasingly challenged. Intra-professional competition is being intensified with the increased supply of medical providers (Barnett et al. 1998). In America medicine's authority is being increasingly challenged from emerging mid-level providers such as nurse practitioners and physician assistants. Mid-level providers are increasingly offering health care that has in the past been provided principally by physicians (Cooper et al. 1998). The consequence of this shift in providers is reshaping the health care division of labor and thus, breaking traditional professional boundaries and altering professional roles. Physicians often view themselves in competition with substitute providers and are often reluctant to support the increased use of advanced practice nurses because many are concerned about their jurisdiction (Mundinger 1994). Substitution of health care providers may arise from the discarding of unwanted tasks to another provider rather than just delegating the work to subordinate grades. This strategy of 'ditching the dirty work' is a tactic that professions often use to deal with encroachment (Hugman 1991; Nancarrow and Borthwick 2005). So why would someone want to enter an occupation that often encounters resistance from the medical profession and where they are often performing the less desirable work?

Although some may argue that these mid-level positions involve deskilled labor (Hugman 1991) in the sense that the work is moving from physicians to lesser skilled health care providers, the work may also be seen as 'upskilling' for those who are moving into the work. For example, occupations such as physician assistants, nurse practitioners and nurse anesthetists may provide the opportunity for men and women to enter an occupation that is better (e.g., higher pay, more autonomy) than the one they were currently in. In this chapter I argue that men and women entered these occupations because it was the best decision amongst the alternatives and it offered the most desirable consequences with the minimum loss.

### Decision-Making

This chapter draws on normative decision theory to frame an analysis of why people chose this career path. The underlying assumption of this theory is that people strive to do what is best for them while choosing the option that offers the most desirable consequences (Beach 1997). "Best" is normally interpreted as deciding on the option that offers the most desirable payoff whether that is maximum benefit or minimum loss. Although people cannot predict what will happen in the future, they tend to opt for the most promising option to see how things turn out. It involves estimating what the consequences or payoffs will be if the option is chosen with a speculation about how valuable these payoffs will be. Ideally people would choose the options that offer the most payoffs and would be the most valuable to them. This theory is often illustrated through the example of gambling (Beach 1997). A person is viewed as a gambler who must place a bet (or choose a course of action) and then observe the outcome—whether win or lose. Decisions often involve doubt, uncertainty and risk. Each profession is a potential option that the decision maker has to choose from and each can be characterized by their potential gains and losses. In the case of substitute health care occupations people must have chosen this career path because it presented the best option for them amongst the alternatives.

## METHODS

The objective of this chapter was to explore why men and women enter substitute health care occupations. To examine this, qualitative semi-structured interviews were conducted with 53 health care providers in New York State, Pennsylvania, U.S., and Ontario Canada (refer to Table 1). These locations were chosen because they provide examples of high utilizations of substitute providers. For example, New York State provides a useful site because it has among the highest proportion of nurse practitioners and physician assistants

(Bureau of Health Professions 2000). Similarly, Pennsylvania was chosen because of its extensive use of nurse anesthetists (AANA 2003). Ontario has Canada's largest provincial primary care reform scheme and has a large number of nurse practitioners (Hutchison et al 2001).

**Table 1. Overview of Interviews**

| Occupation | Study Sites | Male | Female | Total |
|---|---|---|---|---|
| Nurse practitioners | Ontario and New York | 12 | 11 | 23 |
| Physician assistants | New York | 8 | 7 | 15 |
| Nurse anesthetists | Pennsylvania | 8 | 7 | 15 |
| | | | | Total 53 |

Telephone interviews were conducted from August 2003 to January 2004 and lasted between thirty and ninety minutes. Health care providers were identified through college and health association registries and relevant Internet sites. Potential informants were contacted by phone or email and the objectives of the study were conveyed along with the project information form. A date and time for a follow-up phone call was then established.[1]

This research used an unfolding paradigm with general guiding questions and a loosely structured design so that categories and codes can emerge from the data, during analysis aposterioi. Through inductive analysis, patterns and themes were identified around the issues of why they chose the profession. The interview schedule had core questions with probes to allow for comparisons to be made between the interviews. Respondents were asked to describe why they had entered the profession they were currently working in. All interviews were tape-recorded and transcribed verbatim. Data collected through interviews were sorted, coded and categorized according to emergent themes with the aid of NVIVO, a qualitative data analysis software program. This program assisted in condensing the data and identifying relationships among central themes around the issues of reasons for entering the occupation.

The project drew on interpretive traditions within qualitative research, where the researcher seeks an in-depth understanding of the experiences of the participants (Miller & Dingwall 1997; Green & Thorogood 2004). The analysis began by reading through each transcript several times and noting emerging themes and patterns. Analysis gradually evolved into the stage of axial coding, which was concerned with the properties of the themes and their inter-relationships.

## RESULTS

Although there were several factors influencing decisions to enter these occupations the participants in this study chose them because it was the best decision amongst the

[1] This study received ethics approval from a University Research Ethics Board.

alternatives. Table 2 provides an overview of the reasons for entering substitute occupations. Men and women both claimed that role models and exposure to the profession influenced their decision to enter. Many women chose their career because they were in the caring field for a long time and this offered them a challenge. Men, on the other hand, often entered their job as a second career choice as an opportunity to expand their skills and increase their autonomy. Male nurse practitioners often came from diverse backgrounds while many physician assistants and nurse anesthetists had military backgrounds. Men and women both claimed that these occupations offered a comparable alternative to the time consuming and expensive nature of medical training.

## Exposure to the Occupation and Role Models

Several of the health care providers described how role models and various encounters with the occupation influenced their decision to enter. Many of the male physician assistants and nurse anesthetists had a military background prior to starting a health career. For example, several men said: "Pursuing my education as a physician assistant was actually an extension of my military career" (Male physician assistant #6). Others gave similar examples:

> I originally went to nursing school in the mid 1960s and was facing a draft when the Vietnam war was on. So I came into the military out of the army under the student nurse program. Then after basic training I'd applied already for the nurse anesthesia program there (Male nurse anesthetist #1).

The military exposed many men to the physician assistant profession and various other nursing specialties such as nurse anesthesia. Indeed, many men claimed that "the army is pretty good about giving you lots of exposure and chances" (Physician assistant # 8). It was through their exposure to the profession that helped them to decide that this would provide them with an opportunity to advance their career.

Others described how they were introduced to these occupations:

> After I graduated from high school I went in the military and it was there working as an x-ray technician in the operating room that I stumbled quite accidentally across the field of nurse anesthesia…I said to my friend after the case, 'who was that guy up there at the head of the table?' He's a nurse anesthetist. I thought that was intriguing because here was this guy who was an army officer and I knew they made a lot more money than I was making and nobody was bothering him and I thought, 'well I can do that.' (Male nurse anesthetist #2)

For this particular man the autonomous nature of the work and better pay were desirable features influencing his decision to enter. Others described how role models and exposure to these jobs further developed their interest. For example, a male physician assistant described:

**Table 2. Reasons for Entry into Substitute Occupations**

| Type of provider | Gender | Initial career | Reason for going into this career |
|---|---|---|---|
| Nurse practitioner | Female | nurse | continuing education |
| | Female | nurse | continuing education / upgrade skills |
| | Female | nurse | wanted a challenge |
| | Female | nurse | wanted more opportunities and autonomy |
| | Female | nurse | wanted a challenge |
| | Female | nurse | wanted credit for advanced tasks she was already performing |
| | Female | nurse | was performing advanced tasks and wanted further education |
| | Female | nurse | wanted to advance skills |
| | Female | pre-med/nurse | did not want time / expense of medical school; poor grades |
| | Female | engineering | interest in women's health |
| | Female | pre-med | parents sent her to medical school but she did not like it |
| | Male | nurse | did not have the grades to get into medical school |
| | Male | fish biologist | wanted a job that was more secure rather than just contract work |
| | Male | business | wanted a more secure job and was introduced to this career by a role model / initially discouraged from nursing |
| | Male | nurse | was doing advanced skills and wanted further education |
| | Male | nurse | to advance training and more autonomy |
| | Male | rehabilitation | did not have the grades to get into medical school |
| | Male | nurse | wanted more autonomy |
| | Male | nurse | wanted more advanced training / autonomy |
| | Male | nurse | was initially discouraged from nursing |
| | Male | business | wanted to further education |
| | Male | army | was interested in health care |
| | Male | nurse | wanted a more secure job / better pay |
| Physician assistant | Female | medicine | compatible with family |
| | Female | foreign languages | lack of job opportunities in past career |
| | Female | medical lab | wanted something people-oriented/ alternative to nursing |
| | Female | medicine | compatible with family life |
| | Female | social worker | had initially wanted to go into medicine but was too costly and time consuming |
| | Female | political science | better job opportunities |
| | Female | physician assistant | was encouraged to be a nurse but wanted something different |
| | Male | medical sergeant | extension of military career |
| | Male | accounting | interested in health |
| | Male | physician assistant | medicine was costly and time consuming |
| | Male | physician assistant | did not have the grades to get into medical school |
| | Male | aerospace science | health problems and family issues prevented him from continuing on in career |
| | Male | military | extension of military career |
| | Male | navy corpsman | extension of military career |
| | Male | health sciences | less costly and time consuming than medicine |
| Nurse anesthetist | Female | nurse | always wanted to be an anesthetist |
| | Female | nurse | interest sparked by a colleague and role model |
| | Female | nurse | liked focusing on one patient at a time |
| | Female | nurse | wanted more autonomy |
| | Female | nurse | wanted to help patients not to feel pain |
| Nurse anesthetist | Female | nurse | interest in anesthesia |
| | Female | nurse | wanted to advance skills |
| | Male | military nurse | interest in anesthesia |
| | Male | x-ray technician | better pay and autonomy |
| | Male | nurse | exposure to the profession; more autonomy / pay |
| | Male | neurochemistry | wanted further education in critical care |
| | Male | nursing | alternative to medical school |
| | Male | accounting | exposure to the profession |
| | Male | janitorial/business | influenced by colleagues (secure job) |
| | Male | military | exposure and interest in anesthesia |

> I went to college as an undergrad thinking I'll be an accountant and through exposure to medicine I decided that I enjoyed it. When I was in college I ran an ambulance service. I did lots of teaching with the Red Cross regarding first aid. Basically I just followed a path and when I graduated and it came down to saying, 'well, okay, I don't want to sit behind a desk all the time.' I enjoy working with people. So I decided that I would continue on in a career path as a physician assistant. (Male physician assistant #6)

This man, like several other participants in the study, wanted to achieve the maximum benefit from the position that he was currently in.

Several health care providers described how a family member's involvement in health care helped to spark an interest in the area:

> My father is a surgeon and at the small hospital where he was working there was a nurse anesthetist. We would come in and choose the nurse anesthetist to do the cases and so I saw her one day and realized she wasn't one of the anesthesiologists I knew and asked about her, and he told me she was a nurse anesthetist. So I kind of decided right then and there that that's what I wanted to do. (Female nurse anesthetist #1)

During the time that this woman was making a career decision nurse anesthesia the most realistic option instead of the male-dominated field of anesthesiology which is not typically compatible with family life. Many of the women felt limited in their career options but felt that substitute occupations provided them with an opportunity to achieve a more advanced status.

Family influences were also an important factor shaping decisions to enter these occupations. Their mothers and sisters often influenced their decision to enter nursing specialties. For example, "My sister had just graduated as being a nurse. She said look, if you're interested in medicine why don't you look at nursing?" (Male nurse practitioner #10). Indeed, role models and exposure to the profession influenced men and women's decision to enter, which was particularly the case for the nurse practitioner and nurse anesthetist professions.

Others described how a role model influenced their decision to choose that particular occupation. A male nurse anesthetist gives his example:

> I started off being a paramedic and I just truly enjoyed emergency medicine. It was a nurse anesthetist who is usually providing the anesthesia in the room that I was learning how to intubate in. So the nurse anesthetist who taught me how to intubate was like, 'wow, this is what I really want to do.' (Male nurse anesthetist #6)

Many women nurse anesthetists described how they were exposed to their career through several years of experience in critical care.

> I really learned about nurse anesthesia from a colleague who worked with anesthesiologists. Once she got into it and started telling me about it, I was in awe. I couldn't believe these people did what they did--the autonomy, the decision-making. (Female nurse anesthetist #2)

These examples suggest that role models and exposure to these occupations helped participants to see the opportunities they would have for career advancement and thus, influenced their decisions to enter these occupations. Choosing these career paths was the best decision amongst the alternative of staying in their current position. For those who already had a health background choosing to enter one of these occupations would not require a great deal of upgrading.

## Looking For a Challenge and More Autonomous Work

The interviews showed that many of the female nurse practitioners and nurse anesthetists had been in nursing for quite some time and decided to pursue something more challenging. In some cases they also wanted credit for tasks they were already performing. For example, many women reported: "I was a staff nurse for 19 years in the emergency department and then I felt like I needed a challenge. So, I returned to school and did the nurse practitioner program" (Female nurse-practitioner #3). Several male and female providers described how they pursued more advanced practice nursing or physician assistant work because their skills were increasingly being relied upon.

> I was a nurse for 20 years and I found my expertise increasingly being relied on by physicians as assessment and decision-making for the care of the patients. I thought that if I was going to be at that level of independent decision-making then I should have the educational background to back me up. (Female nurse practitioner #1)

Some men and women entered their occupation because they wanted more autonomy or were increasingly being relied upon for more specialized skills. For example, some claimed, "One reason [for becoming a nurse practitioner] was that I was already doing that skill, that scope of practice in here" (Male nurse practitioner #4). Similarly, other female nurse practitioners claimed that after having been in nursing for a long period of time they were up for a challenge of a more advanced scope of practice. These occupations allowed men and women an opportunity to 'upskill' and expand their career. Other nurse practitioners went into the field because their skills were at that level anyhow. In fact, many providers were increasingly being asked to perform advanced skills. For example,

> I was working in an advanced scope within the role of the registered nurse in a women's health clinic. It was through my advanced role that I knew that I wanted to have more autonomy that I needed to complete my role as far as primary health care. So I pursued it. (Female nurse practitioner #5)

Similarly, other women pursued a more advanced role because they wanted more of a challenge and increased autonomy. For example, "I had been a critical care nurse for several years and I wanted more of a challenge" (Female nurse anesthetist #3). Some had been a nurse for several years and felt like they needed a challenge and decided to upgrade their skills. Men and women both claimed that they were drawn into these more advanced occupations because of the autonomy it offered. For example, many of the males claimed how there was

> "a lot of autonomy associated with the work" (Male nurse anesthetist #3). Men were particularly drawn to the "autonomous practice and advanced learning" (Male nurse practitioner #4). Along with autonomy, these occupations provided an avenue for a more secure position. For example, many claimed that they "wanted to become a nurse practitioner because I wanted a profession that was a more versatile field to be in" (Male nurse practitioner #5).

Several people also reported that these occupations offered a good income, which was especially desirable for those who were the breadwinners of the family. For example, some male nurse anesthetists claimed:

Quite honestly, you make a decent buck. You can provide, and it's a good income.

> That's why you see a lot more people going into anesthesia. The money issue is really strong at this point. (Male nurse anesthetist # 3)

> The driving force is that right now we're in a shortage so the salary is very lucrative. The overtime is there, so for a man to be able to support his family it's very desirable. (Male nurse anesthetist # 2)

Men and women entered substitute health care work because it offered them a challenge and an opportunity for more autonomy. Given their current training and background these occupations offered them the best opportunity for more pay and autonomy without a lot of further training. Some providers wanted credit for the advanced tasks that they were already performing so they thought it would be worth the extra effort to get the official credentials. For most, these occupations required just a bit of extra training for much more rewarding work.

## A Second Career Choice

The interviews suggest that these occupations were a second career choice for many of the providers (particularly men) who came from diverse backgrounds such as business, fish biology and the military. Substitute health care occupations offered men and women an opportunity for a career advancement at a time when they may have needed some direction. For example, several people claimed that they were "essentially a lost sheep if you will. I couldn't figure out what I wanted to do. I happened to have an advisor who steered me in this direction" (Male nurse-anesthetist #5). Others gave similar examples:

> I grew up at a time when I couldn't find my focus and I quit school and went into the army corpsman to sort of rekindle things and I when I came back there was the PA profession looking for people like myself. (Male physician assistant #6)

> I was actually in the stockbroker business. I was floundering around in janitorial services for a lot of my life before that. Really didn't do well in college because I really didn't have any direction. A friend sort of twisted my arm and said, 'why don't you go to nursing school?' And I said, 'why not?' (Male nurse anesthetist #7)

For these providers, substitute health care occupations were attractive because they offered more security and rewarding opportunities than the jobs they were currently working in. Interestingly, several men entered nurse practitioner and nurse anesthesia work as their second career because nursing was not a typical 'masculine' career choice and they felt discouraged from such work right after high school. For example, several men shared a similar story:

> In high school I always wanted to be a nurse. Back in the mid to late 70s guys just really didn't do it. So I went into business and hated it. Finally, at about 19 I realized that I really wanted to go into nursing. (Male nurse practitioner #3)

> I applied to nursing which I would never had done from high school but I guess you get a little wiser as you are out in the workforce. I would have never gone from high school because people would have thought I was gay or whatever. (Male nurse practitioner #9)

Another male nurse practitioner described how he did not receive encouragement in high school to enter nursing, despite his interest. He said, "I do remember my guidance counselor not being very happy with me. He thought I was jerking his chain" (Male nurse practitioner #9). Consequently, men often pursued other more 'acceptable' career choices because they were initially discouraged from their first choice, which was nursing. Once some time had passed and they realized they were not enjoying the career they were in they decided to pursue nursing.

Other men entered these occupations because it offered them an opportunity for a secure job. Several providers claimed that they particularly liked the "transferability. You can work anywhere in the English speaking world.

> The job opportunities are good" (Male nurse practitioner #12). Similarly, another health care provider said he decided to pursue nursing because the major attraction was that it was a transportable job. I was able to pick up and leave tomorrow and transfer those skills quite easily. I didn't really know that at the time that it was like a designation like an apprenticeship. (Male nurse practitioner #2)

For this man, nursing was a better option than the occupation that he was currently working in because it offered more security.

Others were in quite diverse backgrounds such as foreign languages, political science and fish biology, but were looking for a more secure position. Given that these substitute health care occupations were in demand and that many of these providers had an interest in health care they decided to pursue this area further.

> My original training was in foreign languages and I really wanted to teach German to teachers and foreign languages. At the time that I graduated there simply were not a lot of jobs in the area. There had been quite a bit of scaling back in many of the school districts. (Female physician assistant #2)

This particular woman was introduced to the physician assistant profession through a volunteer position in a health clinic. Given her lack of opportunities with her previous background in languages she decided to pursue this area which had more options while at the same time developing her interest in women's health.

There were a few examples of people with good educational backgrounds in quite different fields but had chosen this new career either because of limitations experienced from personal health problems or for family reasons.

> My intent was actually to fly in space as a shuttle pilot but 2 factors prevented that. One, I developed high blood pressure when I was in college and second, my dad developed cancer and so I left school prematurely. I subsequently went back to school and graduated with a bachelor of science in physician assistant studies. (Male physician assistant #5)

Choosing the physician assistant profession for this particular man was a compromise as he had planned a much more prestigious career. However, he did so in order to minimize further loss in time with his family.

The results suggest that substitute health care occupations were desirable to both men and women because they offered a secure position, more autonomy and pay. Many people entering these occupations were motivated by a desire to expand their career. Men often encountered barriers when they first entered because of the gendered nature of the work and the stigma associated with men in nursing. Thus, it was often a second career choice where they decided to pursue nursing again once the stigma had calmed down a bit. Others had not decided what they wanted to do for a career and floundered for a bit before deciding that this occupation offered a secure job and good pay for less effort than medical school.

## Alternative to Medical School

Several people chose these occupations (especially the physician assistant profession) because it offered an expanded career choice beyond traditional nursing careers without the time requirements of medical school. Many women were particularly attracted to the physician assistant profession and saw it as an alternate to traditional nursing and 'caring' fields. One female physician assistant captured it best:

> I heard about the PA profession and they were opening up a program and I was very interested in it. I'm too bossy to be a nurse. When I went back to school I was 35 years old and being a doctor wasn't an option. People have asked me why I wasn't a doctor and I tell them when I graduated from high school, women were still one of 3 things: secretaries, teachers or nurses. I was none of the above. (Female physician assistant #3)

This woman, like several others in the study, wanted to achieve a maximum benefit with the options that were available to them. Many women physician assistants and nurse practitioners started off in medical school and later switched to another program after they decided that they no longer wanted to be a physician. For example, one woman claimed:

> I was pre-med for the first couple of years and then decided that isn't what I wanted to do...All of the role models that were put in front of me for women physicians were not people that I saw myself becoming. They were impressive professional role models but it just didn't sound like something I was interested in (Female nurse-practitioner # 4)

For this woman, and several others like her, she wanted to minimize the loss of time with her family that she would have experienced had she continued on in medicine.

Many female physician assistants claimed that the compatibility of work with their family lives was particularly desirable. For example, women reported:

> Like many people that are PAs I had thought at an early stage in life about being in medicine and then life became too complicated to do that. I think there's a lot of people that think about going to medical school and either family issues or economic issues or a variety of things get in the way. (Female physician assistant #5)

This suggests that women's career choices may have been shaped by their desire to balance work with family life. Such constraints can influence women's location within the labor market and reflect traditional notions of gendered work. Although most men did not report choosing their occupation for family reasons, it did provide them with a nice alternative to medical school. The physician assistant profession provides women with an alternative to traditional nursing careers, without the training time and expense of medical school. Many claimed something similar to this: "I didn't really feel the need to put the effort in trying to go to medical school. I knew to be a physician is a lot of hours. I just wasn't looking for that" (Female nurse practitioner #11). These women wanted to have professional careers but also wanted to minimize the clashes that it would have with family life.

Substitute health care occupations also provided an avenue for performing some of the more advanced medical tasks without having the heavy demands of being a physician. For many men and women these occupations provided an alternative opportunity for a medical career.

> At the time I was examining a number of the more traditional careers and leaning towards medicine and sort of by happenstance a friend of mine said, well there's this other thing you can do. You get to do a lot of the same things and it doesn't take nearly as long and you won't be nearly as in debt. (Male physician assistant #8)

Cost and time were major deterrents to entering medical school for both men and women. For instance, many physician assistants claimed something like this:

> I had been interested in medicine when I was in college but was very poor and therefore did not pursue medical school. At that time the PA concept was just arising and

> because of children and family I chose the PA as something that would get me to the practice of medicine sooner than medical school. (Female physician assistant #1)

This occupation provided an opportunity to achieve maximum benefit to practice medicine while minimizing loss of not wanting to go into debt.

Male physician assistants often entered their occupation for similar reasons: "I didn't want to go to medical school and incur the expense and the time, but I still wanted to practice medicine" (Male physician assistant #3). Indeed, the physician assistant profession opened new doors for many men and women because it allowed them to venture beyond traditional feminine careers such as nursing. This was also true of women in nurse anesthesia and nurse practitioner work where they were looking for a more advanced role.

Several men and women were concerned with the cost and training time of medical school. For others, they simply did not have the grades to get into medical school. Several providers described their situation: "Originally I had thought about medicine but I didn't have the marks. So I said 'what can I do next'?" (Male physician assistant #4). A female nurse practitioner had a similar example:

> It's sort of a second career choice. I was pre-med very briefly in college. Didn't do so well in chem. I decided to go another route, both because I didn't want to spend the next 12 years of my life doing medical school and I like the model of nurse practitioner as far as being the complete package. (Female nurse practitioner #9)

For these men and women, becoming a substitute provider allowed them to practice medicine despite the barriers they encountered upon entering medical school. Many of these people were interested in medicine but time, cost and family considerations led them along a different path. These substitute occupations offered a good alternative to be able to practice medicine in an advanced health care role without the time commitment of being a physician.

## Conclusion

Substitute health care providers are increasingly being drawn upon to save costs and help fill gaps in physician shortages. Certainly the interest in increasing the number of non-physician providers is a result of attempts to reduce escalating health care costs (De Leon-Demare et al. 1999). This research offers insight into why people enter these occupations and may also help with recruitment and retention strategies. Most of what is known about career pathways of substitute providers focuses on job satisfaction and experiences while in the occupation and but not why they entered in the first place. This chapter drew on normative decision theory to develop a better understanding why people chose these occupations.

There were several reasons for entering substitute health care occupations including: (1) limited career options for women; (2) interest in nursing but discouraged initially from pursing it (gendered social stigma); (3) compatibility with family life; (4) alternative to medical school; and (5) upskilling in which the participants pursued a better opportunity and more secure position than the one they were in previously.

Role models and exposure to the occupation influenced an interest in the work in many of the participants. Once people became aware of the opportunities for career advancement they started to pursue a path of how to achieve that goal. For those who already had a background in health they did not need much of a push. For several people in this sample these occupations provided a good extension or an alternative to the work they were currently engaged in.

Several women entered nurse practitioner and nurse anesthesia work because they historically had limited career options and this provided them with an avenue to advance their caring career. Women often pursued these more advanced areas of work after spending several years as a registered nurse and felt like they needed a challenge or more autonomy in their work. In other cases, they wanted credit for the tasks that they were already performing at this more advanced level. This is consistent with previous work on gender and nurse anesthetists (Lindsay 2007; Lindsay in press). For most of the participants in this sample, entering these occupations was their best option amongst the alternatives because it offered more autonomy, pay and a secure position for minimum further effort.

This contrasts men's entry into nurse practitioner work, where for many of them it was their second career choice. Several men were in other, and often very different, career paths only to find out that this was not what they enjoyed doing. This may have been partly a result of the occupation not being a typical (masculine) profession and many of the men felt that it would not be acceptable to enter nursing straight out of high school.

Becoming a nurse practitioner was a 'second career' for many men and may be a reflection, in part, of the stereotypes and barriers that men would have encountered if they were to enter nursing right out of high school. This notion of men's 'second career' is also consistent with research on nurses where men often retire early from such work as the military or law enforcement to become nurses (Kleinman 2004). Male nurses often encounter stereotypes that they are gay, low achievers, or feminine (Armstrong 2002; Fisher 1999). For the men in this study their best option was to avoid the stigma of nursing and try to come back to it later on once the stigma had lessened somewhat.

Most physician assistants had various backgrounds prior to entering this occupation. Several health care providers pursued medical school at first, but either because of time, financial constraints or family considerations could no longer continue. Thus, the physician assistant profession offered an attractive alternative to medical school. In fact, many female physician assistants enter the profession because of the compatibility with family life (Lindsay 2005).

Although some may argue that substitute health care providers are doing 'deskilled' work (Hugman 1991) most of the people involved in this work felt that they have been 'upskilled' compared to the job they were doing previously because the work is often more secure, more challenging and autonomous. There was some evidence to suggest that some women moved beyond traditional caring roles and that men are able to move into nursing positions without being stereotyped as a typical 'male nurse.'

Upskilling was not the case for a few people in the sample as they had trained in quite prestigious and lucrative areas; however, for personal reasons (health problems and family responsibilities) they had decided that an occupation such as one of these would be more attractive because of the fewer demands and greater compatibility with family life.

This research suggests that men and women often have different paths into these occupations, which may have important implications for the recruitment of providers. This is particularly essential at a time when there is a shortage of health care providers. These results suggest that it may be useful to recruit men from areas such as the military and business, rather than right out of high school because of the gendered stigma of nursing and carework professions. Women, on the other hand could be recruited from within health care professions. In conclusion, men and women entered these occupations because it was the best decision amongst the alternatives offering the most desirable consequences with minimum loss.

## Acknowledgements

Funding for this research was provided by the Canadian Institutes of Health Research doctoral fellowship. I would like to thank Tracey Adams and Jerry White for their insightful comments on earlier versions of this chapter.

## References

American Academy of Physician Assistants (AAPA). (2003). *Information about PAs.* Online: www.aapa.org/geninfo1.html. (Accessed Jan. 17)

American Association of Nurse Anesthetists. (2003). *About the American Association of Nurse Anesthetists.* Online: www.aana.com/about/default.asp (Accessed April 10).

American Association of Nurse Practitioners. (2003). *Scope of Practice for Nurse Practitioners.* American Academy of Nurse Practitioners.

Amundsen, S. and Corey E. (2000). Decisions behind career choice for nurse practitioners: independent versus collaborative practice and motivational-needs behaviour. *Clinical Excellence for Nurse Practitioners*, 4(5), 309-315.

Armstrong, F. (2002). Not just women's business. *Australian Nursing Journal,* 9(11), 24-26.

Auerbach, D. (2000). Nurse practitioners and primary care physicians. *Harvard Health Policy Review, 1(1)*, 1-4.

Barnett J., Barnett P, and Kearns R. (1998). Declining professional dominance? Trends in the proletarianization of primary care in New Zealand. *Social Science and Medicine, 46(2)*, 193-207.

Beach, L. (1997). *The psychology of decision making: people in organizations.* London: Sage.

Bureau of Health Professions. (2000). *Health Resources and Service Administration State Health Workforce Profiles.* Maryland: U.S. Department of Health and Human Services.

Calpin-Davies P. and Akehurst R. (1999). Doctor-nurse substitution: The workforce equation. *Journal of Nursing Management, 7(2)*, 71-9.

Cooper, R, Henderson T, Dietrich C. (1998). Roles of nonphysician clinicians and autonomous providers of patient care. *Journal of the American medical Association,* 280(9), 795-802.

Deuben, C. (1998). The impact of managed care on labour substitution in the health care workforce. *Michigan Academician, 30(1)*, 69-83.

Fallacaro M , Obst T , Gunn I , Chu M. (1996). The national distribution of certified registered nurse anesthetists across metropolitan and nonmetropolitan settings. *American Association of Nurse Anesthetists Journal 64*, 237-242.

Fisher, M. (1999). Sex role characteristics of males in nursing. *Contemporary Nurse, 8(3)*, 65-71.

Green, J. & Thorogood, N. (2004) *Qualitative Methods for Health Research*, London: Sage.

Hugman R. (1991). *Power in Caring Professions*. London: Macmillan.

Hutchinson, L., Marks T and Pittilo M. 2001. The physician assistant. *British Medical Journal, 323*, 1244-1247.

Kernick D. (2002). Economic approaches to doctor/nurse skill mix: Problems, pitfalls, and partial solutions. *British Journal of General Practice, 474*, 42-6.

Kleinman, C. (2004). Understanding and capitalizing on men's advantages in nursing. *Journal of Nursing Administration, 34(2)*, 78-82.

Lindsay, S. (2005). The feminization of the physician assistant profession. *Women & Health, 41(4)*, 37-61.

Lindsay, S. (2007). Gender differences in the practice location of mid-level health care providers. *Journal of Rural Health* 23(1): 72-76.

Lindsay, S. (in press) Gendering Work: The masculinization of nurse anesthesia. *Canadian Journal of Sociology*

Miller, R. (1996). Anesthesia providers, patient outcomes and costs. *Anesthesia and Analgesia, 82(6)*, 1117-1118.

Miller, G. & Dingwall, R. (1997) *Context and Method in Qualitative Research*, London: Sage.

Mundinger, M. (1994). Advanced-practice nursing--good medicine for physicians? *New England Journal of Medicine, 330(3)*, 211-4.

Nancarrow, S. and Borthwick A. (2005). Dynamic professional boundaries in the healthcare workforce. *Sociology of Health and Illness,* 897-919.

Richards, A., Carley J, Jenkins-Clarke S and Richards D. (2000). Skill mix between nurses and doctors working in primary care-delegation or allocation. *International Journal of Nursing Studies, 37(3)*, 185-197.

Singer, A. and Hooker R. (1996). Determinants of specialty choice of physician assistants. *Academic Medicine, 71(8)*, 917-919.

In: Decision Making in Medicine and Health Care
Editor: P. C. Tolana, pp. 133-151
ISBN: 978-1-60021-870-5


*Chapter VII*

# STRUCTURE OF THE ASSOCIATION BETWEEN PATIENT AND PHYSICIAN EVALUATIONS OF THE LEVEL OF PHYSICIAN EXPLANATIONS

***Akihito Hagihara*[*1], *Kimio Tarumi*[2] *and Minako Nishi*[3]**

[1] Department of Health Services Management and Policy, Kyushu University Graduate School of Medicine, 3-1-1 Maidashi, Higashi-ku, Fukuoka 812-8582, Japan

[2] Postgraduate Guidance Section, University of Occupational and Environmental Health, Iseigaoka, Yahata-nishi-ku, Kita-kyushu 807-0804, Japan

[3] Department of Clinical Psychology, Kyushu University Graduate School of Human Environmental Studies, 6-19-1 Hakozaki, Higashi-ku, Fukuoka 812-8581, Japan

## ABSTRACT

Given that physicians must subjectively judge their level of explanation in actual practice, and that explanations perceived to be inadequate can lead to patients ceasing to use a particular doctor or to the practice of doctor-shopping behavior, physicians need to accurately evaluate patients' perceptions of the sufficiency of physicians' explanations. We studied the association between patient and physician evaluations of the level of physician explanations.

The subjects were 630 physician-patient pairs in Japan. Path analysis was used to reveal the structure of the association between patient and physician evaluations. From a random selection of 190 physicians and 950 patients, 126 physicians and 630 patients returned questionnaires (response rate for both: 66.3%).

We found the following: (1) There was no direct association between physician and patient evaluations of the sufficiency of a physician's explanation; and (2) "Improvement

[*] Address correspondence to: Akihito Hagihara, DMSc, MPH; Kyushu University Graduate School, Department of Health Services Management and Policy, 3-1-1 Maidashi, Higashi-ku, Fukuoka 812-8582, Japan; E-mail: hagihara@hsmp.med.kyushu-u.ac.jp; Fax: +81-92-682-6101

in health and anxiety level", "courtesy", and "being rushed" had the strongest influences on patient understanding and recognition of the sufficiency of a physician's explanation.

In order to promote patient understanding and to provide patients with satisfactory explanations, it is important for physicians to alleviate patient anxiety, to be courteous, and to not rush patients while seeing them. Although these findings are useful for improving doctor-patient communication, some are not consistent with previous findings; more research will be necessary to add to these present findings.

**Keywords:** physician explanation, sufficiency of explanation, physician and patient perception, association.

## INTRODUCTION

As a physician's explanation and a patient's understanding of that explanation can influence subsequent patient behavior, the way that physicians explain health and medical matters to their patients is important. Several studies have found an association between patient understanding of a physician's explanation and patient adherence to a medical regimen [1-3], as well as one between patient understanding of a physician's explanation and patient satisfaction [4-5]. Kasahara et al. reported that patients who were given detailed explanations displayed a better understanding and a more strict adherence to medication [1]. Pitkin reported that information giving is pivotal to developing a working relationship with patients, influencing, for example, long-term adherence to estrogen replacement therapy [3]. David and Rhee reported that in Hispanic communities, the sufficiency of the explanation of a medicine's side effects was correlated with patient satisfaction and compliance [4]. Among Japanese cancer patients, a positive correlation has been reported between a physician's explanation and patient satisfaction [6].

The results of previous studies have indicated that, in Japanese medical settings, poor patient-physician communication is evident. Comparative studies of patient-physician interaction patterns in the United States and Japan have revealed several characteristics of patient-physician interaction in Japanese medical settings [7-9]. In patient-physician communication about terminal care, physicians had practically no knowledge of their patients' preferences regarding (1) information about diagnosis and prognosis, (2) the place of death, and (3) life-prolongation *vs.* pain-control strategies at a terminal stage [7]. Japanese patients were less satisfied than American patients with physicians' explanations of their condition and drug prescriptions. In addition, the mean length of time physicians spent seeing a patient was significantly longer in the United States than in Japan [8]. In Japan, while the majority of patients favor patient-centered decision-making in relation to the treatment of chronic adult diseases such as diabetes, in a terminal care setting, patient-centered decision-making is unpopular among many Japanese patients, and the role of the family is very important [10-11]. In view of the clinical importance of medical explanations and patient-physician communication in Japanese medical settings, it is necessary to examine how the level of detail in a physician's explanation affects the working relationship in patient-physician pairs.

To date, very few studies have examined how physician explanations are related to patient perceptions of sufficient information being offered by the physician. Only one study, using quantitative measurements, has reported negative findings with respect to physician explanations and patient perceptions [12]. To the best of our knowledge, no studies have examined how physician and patient perceptions of the level of physician explanations are related. This relationship is very important in a medical setting, because if a patient cannot understand a physician's explanation, the patient may evaluate the physician's explanation as 'insufficient'; if a patient readily understands a physician's explanation, the patient may evaluate the physician's explanation as 'sufficient' [12]. Similarly, if a physician judges that a patient cannot understand an explanation, the physician may evaluate the explanation as 'insufficient', and if a physician judges that a patient readily understands an explanation, the physician may evaluate the explanation as 'sufficient' [12]. If subjective evaluations of the sufficiency of a physician's explanation during a medical encounter are the same for patient and physician, then patient-physician communication may be considered good. However, if a patient's evaluation is better than a physician's evaluation, meaning that the patient rates the physician's explanations as more substantial than does the physician, this situation may lead to a patient misunderstanding the physician's explanation. If a physician's evaluation is better than a patient's evaluation, meaning that the physician rates his/her explanation as more substantial than the patient does, this situation may lead to a patient's inability to understand the physician's explanation.

In actual practice, in order to provide adequate explanations, physicians need to determine the level of a patient's understanding by asking questions such as "Do you understand me?" and "Do you have any questions?" Based on the patient's response, attitude, statements, questions, and other factors, including his or her clinical experience, the physician *subjectively* judges whether or not the explanation he or she has given to the patient is sufficient. Thus, the physician explains matters more or less fully, according to his or her subjective judgment. Since the above constitute theoretical characterizations about patient-physician interaction in a Japanese medical setting, we have no information about how one set of activities affects the other. Therefore, this study examined physician-patient pairs to reveal the structure of the association between patient and physician evaluations of the level of physician explanations during medical encounters. The findings should be helpful in improving patient-physician communication in Japan.

## METHODS

### Subjects

The subjects of this study were physicians and their patients in Fukuoka Prefecture, Japan. The physicians were members of the Fukuoka Prefecture Internal Medicine Association (FPIMA), which has 20 branches. Based on the number of member physicians in each FPIMA branch, 5 to 70 physicians per branch were selected randomly (selection rate: 10.4%). Five patients per physician were also selected randomly, for a total of 950 patients.

## Study Period and Procedure

The study was performed between July and September 2002.

In order to ensure physician and patient confidentiality, FPIMA branches randomly selected the physicians, independently of the research team. Since we did not know the identity of participating physicians, we sent 5 to 70 packages to each FPIMA branch, each of which included five questionnaires for the physician, *i.e.*, one per patient, and five packages for patients, and the FPIMA branch forwarded the packages to the selected physicians.

Five patients per physician were selected in the following manner: on one working day during the study period, the physician gave a questionnaire package to the patient who happened to be there at a given timeslot within each office hour (*i.e.*, the second patient for hours beginning 9, 10, 11 a.m., etc.); up to five patients were given a package. For each patient questionnaire, the physician filled out a corresponding questionnaire immediately following his/her meeting with the patient. After the physician answered each questionnaire item, he or she returned the completed questionnaire to us by mail.

After receiving the questionnaire from the physician, with an explanation of this survey, each patient answered the questionnaire at home, to ensure that the physician's presence did not influence his/her answers. Each patient returned the completed patient questionnaire to us directly by mail. In summary, since the FPIMA randomly selected physicians, we did not know the identity of participating physicians and, since the participating physicians randomly selected patients, neither we nor the FPIMA knew the identity of participating patients.

**Table 1. Descriptive statistics of the variables included in the Structural Equation Model of patient-physician communication**

| | Mean ± SD | Range | Cronbach |
|---|---|---|---|
| 1. Patient's age (year) | 61.82±14.72 | 15.00-94.00 | |
| 2. Patient's gender (Male=1, Female=0) | 0.45±0.50 | 0-1 | |
| 3. Physician's age (year) | 53.37±9.18 | 30.00-77.00 | |
| 4. Physician's gender (Male=1, Female=0) | 0.97±0.17 | 0-1 | |
| 5. Improvement in health and anxiety level | 6.08±1.83 | 2.00-10.00 | 0.81 |
| 6. Courtesy | 20.59±3.95 | 5.00-25.00 | 0.93 |
| 7. Being rushed | 5.26±2.83 | 3.00-15.00 | 0.92 |
| 8. Patient understanding | 20.42±2.71 | 10.00-25.00 | 0.90 |
| 9. Physician recognition of the sufficiency of his/her explanation | 15.15±2.11 | 4.00-20.00 | 0.91 |
| 10. Patient recognition of the sufficiency of a physician's explanation | 16.16±2.63 | 4.00-20.00 | 0.86 |
| 11. Patient satisfaction | 15.31±3.28 | 4.00-20.00 | 0.90 |

*n* = 584.

## VARIABLES

Table 1 shows the variables used in the study. In order to analyze the association between physician and patient perceptions of the level of physician explanations of medical testing (Numbers 9 and 10), the physician and patient questionnaires included the same items, with the same response categories. In each case, a five-item Likert scale was used to examine the responses. The "explanation of medical testing" category allowed responses between 1 (very insufficient) and 5 (very sufficient) to measure respondents' perceptions of the level of physician explanations with respect to a medical test, test results, disease, and prognosis of the disease (Appendix 1). Larger values indicated more complete physician explanations. Reliability indices (Cronbach's α) of the measure exceeded 0.8 for patients and 0.9 for physicians.

As patient outcome variables, the patient questionnaire also included the patient's understanding of the physician's explanation (Number 8), measures of the improvement in health and anxiety levels (Number 5), satisfaction with care (Number 11), and their impression of the physician (Numbers 6 and 7). Five responses between 1 (do not understand at all) and 5 (understand very well), measured "patient understanding" (Number 8) by focusing on the respondents' perceptions of how well they, as patients, understood physician explanations of medical test items (Appendix 1). The reliability indices (Cronbach's α) were 0.90, showing a high level of reliability. Higher values indicated greater understanding. A scale of five responses from 1 (very bad) to 5 (very good) was used to measure the respondents' perceptions of "improvement in health and anxiety level" (Number 5) (Appendix 2). The reliability index (Cronbach's α) was 0.81, and a higher value indicated a greater improvement in health and anxiety level. "Satisfaction with care" (Number 11) was measured on a scale of five responses between 1 (strongly disagree) and 5 (strongly agree) to determine the respondents' satisfaction with care (Appendix 3). A greater value indicated more satisfaction with care.

Factor analysis (principle components with Varimax rotation) isolated multiple clean, strong clusters to analyze patient impressions of physicians (Numbers 6 and 7). The first was labeled "courtesy" and consisted of five items; the second was labeled "being rushed" and consisted of three items (Appendices 4 and 5). The first and second measured courteousness (*i.e.,* treating a patient as an individual rather than as a case), and impatience as expressed in the physician's attitude (*i.e.,* rushing a patient while seeing the patient), respectively. A higher value indicated that the physician's attitude exhibited a higher level of that particular feature.

In addition, the patient and physician questionnaires asked questions about the patients' and the physicians' age (Numbers 1 and 3) and gender (Numbers 2 and 4).

## THEORETICAL MODEL

Based on a theoretical model shown in figure 1, the structure of the association between patient and physician evaluations of the level of physician explanations was analyzed using path analysis. As noted previously, in actual practice, a physician always subjectively judges whether or not the explanation given to the patient is sufficient, and tries to provide an adequate explanation. Thus, there is a hypothetical association between patient and physician recognition of the sufficiency of a physician's explanation. As an association between patients' perception of sufficient physician explanation and patient satisfaction has been reported, there is also a hypothetical association between these variables [6]. Along with this "physician recognition of the sufficiency of explanation" → "patient recognition of the sufficiency of explanation" → "patient satisfaction" pathway, other relevant variables were also included in the model for the following reasons.

According to Maeda et al., physicians must develop certain communication techniques when interviewing patients [13]. They should learn: (1) not to interrupt when a patient speaks, (2) not to use excessive medical jargon, (3) to ensure that they do not suffer from bad breath or emit cosmetic odors, (4) to ensure that their clothes are neat and that they are well-groomed, (5) to offer a polite greeting, (6) to listen and nod while a patient speaks (7) to make eye contact while explaining things to a patient, and (8) to provide a summary of the patient's questions and to be empathetic. From a patient's perspective, the development of these communication techniques on the part of physicians is to be desired: the physician should wear neat clothes, greet patients politely, explain things using non-professional terms, and show an interest in the patient. Variables concerning doctor and patient attributes are shown in the first column of figure 1. In addition, it has been reported that the status of a patient's physical and mental health also influences patient-physician communication [14-15]. Thus, "improvement in health and anxiety level" was also included in the first column of the theoretical model (figure 1).

Human communication has two dimensions, interpersonal and intrapersonal [16-17]. In the interpersonal dimension, a patient's impression of a doctor is shaped by the physician's interviewing techniques (*e.g.*, greeting style, manner of listening, or form of explanation to a patient) and attributes (*e.g.*, age and gender). Additionally, one of the parties involved in such communication will try to control the content of the message, with respect to attitude and knowledge ('tuning'), so that the message will be clear to the other party. Each party also monitors him/herself and communicates in such a way as to be socially desirable ('self-monitoring'). Thus, variables concerning a patient's immediate impression of a doctor (*i.e.*, "courtesy", "being rushed") were placed in the second column of the theoretical model (figure 1). The figure's third column includes a variable related to whether a doctor's explanation was easy to understand (*i.e.*, whether or not tuning and self-monitoring were good).

In the intrapersonal dimension, a patient communicates with a doctor using a process consisting of: (1) persuasive communication on the part of a doctor, such as information giving; and (2) decision-making on the part of the patient. The patient's ultimate decision

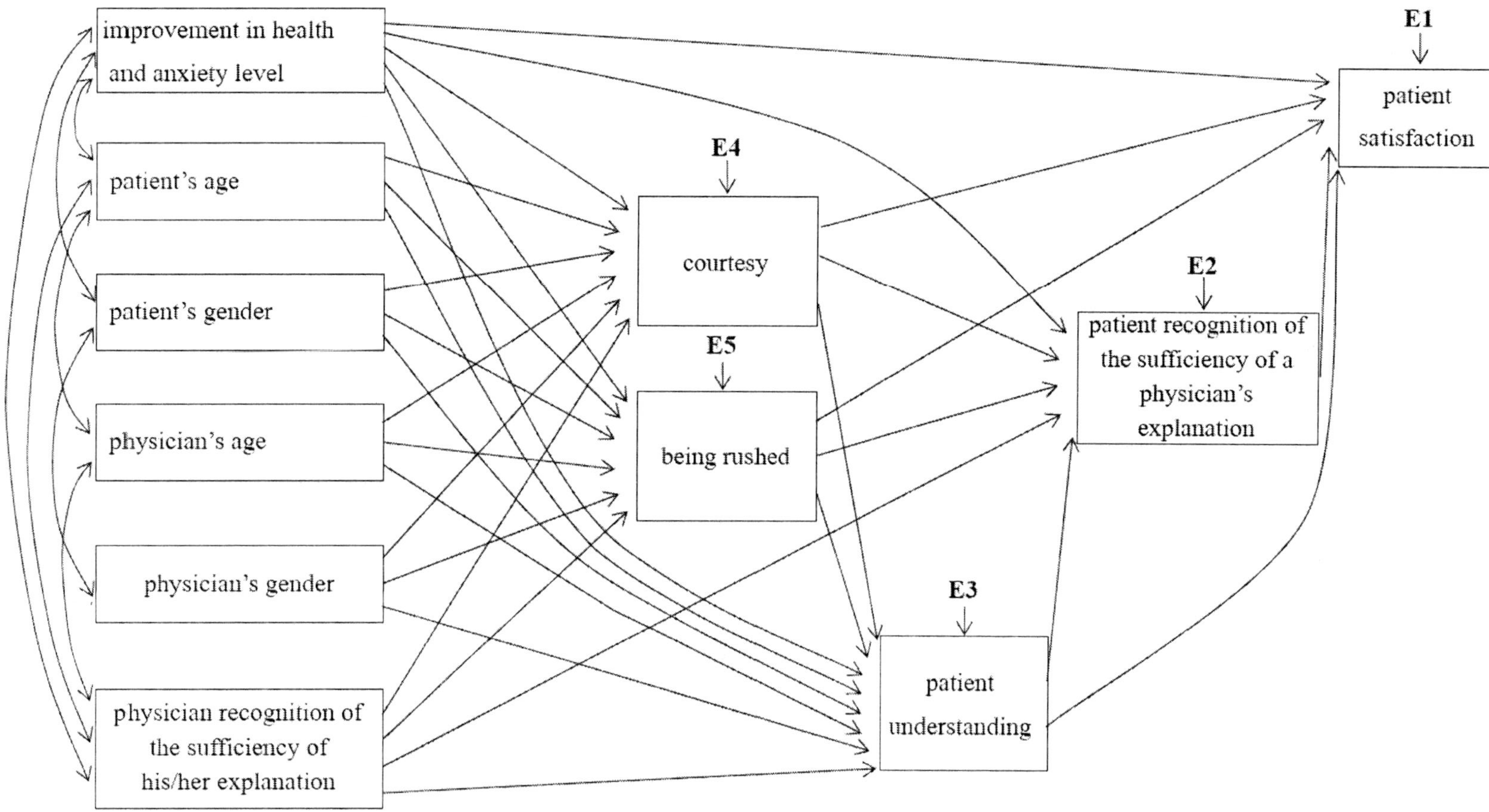


Figure 1. Path diagram of the initial theoretical model.

concerning whether to accept the advice offered depends upon the patient's judgment as to whether the advice is affirmative [16, 18]. In the decision-making process, the question of whether the patient likes the advice or not is very important [19]. In Japan, paternalism seems to be an important factor of the process by which a patient decides whether to accept a physician's advice [20]. This means that, along with liking the doctor's advice, a patient's definition of his/her or the doctor's role in the patient-doctor interaction, and what he/she expects from the doctor, might equally influence patient understanding of a physician's explanation, patient recognition of the sufficiency of this explanation, and patient satisfaction. Thus, there is a hypothetical association between a patient's impression of a doctor (*i.e.*, "courtesy", "being rushed") and subsequent variables (*i.e.*, "patient understanding," "recognition of the sufficiency of a physician's explanation", "patient satisfaction"). "Patient recognition of the sufficiency of a physician's advice" and "patient satisfaction" were placed individually in the fourth and fifth columns of the model (figure 1).

Curved lines with arrows at both ends linking two boxes indicate correlations between two variables. Straight lines with arrows at the right end, linking two boxes, indicate that a variable in the left box influences a variable in the right box. E1 to E5 are error terms (figure 1).

## Analysis

The unit of analysis consisted of a pairing of a physician and his/her patient. Since five patients were allocated to each physician, the data were structured in a hierarchical manner. However, an analysis based on the HLM model (Version 5) revealed that the frequency of concordance between patient and physician recognition of the sufficiency of the physician's explanation was independent among doctors ($\chi^2 = 121.00$, $df = 119$, $p = 0.43$) [21]. Therefore, the study did not analyze the hierarchical structure of the data.

A path analysis was performed to test the theoretical model presented in figure 1. All analyses were conducted using the CALIS procedure in SAS [22]. These estimates and all the analyses were performed on a variance-covariance matrix.

After fitting the theoretical model (see figure 1) to the data, we revised the initial model in the following way: first, if both the absolute value of the $t$ statistic for a path did not exceed 1.96, and the standardized path coefficients were trivial in magnitude (*i.e.*, the absolute values did not exceed 0.05) [23], we deleted the path. Then, the data were fitted to the revised model. If the absolute value of entries in the normalized residual matrix did not exceed 2.00, the model was further evaluated using the following goodness-of-fit indices: the model chi-square test, the normed fit index (NFI) [24], the non-normed fit index (NNFI) [24], and the comparative fit index (CFI) [25]. The chi-square statistic provided a test of the null hypothesis: it showed that the reproduced covariance matrix has the specified model structure, *i.e.*, that the model fits the data. Thus, the closer to 1.00 the $p$ value is, the better the fit of the model to the data. The NFI ranges in value from 0 to 1, where 0 represents the goodness-of-fit associated with a 'null' model (one specifying that all variables are uncorrelated), and 1 represents the goodness-of-fit associated with a 'saturated' model (a model with 0 degrees of freedom that perfectly reproduces the original covariance matrix).

The NNFI and CFI are variations on the NFI that are less biased in small samples [25]. NFI, NNFI, and CFI values over 0.9 indicate an acceptable fit between the model and data. In refitting a model to the data, we used the Lagrange multiplier test or the Wald test to seek paths that need to be added to or eliminated from the model, in order to improve the model fit significantly [25].

# RESULTS

Of the 190 randomly selected physicians, 126 returned questionnaires (response rate: 66.3%). Of the 950 randomly selected patients, 630 returned questionnaires (response rate, 66.3%).

Table 1 shows the mean, SD, range, and Cronbach α of the variables used in the analysis. Generally, reliability indices of the composite variables are larger than 0.8, showing a high reliability. Table 2 shows correlation coefficients among study variables. The most striking finding was that there was a very weak relation between doctor and patient recognition of the sufficiency of a physician's explanation (r=0.09, $p<0.05$). On the other hand, patient recognition of the sufficiency of a physician's explanation was closely related to patient understanding of a physician's explanation (r=0.74, $p<0.001$), as well as sense of improvement in health and anxiety level (r=0.46, $p<0.001$), courtesy (r=0.48, $p<0.001$), and being rushed (r=-0.35, $p<0.001$), and to patient satisfaction (r=0.62, $p<0.001$).

Figure 2 shows the results of the initial theoretical model in figure 1. Table 3 shows the goodness-of-fit indices of the initial model. Estimates of this model revealed a significant chi-square value ($\chi^2 = 42.700$ ($df = 10$), $p = 0.000$). Although NNFI and CFI values exceeded 0.9, the NFI value for this model was only 0.845. Chi-square and NHI values indicated that the fit between the model and the data could be substantially improved. In addition, the absolute value of $t$ statistics for several path coefficients did not exceed 1.96, and the standardized path coefficients were less than 0.05. Therefore, we rejected the initial model, and attempted to identify modifications that would improve the model's fit.

**Table 3. Goodness-of-Fit indices for the Structural Equation Model of patient-physician communication**

| Model | Chi-square | *df* | *p* | NFI | NNFI | CFI |
|---|---|---|---|---|---|---|
| Null model | 263.988 | 13 | 0.000 | 0.292 | | |
| Initial model (Figs. 1 and 2) | 42.700 | 10 | 0.000 | 0.845 | 0.965 | 0.972 |
| Revised model (Figure 3) | 19.867 | 23 | 0.650 | 1.007 | 0.984 | 1.000 |

Note: $N = 584$. NFI = Normed fit index; NNFI = Non-normed fit index; CFI = Comparative fit index.

First, non-significant paths were eliminated from the initial model, and the data were fitted to the revised model. Since a Lagrange multiplier test showed that adding a path from "being rushed" to "courtesy" significantly improved the fit of the data to the model ($\gamma = 34.527$, $p = 0.000$), this path was added to the revised model. Figure 3 shows the revised model. Table 3 shows the goodness-of-fit indices of the revised model. The model chi-square statistics were non-significant ($\chi^2$ = 19.867 ($df$ = 23), $p$ = 0.650), and NFI, NNFI, and CFI values all exceeded 0.9. The absolute magnitudes of all the path coefficients were also meaningful, and $t$-tests revealed that, in the revised model, all were significant at $p<0.05$. Therefore, we accepted the revised model in figure 3 as the final model. Analysis revealed $R^2$ values of 0.21 for "courtesy", 0.02 for "being rushed", 0.35 for "patient understanding", 0.61 for "patient recognition of the sufficiency of a physician's explanation", and 0.49 for "patient satisfaction." In the final model, we could find no path whose addition (tested using the Lagrange multiplier test) or deletion (tested using the Wald test) significantly improved the model.

## Discussion

This study revealed several notable findings. Most importantly, there was no direct association between physician and patient evaluations of how substantial a physician's explanation was (figure 1). Several points should be made with respect to this finding. First, although there was a weak correlation between "patient recognition of the sufficiency of a physician's explanation" and "physician recognition of the sufficiency of the physician's explanation" ($r$=0.09, $p$<0.05) (table 2), there was no direct association between these two variables. Thus, our findings imply that a physician's judgment regarding the level of his/her explanation does not always agree with that of the patient. This finding supports previous studies, which showed that patient-physician communication was very poor, and that physicians' explanations tended to be insufficient [7 ,8]. Numerous studies have reported the need for adequate explanations on the part of physicians [26, 27]. A doctor-patient pair in which there is discord with respect to recognition of the sufficiency of the doctor's explanation is likely to lead to a situation in which the patient is unable to understand the explanation or is likely to misunderstand the physician's explanation. When Japanese patients are in a situation of disagreement about medical care, they respond in diverse ways that may include ceasing to use a particular doctor and doctor-shopping behavior (*i.e.*, seeing multiple doctors for the same illness) [28-30]. This study shows that, in order to prevent this, physicians must improve physician-patient communication, especially when explaining the results of tests, so that patients are satisfied with their explanations.

Second, although there was a weak correlation between "patient recognition of the sufficiency of a physician's explanation" and "physician recognition of the sufficiency of the physician's explanation" ($r$=0.09, $p$<0.05) (table 2), the correlation was split into three pathways; (1) "physician recognition of the sufficiency of the physician's explanation" → "patient understanding" →"patient recognition of the sufficiency of a physician's explanation" [indirect effect: 0.054 (=0.09 x 0.60)], (2) "physician recognition of the sufficiency of the physician's explanation" → "courtesy" →"patient recognition of the sufficiency of a physician's explanation" [indirect effect: 0.014 (=0.09 x 0.16)], and (3) "physician recognition of the sufficiency of the physician's explanation" → "courtesy" → "patient understanding" →"patient recognition of the sufficiency of a physician's explanation" [indirect effect: 0.014 (=0.09 x 0.25 x 0.60)]. Incidentally, the sum of the three effects was 0.082; this was very close to 0.09, which was the correlation coefficient between physician and patient recognition of the sufficiency of a physician's explanation (table 2).

Third, "improvement in health and anxiety level", "courtesy", and "being rushed" had stronger influences upon patient understanding of a physician's explanation than did "physician recognition of the sufficiency of an explanation" (figure 3). Along with "patient understanding", "improvement in health and anxiety level", "courtesy", and "being rushed" also influenced "patient recognition of the sufficiency of a physician's explanation" (figure 3). With regard to "improvement in health and anxiety level", Ben-Sira has reported that a patient's immediate perception is influenced by the mode of response manifested by the physician, which includes the physician's style of affective behavior [14-15]. Street has reported that anxiety levels influence the relationship between physician behavioral measures and patient perceptions [12]. The findings from this study support these previous findings.

With regard to the courtesy scale, the scale was very similar to Ben-Sira's scale that measures a type of physician behavior by which a patient is treated as an individual rather than as a 'case' [14]. The "being rushed" variable was related to the degree to which a doctor rushed patients while seeing them. It appears reasonable that "being rushed" influences "courtesy" in the path diagram (figure 3). However, why do "being rushed" and "courtesy" influence patient understanding or recognition of the sufficiency of a physician's explanation? The paternalistic patient-physician interaction mode and the respective social status and roles of the physician and the patient in Japanese medical settings might contribute to these findings. Japanese culture has developed a particular communication feature, one that may be described as 'a mutual collaboration system'. Japanese speakers have developed a unique conversation style; this style involves the use of sentences without a subject, the frequent use of connotative messages, and a high dependence on situation [31]. Fukada has called Japanese communication 'high context communication' and has pointed to the fact that, since Japanese communication depends on situation, context, and circumstances, connotative messages can be more important than spoken messages [16]. Given the continued existence of a paternalistic patient-physician relationship in Japan, in combination with this unique communication style, a patient is likely to have a fixed view with respect to a doctor's role or status during patient-physician interaction. It is probable that a stereotypical idea of doctors, one that includes attributes such as treating the patient as an individual rather than as a case, and not rushing patients, influences patient understanding and recognition of the sufficiency of a doctor's explanation more strongly than does the quantity of information provided by a doctor.

**Table 2. Intercorrelations of variables for the Structural Equation Model of patient-physician communication**

| Variable | 1 | 2 | 3 | 4 | 5 | 6 | 7 | 8 | 9 | 10 |
|---|---|---|---|---|---|---|---|---|---|---|
| 1. Patient's age (year) | | | | | | | | | | |
| 2. Patient's gender (Male=1, Female=0) | 0.13† | | | | | | | | | |
| 3. Physician's age (year) | 0.17‡ | 0.09* | | | | | | | | |
| 4. Physician's gender (Male=1, Female=0) | 0.09* | 0.00 | 0.10* | | | | | | | |
| 5. Improvement in health and anxiety level | 0.01 | 0.02 | 0.03 | 0.06 | | | | | | |
| 6. Courtesy | 0.18‡ | 0.03 | -0.03 | -0.02 | 0.33‡ | | | | | |
| 7. Being rushed | -0.02 | 0.01 | 0.06 | 0.06 | -0.12† | -0.30‡ | | | | |
| 8. Patient understanding | 0.10* | 0.04 | 0.00 | 0.01 | 0.44‡ | 0.44‡ | -0.35‡ | | | |
| 9. Physician recognition of the sufficiency of his/her explanation | 0.10* | 0.03 | 0.10* | 0.04 | 0.01 | 0.11* | 0.03 | 0.12† | | |
| 10. Patient recognition of the sufficiency of a physician's explanation | 0.08 | -0.04 | 0.03 | 0.03 | 0.46‡ | 0.48‡ | -0.35‡ | 0.74‡ | 0.09* | |
| 11. Patient satisfaction | 0.08* | 0.01 | 0.03 | 0.02 | 0.52‡ | 0.51‡ | 0.28‡ | 0.55‡ | 0.09* | 0.62‡ |

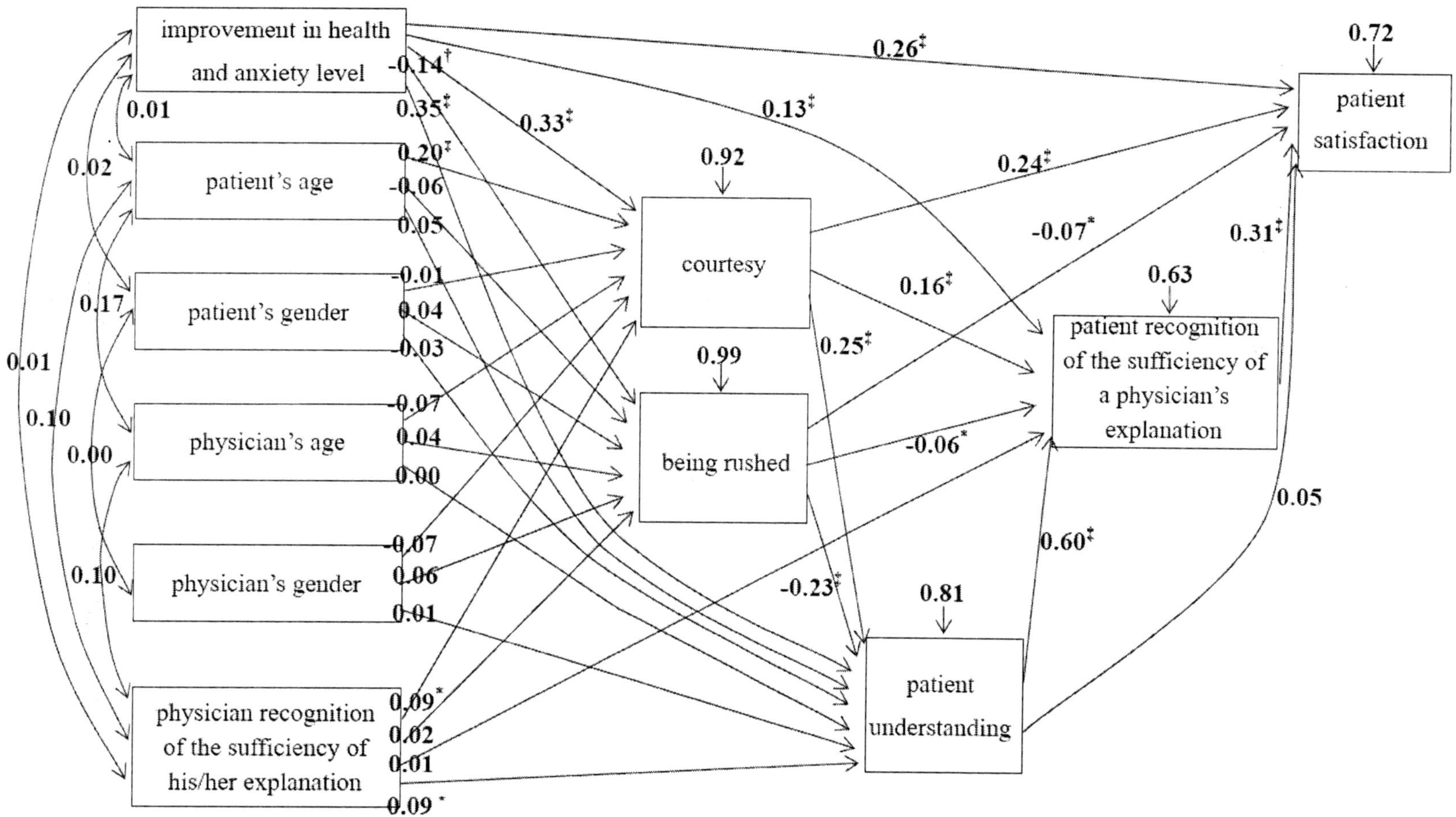


*$p < 0.05$, †$p<0.01$, ‡$p<0.001$.

Figure 2. Initial model: Standardized path coefficients are shown by single-headed straight arrows, and double-headed curved arrows show correlations.

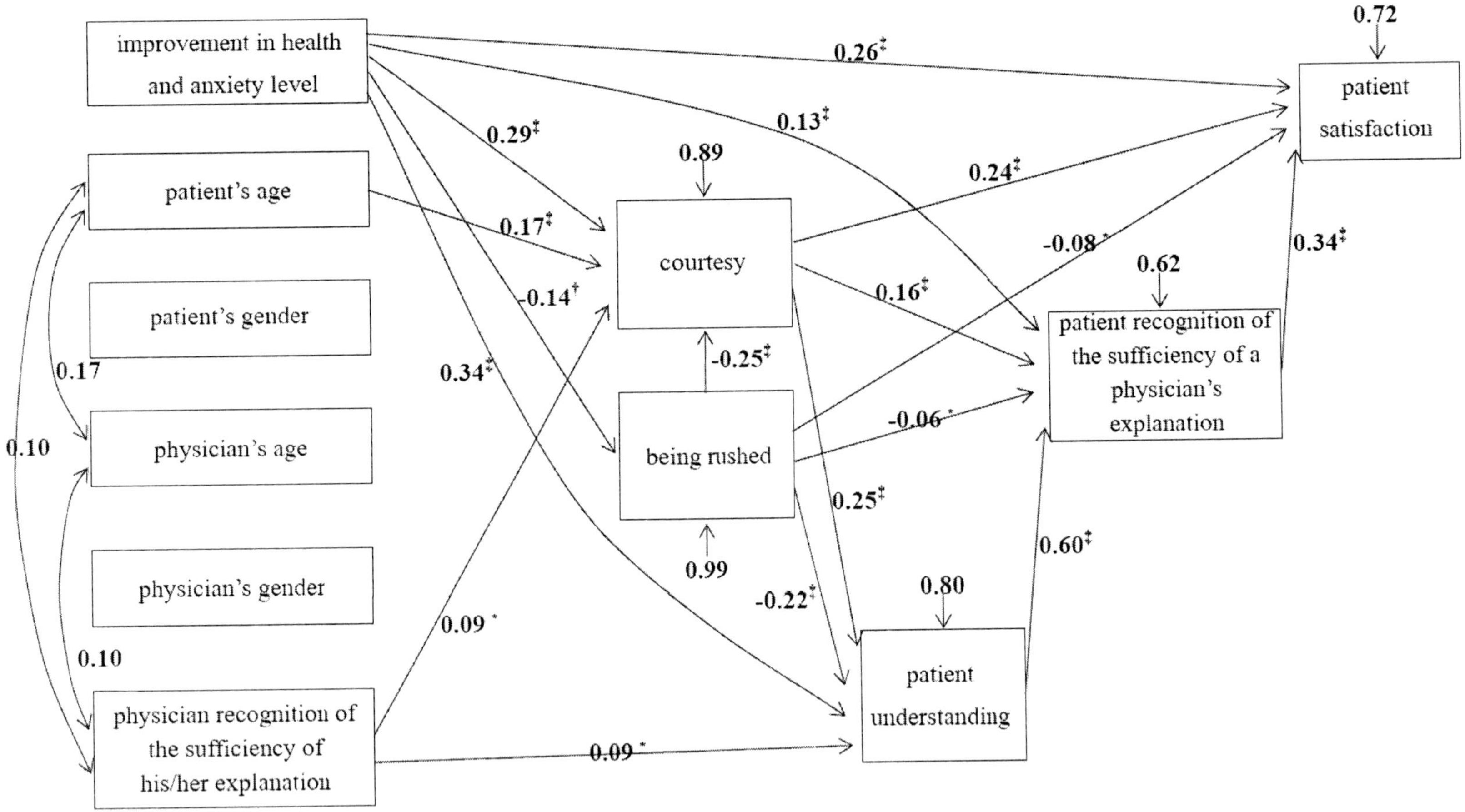


*$p < 0.05$, †$p<0.01$, ‡$p<0.001$.

Figure 3. Revised model: Standardized path coefficients are shown by single-headed straight arrows, and double-headed curved arrows show correlations.

There were findings related to differences between the theoretical and revised models. (1) In the revised model, patient age was related to "courtesy" (figure 3). Elderly patients had also been seeing their physicians for longer ($r$=0.18, $p$<0.01) (table 2). The length of the doctor-patient relationship might influence the finding. (2) No other variables concerning patient or doctor attributes were related to any other variables in the analysis (figure 3). A meta-analysis of patient gender examined the question of whether men and women differed with respect to how easily they were influenced; it revealed that women were more persuadable than men, and that they conformed to a greater extent than did men in a group pressure situation [32, 33]. It is possible that this variable relates to other variables. Older doctors generally have more clinical experience; they also tend to have more skill and better practical techniques for explaining things to patients [28]. It has been reported that older physicians tend to be less aggressive toward patients, as compared to younger physicians [34]. However, doctor age was not related to any variables. These points will also need to be verified in future studies.

It is important to point out some of the practical implications of the findings. (1) A patient's understanding of a physician's explanation is largely influenced by the physician's attitude toward the patient and by an improvement in the patient's health and level of anxiety (figure 3). In other words, if a physician focuses on the quantity of explanation delivered to a patient, and ignores his/her own or the patient's attitudes, he/she cannot accurately recognize the sufficiency of the explanation or the level of patient understanding. In order to promote patient understanding and help patients feel that explanations are sufficient, it is important that physicians reduce or ameliorate problems relating to precedent variables to patient understanding and recognition of the sufficiency of a doctor's explanation. Specifically, it is important to be courteous, to treat patients as individuals rather than as cases, to not rush patients, and to alleviate patients' anxieties. (2) 'Tuning' is a communication technique used to ensure that a message is presented clearly to the other party with respect to attitude and knowledge. Useful information was obtained in this study by looking at this technique; specifically, when controlling the content of information, physicians should focus on being polite. Being polite to patients might be more important to patients than explaining things in a logical, persuasive, and fluent manner. (3) Since a stereotypical image of doctors, as well as forms of paternalism, persist in Japan, alongside a communication style that has been described as 'a mutual collaboration system' and as 'high context communication', physicians should be aware of factors relating to their role or status, such as their attitude toward patients, their appearance, and their clothing.

There are limitations to this study. First, the physician and patient response rates were both 66.3%; however, the age distribution of the physicians in the study was very close to that of FPIMA member physicians. Therefore, our findings apply to other internists and their patients in Japan, as well as to FPIMA member physicians and their patients. Second, in this study physician specialty was limited to internal medicine; therefore, our findings can only be applied to other internist-patient interactions. Interactions between patients and medical doctors with other specialties need to be examined in the future. Third, with respect to important factors in medical conversations, it has been reported that the assessments of physicians and patients differ [35]. Factors prompting physicians to ask patients significantly more questions have also been reported; these include race, income level, and ongoing use of medications [36]. Explanations of a diagnosis may include an element of 'bad news' more frequently than explanations of medical testing; since our results were based on physician explanations of medical testing, the findings may be applicable to other doctor-patient interactions dealing with medical tests.

In conclusion, the following findings were obtained in this study: (1) there was no direct association between physician and patient evaluations of the sufficiency of a physician's explanation. (2) "Improvement in health and anxiety level", "courtesy", and "being rushed" had the strongest influence on patient understanding and recognition of the sufficiency of a physician's explanation. In order to promote patient understanding and to provide patients with explanations that are perceived to be satisfactory, it is important that physicians alleviate patient anxiety, that they behave in a courteous manner, and that they do not rush patients. Although these findings are useful for improving doctor-patient communication, some are not consistent with previous findings; more research will be necessary to verify these findings.

## REFERENCES


[1] Kasahara S, Ohno Y, Sugo A. A report on medication adherence among outpatients. *Nippon Koshu Eisei Zasshi (Japanese Journal of Public Health)* 2002; 49: 1259-1267. (in Japanese)

[2] MacGregor EA. The doctor and the migraine patient: improving compliance. *Neurology.* 1997; 48 (3 Suppl 3): S16-S20.

[3] Pitkin J. Compliance with estrogen replacement therapy: current issues. *Climacteric* 2002; 5 (Suppl 2): 12-19.

[4] David RA, Rhee M. The impact of language as a barrier to effective health care in an underserved urban Hispanic community. *Mount Sinai Journal of Medicine.* 1998;65: 393-397.

[5] Zebiene E, Razgauskas E, Basys V, Baubiniene A, Gurevicius R, Padaiga Z. Meeting patient's expectations in primary care consultations in Lithuania. *International Journal for Quality in Health Care.* 2004; 16: 83-89.

[6] Takayama T, Yamazaki Y, Katsumata N. Relationship between outpatients' perceptions of physicians' communication styles and patients' anxiety levels in a Japanese oncology setting. *Social Science and Medicine.* 2001; 53: 1335-1350.

[7] Kai I, Ohi G, Yano E, Kobayashi Y, Miyata T, Niino N. Communication between patients and physicians about terminal care: a survey in Japan. *Social Science and Medicine.* 1993; 36: 1151-1159.

[8] Kurata JH, Watanabe Y, McBrige C, Kawai K, Andersen R. A comparative study of patient satisfaction with health care in Japan and the United States. *Social Science and Medicine.* 1994; 39: 1069-1076.

[9] Ohtaki S, Ohtaki T, Fetters MD. Doctor-patient communications: a comparison of the USA and Japan. *Family Practice.* 2003; 20: 276-282.

[10] Sekimoto M, Asai A, Ohnishi M, Nishigaki E, Fukui T, Shimbo T. Patients' preference for involvement in treatment decision making in Japan. *BMC Family Practice.* 2004; 5: 1-10.

[11] Ruhnke GW, Willson SR, Akamatsu T, Kinoue T, Takashima Y, Goldstein M K. Ethical decision making and patient autonomy: a comparison of physicians and patients in Japan and the United States. *Chest.* 2000; 118: 1172-1182.

[12] Street RL. Communicative styles and adaptations in physician-parent consultations. *Social Science and Medicine.* 1992; 34: 1155-1163.

[13] Maeda I, Tokuda S. *Patient satisfaction: communication and dynamism of care-seeking behavior.* pp.105-109, Tokyo: Nihon-Hyoron-Sya, 2003.

[14] Ben-Sira Z. The function of the professional's affective behavior in client satisfaction: a revised approach to social interaction theory. *Journal of Health and Social Behavior.* 1976; **17:** 3-11.

[15] Ben-Sira, Z. Affective and instrumental components in the physician-patient relationship: an additional dimension of interaction theory. *Journal of Health and Social Behavior.* 1980; **21:** 170-180.

[16] Fukada K. *Interpersonal communication.* pp. 14-15, 144, 211-212. Kyoto: Kita-ohji Syobou, 1998.

[17] Northouse PG., Northouse LN. *Health communication. Strategies for health professionals.* pp. 1-20. Connecticut, Norwalk: Appleton and Lange, 1992.

[18] Mutoh T, Mori T, Endoh Y, Tamase K.*Psychology.* pp.381-382, 356. Tokyo: Yuuhi-kaku, 2004.

[19] Takemura K. Decision-making and support. In S. Ichikawa. (Ed.) *Cognitive psychology.* pp. 100-103. Tokyo: University of Tokyo Press, 1996.

[20] Leflar R. *Medical care and law in Japan.* pp. 15-61. Tokyo: Keisoshobo, 2003.

[21] Bryk A, Rausenbush S, Congdon R. *Hierarchical linear and nonlinear modeling with the HLM/3L programs.* Chicago: Scientific Software Intl, 1996.

[22] SAS Institute Inc. SAS technical report P-200. SAS/STAT Software: CALIS and logistic procedures. Release 6.04. pp. 53-174. Csary, NC: SAS Institute, 1990.

[23] Billings RS, Steve P, Wroten SP. Use of path analysis in industrial/organizational psychology: Criticism and suggestions. *J. Appl. Psych.* 1978; 63: 677-688.

[24] Bentler PM, Bonett DG. Significance tests and goodness-of-fit in the analysis of covariance structures, *Psych. Bull.* 1980; 88: 588-606.

[25] Hatcher L. A step-by–step approach to using the SAS system for factor analysis and structural equation modeling. pp. 141-248. Cary, NC: SAS Institute, 1994.

[26] Garrity TF, Lawson EJ. Patient-physician communication as a determinant of medication misuse in older, minority women. *Journal of Drug Issues.* 1989; 19: 245-259.

[27] Levinson W, Stiles WB, Inui TS, Engle R. Physician frustration in communicating with patients. *Medical Care.* 1993; 31: 285-295.

[28] Asai A, Kishino M, Fukui T, Masano T. Postgraduate education in medical ethics in Japan. *Medical Education.* 1998; 32: 100-104.

[29] Asai A, Kishino M, Fukui T, Sakai M, Yokota M, Nakata K. Choices of Japanese patients in the face of disagreement. *Bioethics.* 1998; 12: 162-172.

[30] Guo Y, Kuroki T, Yamashiro S, Koizumi S. Illness behavior and patient satisfaction as correlates of self-referral in Japan. *Family Practice.* 2002; 19: 326-332.

[31] Kitayama S, Miyamoto Y.Cultural psychologies and macro level comparison from the Eastern and Western viewpoint. *Japanese Psychological Review*. 2000; 43: 57-81.

[32] Hall JA, Roter DL. Do patients talk differently to male and female physicians? A meta-analytic review. *Patient Education and Counseling*. 2002; 48, 217-224.

[33] Ishikawa H, Takayama T, Yamazaki Y, Seki Y, Katsumata N, Aoki Y. The interaction between physician and patient communication behaviors in Japanese cancer consultations and the influence of personal and consultation characteristics. *Patient Education and Counseling*. 2002; *46:* 277-285.

[34] US Department of Health, Education, and Welfare. *Diagnosis and management of hypertension: a nationwide survey of physicians' knowledge, attitudes, and reported behavior.* (DHEW Publication No. NIH 79-1056). Washington, DC: U.S. Government Printing Office, 1979.

[35] Laine, C., Davidoff, F., Lewis, C. E., Nelson, E. C., Nelson, E., Kessler, R. C., et al. Important elements of outpatients' care: a comparison of patients' and physicians' opinions. *Annals of Internal Medicine*. 1996; 125: 640-645.

[36] Sleath B, Roter D, Chewning B, Svarstad B. Asking questions about medication. Analysis of physician-patient interactions and physical perceptions. *Medical Care*. 1993; 37: 1169-1173.

## Appendix 1. Understanding of Physician Explanations

When measuring patient and physician awareness of the sufficiency of a physician's explanation, items 1, 2, 3, and 5 were used. When measuring patient understanding, all five items were used.

1. Physician explanation of the testing method.
2. Physician explanation of the test results.
3. Physician explanation of the name of the disease.
4. Physician explanation of the severity of the disease.
5. Physician explanation of the prognosis of the disease.

## Appendix 2. Improvement of Health

1. How is your physical condition, mental condition, or pain control?
2. How is alleviation of your worry or anxiety progressing?

## Appendix 3. Patient Satisfaction

1. I am satisfied with the care.
2. I am satisfied with the consequences of the treatment.
3. If I need care again in the future, I will consult with my physician.
4. If my family or friends need care in the future, I will recommend my physician.

## Appendix 4. Courtesy

1. My doctor keeps me informed of ongoing changes.
2. My doctor is modest.
3. My doctor does not attribute the cause of a poor outcome to the patient.
4. My doctor pays a lot of attention to me when talking about an important topic.
5. My doctor frequently talks in a social manner.

## Appendix 5. Being Rushed

1. The physician rushes me while seeing me.
2. The time a physician spends in seeing me is short.
3. The physician does not speak much while seeing me.

In: Decision Making in Medicine and Health Care
Editor: P. C. Tolana, pp. 153-167
ISBN: 978-1-60021-870-5


*Chapter VIII*

# DECISION MAKING IN THE PATIENT-PHYSICIAN RELATIONSHIP

***Dennis J. Mazur[1,2] and Marcus D. Mazur[3]***
[1]Center for Ethics in Health Care, Oregon Health and Science University Portland, Oregon, USA;
[2]Department of Veterans Affairs Medical Center, 3710 S.W. U.S. Veterans Hospital Road Portland, Oregon, USA;
Case Western Reserve University School of Medicine, Cleveland, Ohio, USA.

## ABSTRACT

Decision making in the patient-physician relationship was first addressed by courts in England in 1767. The courts first viewed the issues of decision making under the concept of "consent" and asked whether the profession of medicine held physicians to a duty of securing an individual patient's consent prior to performing a medical intervention. Although there was a presumption that some sort of discussion related to the physician obtaining consent from the patient took place, this first British court focused on whether the profession of medicine held such a duty as an obligation of physicians.

Courts in our four countries of interest—England, the United States, Canada, and Australia—hear cases in consent or informed consent under two different standards. Courts in Great Britain hear informed consent cases under a professional standard. Courts in Canada and Australia hear them under a reasonable person standard. And in the United States, about half of the states hear them under a professional standard and the others hear them under a reasonable person standard.

In court decision making under a professional standard, a physician must disclose to a patient what other physicians with the same or similar training would commonly disclose to their patients. Under a reasonable person standard, a physician must disclose what a reasonable person in the patient's position would want to know.

In their formulation of the concepts of consent (Great Britain and Australia) and informed consent (the United States and Canada), courts have focused on the physician's obligation to disclose information about the risks of physician-recommended interventions. Ethicists and cognitive psychologists have gone beyond court decision making, focusing on forms of shared and participatory decision making in which patients are encouraged to take more active roles.

This paper reviews the challenges patients face as they decide whether to take more active roles in decision making, and the challenges physicians face as non-physicians propose alternative frameworks for the patient-physician relationship. This review examines four perspectives on decision making in the patient-physician relationship: judicial, ethical, decision analytical, and cognitive psychological. Patient challenges include issues of literacy and numeracy, and the level of comfort patients have with the words, numbers, tables, and graphs used to portray scientific evidence in discussions related to their medical care. Physician challenges include following the laws of consent and informed consent in their respective countries. Challenges for both patients and physicians include: (1) deciding which decision making strategy to adopt in the patient-physician relationship—patient-based, physician-based, or some form of shared or participatory decision making, and (2) determining how decisions are to be made in the absence of high quality scientific information.

## INTRODUCTION

More optimal decision making is always a noble goal in the practice of medicine. Yet there is a disparity of thought among patient and physician experts regarding what this goal entails. This paper analyzes the arguments from four perspectives: judges, ethicists, expert decision makers, and cognitive psychologists.

We will focus on three questions: What are the goals of more optimal decision making from each of the four perspectives? How are the goals achieved within the constraints of the patient-physician relationship? Can the goals be achieved while accommodating patient and physician preferences within the context of decision making?

## VIEWPOINTS FROM THE COURTS

Decision making in the patient-physician relationship was first addressed by courts in England in 1767 [1]. The courts first viewed the issues of decision making under the concept of "consent" and asked whether the profession of medicine held physicians to a duty of securing the individual patient's consent prior to performing a medical intervention. Although there was a presumption that some sort of discussion related to the physician obtaining consent from the patient took place, this first British court focused on whether the profession of medicine held such a duty as an obligation of physicians. In 1957, the term *informed consent* entered the judicial lexicon in a California appellate court opinion [2].

In 1972, Judge Spottswood Robinson, in a landmark United States federal opinion, created a *reasonable person standard* of informed consent to replace the *professional standard* [3]. Judge Robinson's opinion became a key point in the discussion of subsequent high court decisions in Great Britain, Canada, and Australia. Today, British courts hold onto *a professional standard* [4], the Supreme Court of Canada and the High Court of Australia have adopted *a reasonable person standard* [5], [6], and in the United States, about half of the states hold a professional standard, and the others hold a reasonable person standard [7].

Under a professional standard, a physician must disclose to a patient what other physicians with the same or similar training would commonly disclose to their patients. Under a reasonable person standard, a physician must disclose what a reasonable person in the patient's position would want to know. Each of the high courts has focused on the physician's obligation to disclose the *risks* of the physician-recommended intervention.

In the landmark cases within their respective countries, each of the high courts has focused on one specific type of decisional context in medicine—one patient and one surgeon in a patient-physician relationship where four conditions held:

1. The surgeon had recommended a surgical intervention in the patient's care.
2. The surgeon had disclosed some but not all risk information to the patient.
3. One of the risks that had not been disclosed actually materialized in the patient's case.
4. The patient argued that had the risk been disclosed the patient would never have agreed to the surgical intervention.

Ethicists and cognitive psychologists have attempted to go beyond court decision making, with its focus on physician obligations to disclose risk information to the patient, to issues of whether the patient understands the disclosed information and what information the patient is going to receive for decision making.

## VIEWPOINTS FROM ETHICISTS

While courts focused physician attention on risk disclosure to patients, ethicists declared a need to check that the patient understood the disclosed risk information. R.R. Faden and T.L. Beauchamp, for example, argued that patients needed to have "substantial understanding" of disclosed information [8]. But ethicists need approaches to secure this goal in ways that are acceptable to patients and their physicians.

When approached from neurocognitive perspectives, determining the level of understanding a patient has when asked to make a decision in medicine is much more complex than ethicists have recognized. Decisions need to be considered *at a time* and *over time*. Let us consider two examples of decision at a time that become decisions over time.

In clinical care, whether to perform a coronary angiogram to evaluate chest discomfort is an example of a decision *at a time*. If the coronary angiogram is not performed but instead the patient is started on a trial of sublingual nitroglycerine, the decision of when to perform a coronary angiogram becomes a decision *over time*. Although the physician and patient may wait and see how the patient responds to medical management, at some point they may decide to do the coronary angiogram. How will that time point be decided upon?

In research on human subjects, an example of a decision *at a time* is whether a patient with Alzheimer's disease wants to volunteer for a study tracking cognitive thought processes and emotions to see how his or her cognitions and emotions change over time as his or her disease progresses. This is a decision a patient with early Alzheimer's disease may very well want to consider. However, this decision *at a time* has ramifications *over time*. If this patient loses his or her cognitive abilities to make decisions on his or her own behalf because of progressive Alzheimer's disease, will the patient then be able to continue to participate in the present study considering that he or she does not remember agreeing to participate in the study in which he or she had been enrolled?

When one considers Faden and Beauchamp's notion of substantial understanding, how does that notion change over time as the patient ages? And how does the concept of substantial understanding further change when the patient sustains a mild stroke or develops dementia? In post-stroke states and in early dementia in Alzheimer's disease, do we understand enough about executive function of the brain to know when a successful discussion has met the ethicists' criteria of "substantial understanding"? Further research is needed in the area of substantial understanding over time as aging takes places and as progressive diseases affecting cognition and emotions go from mild to more severe forms.

## Impact of Stroke on Patient Decision Making Capacity

D. Mukherjee and colleagues investigated the psychological aspects of stroke and success or failures of patient adaptation after sustaining a stroke. These psychological processes include: risk for depression and anxiety, changes in identity and personality processes, and potential for social isolation [9]. The authors note that:

> Depression and anxiety are heterogeneous constructs and can affect individuals' emotional functioning and cognitive abilities. Executive function, self-agency, and volition may be affected. Alterations in identity and personality may also result from the interaction of fluctuating emotional, cognitive, and physical abilities as well as from changes in social context and family dynamics. Social isolation, or lack of access to social contact or resources, can be a consequence of difficulties in cognitive and emotional function that influence interpersonal relationships, changes in social roles, communication difficulties, and challenges in transportation and employment. Social stigma and marginalization also contribute to isolation [9].

The authors describe these psychological phenomena in the context of brain damage and recovery and raise ethical concerns, including impact on decision-making capacity, pre- and post-injury selves and interests, and the social milieu in which strokes are experienced [9].

## Impact of Vascular, Neuropsychiatric, Social, and Frailty-Related Factors in Decision Making

Current research is uncovering various factors that may induce cognitive impairment in otherwise non-demented adults. For example, R. Monastero and colleagues investigated the relation of vascular, neuropsychiatric, social, and frailty-related factors with cognitive impairment, no dementia (CIND) to future progression to Alzheimer disease (AD) [10].

The investigators followed 718 study participants aged 75 years and older who attended baseline, 3-, and 6-year follow-up examinations. CIND was defined according to the performance on the Mini-Mental State Examination. The investigators surveyed potential risk factors at baseline and clustered them according to four research hypotheses (frailty, vascular, neuropsychiatric, and social hypothesis); each representing a possible pathophysiological mechanism of CIND independent of subsequent development of AD [10].

The authors found that after 3.4 years of follow-up, 82 participants (11.4%) developed CIND. When the population was subsequently followed for 2.7 years, subjects with CIND had a threefold increased risk to progress to AD. After multiple adjustments, including adjustment for the development of AD at the 6-year follow up, risk factors for CIND were hip fracture, polypharmacy, and psychoses [10].

The authors concluded that not only the AD-type neurodegenerative process, but also neuropsychiatric- and frailty-related factors may induce cognitive impairment in non-demented elderly persons [10]. Thus, the search for cognitive impairments is much more complex than simple identification of an early stage of a neurodegenerative process. Ethical frameworks need to be expanded to ensure that all relevant factors of cognition and its impairment are better understood as the individual approaches the decision making tasks he or she will be asked to perform in relation to his or her own health and medical care.

## Viewpoints from Decision Analysts

The decision sciences offer a perspective of how to display and analyze decision making in medicine. Decision trees are often used to depict a decision problem as paths of choices and alternatives. This representation of an increasingly branching tree is used to communicate outcomes (benefits and risks) and their estimated chance (probability) of occurring.

Decision analysis emphasizes two perspectives: the elicitation of patient preferences for outcomes and the evaluation of outcome by expected utility. According to R.J. Lilford, "The great strength of decision analysis is that it is based not just on probabilities but also on the value placed on various outcomes. It therefore represents a method for synthesizing both medical facts (probabilities) and human values (utilities), which together determine the best course of action—that is, the course that stands to maximize expected utility" [11].

These authors further state that "although it is currently unrealistic to do a separate decision analysis for each patient, computer programs may soon overcome this problem. In the meantime, decision analysis can be used to provide guidelines for managing groups of patients with similar clinical features" [11].

The use of computer programs to help elicit patient preferences is a part of current attempts to develop decision tools to engage patients in shared and participatory decision making processes. But the ethical focus on patient "substantial understanding" of the basic concepts and methodologies employed in a decision analysis may not be realizable because of the absence of simple techniques to check on how much the patient actually understands once engaged in these shared and participatory decision making processes.

Let us consider the example of a computerized decision support tool that is being tested as an aid for patient decision making. In this research study, specific types of information should be gathered from study volunteers using the system, such as problems and levels of satisfaction or dissatisfaction with the system. If a volunteer begins the study exercise but later asks to stop participation or is stressed or offended by the process, investigators need to determine what specifically the volunteer found objectionable.

If study participants and patients in clinical care are willing to provide feedback on their exposure to decision support systems, researchers can learn not only whether participants were dissatisfied with the process but also the specific aspects that they were dissatisfied with. If participants were offended by the computerized decision support process itself, researchers can find out precisely how and in what way. After all, what is being studied in these computerized decision processes is information that usually takes place as a part of discourse between a patient and a physician. This information shared is traditionally treated with a high degree of respect and confidentiality.

Yet key questions remain related to both the basic concepts of decision analysis as applied to an individual's setting and the use of certain methodologies to elicit patient preferences. What it means for an individual to understand expected utility is a key point in explaining why expected utility should be sought after as a guide in individual decision making. Another research issue centers on what explanations regarding expected utility are necessary and sufficient to communicate the concept so the individual understands its meaning and uses. Does one exposure to the concept, for example in a preference elicitation session with the patient, count as sufficient experience with the concept? Do five such exposures count as sufficient experience with the concept? This becomes a key question in all decision support systems and tools that rely on expected utility. What is to count as the necessary and sufficient criteria for an individual to understand expected utility enough so that the results of a decision analysis should be applied to the individual's care?

When eliciting an individual's preferences in a health or medical context, the same question holds: What does it mean to understand a methodology that is being employed in an individual's case? How do we know whether the preferences elicited can be used in the decision making related to the patient's care? For example, while we may not encounter a participant's volunteered comments about his or her religious objections to the use of expected utility, there may indeed be religious objections to the use of any methodology that requires consideration of gambles (or trade-offs).

If an individual has religious objections to gambling, any technique phrased as a gamble may well cause problems for the individual and the preference elicitor [12,13]. There may be patients reluctant to answer a question that asks them how much life they are willing to trade off to get to another health care state [14]. Cognitive psychologists need to research these conceptual and methological issues.

## Viewpoints from Cognitive Psychologists

While the decision analyst is attempting to optimize decision making through the use of expected utility, cognitive psychologists have identified cognitive biases as they impact decision making. Cognitive biases can be manifested by both professionals and non-professionals in decision making and are argued to be based on *heuristics* (*short-cuts* or *rules of thumb*), which the decision maker uses in coming to a decision instead of performing a full analysis of the decision [15,16].

One such short-cut or rule of thumb is illustrated in the "availability bias" [17]. Here, the decision maker bases his or her choice "on ideas that come most readily to mind, irrespective of the validity of these ideas" [18]. An extension of this availability bias enters in the assessment of frequency of event occurrence. Here, instead of basing estimates on how frequently an event occurs, individuals base their estimates on the vividness and the emotional impact of the event itself. Events that are easy to imagine or recall will be perceived as relatively more frequent than events that are less easily imagined or recalled.

I.I. Benbasat and J. Lim asked whether availability bias could be reduced in a group context [19]. The authors report research findings on two computer-based support facilities—electronic brainstorming and electronic mail. These techniques were tested for their contributions to reducing the availability bias. The authors report the following:

> A 2 x 2 experimental design was used: electronic brainstorming (available or not) and communication mode (electronic or verbal). Forty teams of three members each were asked to work on a task involving the rating of the importance of a number of items associated with a secretary's task. Both electronic brainstorming and electronic communication helped reduce the availability bias. In both cases, the reduction in bias was due to increased attention paid to items that were found to have low availability in the absence of these support tools [19].

## Risk Disclosures

One of the basic questions underlying decision making in the patient-physician relationship is one the courts first considered in their development of the concept of "consent" and then "informed consent." Do patients want risks disclosed? Two studies have been done to answer this question. The first focused on disclosures of risks related to invasive medical interventions; the second study focused on the risks of prescription medicines.

My colleague and I have studied patient preferences for risk disclosure regarding medical interventions. We have found that the vast majority of patients wanted the risks of medical interventions their physicians were recommending in the care disclosed to them by their physicians. Of 467 subjects interviewed, 436 (93.4%) preferred that their physician disclose risk information [20].

D.K. Ziegler and colleagues have studied risk disclosure regarding prescription medicines and have found that patients want all the risks of prescription medicines disclosed to them [21]. So, in terms of risks of medical interventions and risks of prescription medicines, the vast majority of patients want risk disclosure. The questions that now have to be addressed in relation to the risks of medical interventions and prescription medicine are questions of words and numbers:

- Do patients understand what is involved in the medical intervention that is being proposed?
- Do patients understand the terminology being used in the risk disclosure?

- Do patients understand the problems with the use of words as qualitative expressions of chance?
- Do patients understand what the risk numbers mean in terms of frequency of event occurrence?

## Words (Terminology)

The terminology used in consent, informed consent, and decision making is problematic. Do patients understand the medical terminology describing disease states and medical conditions? Do patients understand the terminology used in screening, diagnosis, therapeutics, and their respective risks of adverse outcomes? Do patients understand qualitative expressions of chance (probability)? The challenge patients face with the language used in clinical care goes well beyond the problem of understanding medical terminology to fighting common-place misconceptions about the nature and risks of specific therapies. Patients may have misconceptions because they may not understand the terms being used.

## Understanding the Beliefs Upon which Participants are Basing their Preferences

The description of a medical intervention is important for decision making in the patient-physician relationship because the patient may have conceptions about the nature of a medical intervention that are simply false and will need to be corrected by the physician.

In a study of 238 men with chronic medical problems, 424 radiologists, and 491 business school graduate students, B.J. McNeil and colleagues studied the impact of "identification of treatment" on participant choice [22]. Here, the identification of treatment means that the treatment's "name" was placed on the treatment modality. Naming a treatment modality directly is to be contrasted with the provision of an "unnamed" therapy for consideration. Whether the therapy is named or unnamed, all study participants are presented with the same survival and mortality data.

The identified treatments were "surgery" and "radiation therapy". All subjects were asked to consider themselves as the patient deciding on treatment for operable lung cancer. Half of respondents received data on treatments identified as "surgery" or "radiation therapy"; the other half received data that were simply labeled as "A" and "B". The authors wanted to determine the extent to which "choices are determined by prior conceptions (or misconceptions) about surgery and radiation therapy." The authors found that radiation therapy was chosen 42 per cent of the time when it was not identified and only 26 per cent of the time when it was identified [22]. The authors argued that "Evidently, identification of the two treatments favors surgery over radiation therapy" [22]. The authors continued their argument as follows:

> The finding that radiation therapy was less attractive when the treatments were identified indicates that people relied more on pre-existing beliefs regarding the treatments than on the statistical data presented to them. We do not know, however,

whether these beliefs were based on valid evidence or reflected a widely shared bias against radiation therapy [22].

What is important here is the recognition that one cannot simply assume that a patient is examining data provided to him or her and using that data in making his or her decision. Physicians must also ask questions about the beliefs patients hold about the therapeutic options, as well as determine whether the patient understands the numbers being presented.

Yet, in the above study, there may have been another misconception regarding the impacts of therapy beyond labeling the treatment "radiation therapy." The other misconception, not mentioned by the authors, was the participant reacting to the descriptor "surgery". Some patients may have held the belief that exposure of their tumor to air will cause the tumor to spread. This is a folk belief that one of the authors (DJM) has heard in interviews with patients when discussing issues related to surgical removal of cancer and how patients viewed surgical intervention for cancer contrasted with other interventions. McNeil and colleagues could not distinguish the rejection of the choice of surgery because of patient misconceptions from other reasons why the patient did not select the surgical option (for example, the patient was not willing to accept the initial risks of death from surgery itself or death from the general anesthesia used with the surgery).

## Numbers

When asked directly whether patients preferred to receive risk information about the chance of adverse outcomes from their physicians in terms of words (i.e., *rare*, *possible*, or *probable*) or in terms of numbers (percents), 32% of patients reported that they wanted risk information only numerically; 35.3% wanted it only qualitatively; 21.8% wanted the information either way; and 8.3% wanted the information both ways [23].

The fact that such a large number of patients preferred to receive risk information qualitatively in terms of words is problematic to the cognitive psychologist who understands that individuals will place different numeric meanings onto verbal probability expressions [23]. For example, the term "rare" may be intended to mean occurring in "< 1 in 100 patients" when communicated by a physician, but the term "rare" as interpreted by the patient may mean occurring in about "< 1 in 1,000,000 patients" [23].

## Five-Year Survival Curves

Studies using five-year survival curves show the importance of providing risk information beyond the risks of the initial procedure. In judicial decision making, a physician is obligated to disclose the risks of the recommended procedure to his or her patient. In surgical interventions, these risks occur either at the time of the surgery or shortly thereafter. Judicial decision making has not yet addressed risks that occur in the short term, medium term, or long term.

Patients have been shown to base their own decisions not only on short-term data, but also on data in the medium and long terms [24]. Yet, the amount of explanation provided by physicians can also influence patients' use of five-year survival data in decisions [25].

In a study of 136 patients, my colleague and I randomized patients to two groups: one receiving limited explanation (LE) and one receiving extensive explanation (EE) and asked patients to choose between two alternative treatments (differing in short-term vs. long-term survival benefits) for an unidentified medical condition, based on the information given in the explanations. Patients randomized to LE received a brief orientation to graphs summarizing the treatment results; patients randomized to EE received a detailed verbal description of the graphs. We found that significantly ($p < 0.001$) more patients receiving EE changed their preferences across the three pairs of five-year survival curves, compared with patients receiving LE. Of the patients receiving EE, 57% reported either medium-term (year 0-to-intercept or intercept-to-year 5) data or the average life expectancy for the five-year period contained in the curves (ALE-5) as most influencing their decision making; whereas 78% of patients receiving LE reported only endpoint (year 0 or year 5) data as most influencing their preferences [25]. We concluded that:

> The patients' treatment preferences for long-term vs. short-term survival benefits were influenced by the amounts of verbal explanation provided to them about five-year survival graphs summarizing treatment results. The patients appeared to minimize the importance of medium-range data when those data were not specifically pointed out to them [25].

# Challenges in Decision Making

## Challenges Facing Patients

While many parties may be interested in involving patients more in decision making related to their care, there are basic obstacles in terms of words and numbers that need to be better understood not only in discussions between patients and physicians, but in interactions between patients and tools developed to facilitate patient decision making.

In some decision making frameworks that are billed as "shared decision making," the physician's sole role is to provide information to patients while the patient takes on the role of decision maker [26,27]. This perspective does not take into account the wide variety of preferences patients report they have in whom they want to make decisions in their care. In a study of 467 subjects interviewed, 318 (68%) preferred shared decision making; 100 (21.4%) preferred physician-based decision making; and 49 (10.5%) preferred patient-based decision making [28].

Patients also value their physician's opinion. In a study of 200 consecutive patients, over half of all participations selected physician opinion as the most important type of information that they use to base their decisions [29]. Here, physician opinion was ranked over risk and benefit information in terms of what the patient reported using as information to base their decisions in medical care.

## Challenges Facing Physicians

Physician challenges include following the laws of consent and informed consent in their respective countries. Let us take the case where a physician attempts to turn over the legal obligation of risk disclosure to a shared decision making system. Such a physician must make certain that this shared decision making system optimally satisfies the applicable consent and informed consent laws of the state or country in which the system is used. Each physician has legal disclosure obligations in consent or in informed consent that he or she must respect in the patient-physician relationship. The physician is responsible for ensuring that the ways in which physician conducts his or her disclosure to patients are consistent with what is required by the law.

## Challenges Facing Patients and Physicians

Challenges facing both patients and physicians include: (1) selecting a preferred decision making strategy in the patient-physician relationship, (2) understanding each other's perspective on the benefits and risks of each strategy (patient-based, physician-based, or some form of shared or participatory decision making), and (3) when a discussion of medical and scientific information is the key point of the decision, understanding the difficulties each party faces when there is a lack of high quality scientific evidence available.

Physicians must be responsive to the wants and needs of their patients. Physicians need to be sensitive to changes in the patient and his or her thinking as the patient ages and as the patient's thinking is affected by trauma, vascular, neuropsychiatric, social, and frailty-related factors at any point in their lives.

## Trust in the Designers of Decision Support Systems and Tools

Much is discussed about the need for patients to become more responsible for the decision making that is conducted in their own care. Effort is going into systems designed to help patients make decisions that obviate the physician's role in the decision making process [30]. Even when there is recognition that some patients do not want to use such tools, this recognition may not be respected in the patient-physician relationship. For example, A. Robinson and R. Thomson argue as follows:

> While there is an increasing emphasis on patient empowerment and shared decision making, evidence suggests that many patients do not wish to be involved in decisions about their own care. Previous research has found patient preferences for involvement in decision making to vary with age, socioeconomic status, illness experience, and the gravity of the decision. Furthermore, there is evidence that certain patients may experience disutility from being involved in decision making about the treatment of their health problems . . . [P]atients may be ill-informed about what participation in decision making actually entails and unaware of the benefits they stand to gain by articulating their preferences to their clinician. Furthermore, clinicians are not good at accurately

assessing patients' preferences, while patients may have unrealistic expectations about their clinician's ability to "know what is best" for them [31].

Little has been said about the trust that patients and physicians are asked to place in such systems. This is particularly true when patients use decision support tools to assist them in making decisions but their physicians do not play a role. In addition, little work has been done surveying physicians' opinions about using decision tools with their patients. Key issues need to be addressed with each such tool and system, including the issue of how the tool or device's information will compare with respect to the most available peer-reviewed medical literature available at sites that can be accessed by the public like PubMed Central (PMC) [32].

The notion of trust and up-to-date medical knowledge is important not only to patients who are asked to use these tools in their decision making, but to physicians who must be ready to substantiate the importance of these tools that are impacting the patient-physician relationship. According to E.Z. Silfen and C.O. Patel, in the use of Web resources, "physicians face the dual challenge of judging the relevance of the information and trusting its Web source" [33]. These authors argue for the need to develop a "trust-relevance" framework for evaluating these information resources on the Web. The authors argue for physicians that:

> By demystifying the concepts associated with information resources, search engines, and retrieval tools, and presenting a reasonable view of current opportunities as well as future possibilities, the authors hope to provide guidance so physicians can more rapidly adopt innovative computer-assisted search tools for acquiring information that facilitate patient care decision-making [33].

But what needs to be recognized is the fact that physicians' and patients' trust needs to be engendered in information retrieval and decision support tools and systems before they will be found to be truly useful in decision making in the patient-physician relationship.

Onora O'Neill argues that there must not only be trust, but there must also be accountability in areas of clinical practice and public health policy [34]. O'Neill makes the distinction between older public policy cultures and their "reliance on trust between professionals and the public" and "a new public culture based on accountability and transparency" [34]. Transparency relates to decision making so all participants understand what is being done in a decision and for what reason(s) the decision is being made in the way that it is being made.

## CONCLUSION

The issues of decision making go beyond consideration of risk and benefit as emphasized in decision sciences. All terminology must be reassessed continuously as new approaches to information retrieval need to be parsed, analyzed, and translated into the language of both the patient and the physician in the patient-physician relationship. This language of the patient-physician relationship is one which at its very basis depends on understanding words (terminology) and numbers both in decision making and in any decision tools used in such decision making. Yet the patient-physician relationship is a relationship where literacy and numeracy has yet to be achieved adequately enough to achieve a basic understanding of elements of a decision that is composed of four elements: risk, benefit, physician's opinion, and patient's preference. Each element needs more clarity in terms of how to best allow each party to do their best in this unique joint decision-making relationship we have in the patient-physician relationship.

## REFERENCES


[1] *Slater v. Baker and Stapleton.* (1767). 95 Eng. Rep. 860, 2 Wils. KB 359.

[2] *Salgo v. Leland Stanford Junior University Board of Trustees.* (1957). 154 Cal. App. 2d 560; 317 P.2d 170.

[3] *Canterbury v. Spence.* (1972). 464 F.2d 772.

[4] *Sidaway v Board of Governors of the Bethlam Royal Hospital and The Maudsley Hospital* (1985) 1 AC 871.

[5] *Reibl v. Hughes.* (1980). 2 SCR 885.

[6] *Rogers v. Whitaker.* (1992). 67 ALJR 47.

[7] Mazur, D.J. (2007). *Evaluating the science and ethics of research on humans: a guide for IRB Members.* Baltimore, MD: Johns Hopkins University Press.

[8] Faden, R.R., & Beauchamp, T.L. (1986). *A history and theory of informed consent.* New York: Oxford University Press, at pp. 300-330.

[9] Mukherjee, D., Levin, R.L., & Heller, W. (2006). The cognitive, emotional, and social sequelae of stroke: psychological and ethical concerns in post-stroke adaptation." *Topics in Stroke Rehabilitation 13* (4), 26-35, p. 26.

[10] Monastero, R., Palmer, K., Qiu, C., Winblad, B., & Fratiglioni, L. (2007). Heterogeneity in risk factors for cognitive impairment, no dementia: population-based longitudinal study from the Kungsholmen Project. *The American Journal of Geriatric Psychiatry 15* (1), 60-69.

[11] Lilford, R.J., Pauker, S.G., Braunholtz, D.A., & Chard, J. (1998) Decision analysis and the implementation of research findings. *British Medical Journal 317* (7155), 405-409.

[12] van der Donk, J., Levendag, P.C., Kuijpers, A.J., Roest, F.H., Habbema, J.D., Meeuwis, C.A., Schmitz, P.I. (1995). Patient participation in clinical decision-making for treatment of T3 laryngeal cancer: a comparison of state and process utilities. *Journal of Clinical Oncology 13* (9), 2369-2378.

[13] Mazur, D.J. (2001). *Shared decision making in the patient-physician relationship: challenges facing patients, physicians, and medical institutions.* Tampa, FLA: American College of Physician Executives, pp. 219-222.

[14] Fowler, F.J., Jr., Cleary, P.D., Massagli, M.P., Weissman, J., & Epstein, A. (1995). The role of reluctance to give up life in the measurement of the values of health states. *Medical Decision Making 15* (3), 195-200, at p. 195.

[15] Kahneman, D., & Tversky, A., (1973). On the psychology of prediction. *Psychological Review 80* (4), 237-251.

[16] Kahneman, D., & Tversky, A. (1996) On the reality of cognitive illusions. *Psychological Review 103* (3), 582-591; discussion 592-596.

[17] Tversky, A., & Kahneman, D. (1973). Availability: a heuristic for judging frequency and probability. *Cognitive Psychology 5*, 207-232.

[18] Waddington, L., & Morley, S. (2000). Availability bias in clinical formulation: the first idea that comes to mind. *British Journal of Medical Psychology 73* (pt. 1), 117-127.

[19] Benbasat, I.I., & Lim, J. (2000). Information technology support for debiasing group judgments: an empirical evaluation. *Organizational Behavior and Human Decision Processes 83* (1), 167-183, at p. 167.

[20] Mazur, D.J., & Hickam, D.H. (1997). Patients' preferences for risk disclosure and role in decision making for invasive medical procedures. *Journal of General Internal Medicine 12* (2), 114-117, at p. 114.

[21] Ziegler, D.K., Mosier, M.C., Buenaver, M., Okuyemi, K. (2001). How much information about adverse effects of medication do patients want from physicians? *Archives of Internal Medicine 161* (5), 706-713.

[22] McNeil, B.J., Pauker, S.G., Sox, H.C., Jr., Tversky, A. (1982). On the elicitation of preferences for alternative therapies. *New England Journal of Medicine 306* (21), 1259-1262., at p. 1261.

[23] Mazur, D.J., & Hickam, D.H. (1991). Patients' interpretations of probability terms. *Journal of General Internal Medicine 6* (3), 237-240.

[24] Mazur, D.J., & D.H. Hickam. (1993). Patients' and physicians' interpretations of graphic data displays. *Medical Decision Making 13* (1), 59-63.

[25] Mazur, D.J., & Hickam, D. H. (1994). The effect of physician's explanations on patients' treatment preferences: five-year survival data. *Medical Decision Making 14* (3), 255-258.

[26] McNutt, R.A. (2004). Shared medical decision making: problems, process, progress. *Journal of the American Medical* Association *292* (20), 2516-2518.

[27] Coulter, A. (2005). Shared decision-making: the debate continues. *Health Expectations 8* (2), 95-96.

[28] Mazur, D.J., & Hickam, D.H. (1997). Patients' preferences for risk disclosure and role in decision making for invasive medical procedures. *Journal of General Internal Medicine 12* (2), 114-117.

[29] Mazur, D.J., Hickam, D.H., Mazur, M.D., & Mazur, M.D. (2005). The role of doctor's opinion in shared decision making: what does shared decision making really mean when considering invasive medical procedures? *Health Expectations 8* (2), 97-102.

[30] Gafni, A., Charles, C., & Whelan, T. (1998). The physician-patient encounter: the physician as a perfect agent for the patient versus the informed treatment decision-making model. *Social Science and Medicine 47* (3), 347-354.

[31] Robinson, A., & Thomson, R. (2001). Variability in patient preferences for participating in medical decision making: implication for the use of decision support tools. *Quality in Health Care 10* (suppl 1), i34-i38.

[32] http://www.pubmedcentral.nih.gov. Accessed on January 26, 2007.

[33] Silfen, E.Z., & Patel, C.O. (2006). Trusted and relevant medical knowledge: the promise of information retrieval in biomedicine. *Journal of Healthcare Information Management 20* (4), 74-82.

[34] O'Neill, O. (2004). Accountability, trust and informed consent in medical practice and research. *Clinical Medicine 4* (3), 269-276.

In: Decision Making in Medicine and Health Care
Editor: P. C. Tolana, pp. 169-183
ISBN: 978-1-60021-870-5


*Chapter IX*

# EMPOWERING CANCER PATIENTS TO MAKE INFORMED DECISIONS

***Robert J Thomas[1,2,*] and Madeleine Williams[3]***
[1]Cranfield University Post-graduate Medical School, UK;
[2]Addenbrooke's Hospital Cambridge University NHS Trust and The Primrose Oncology Research Unit Bedford Hospital, UK;
[3]The Primrose Oncology Research Unit, Bedford Hospital, UK.

## ABSTRACT

The benefits of good quality patient information are now firmly established. Adequately informed patients are able to share decision making with their medical team whilst exercising their own autonomy. Providing higher levels of information and involving patients in their own treatment decisions has been shown to have a protective effect on patients' psychological and physical wellbeing. In both randomized [1-5] and prospective observational studies [6-8] patients with a variety of cancer types offered higher levels of information were significantly more satisfied, had improved compliance, and reduced anxiety and depression. In order to empower patients with enough understanding to have a truly informed input into their management, many oncology units around the world have introduced a wide selection of educational tools, which aim to provide multifaceted education programmes, addressing a range of cultural and educational levels. In order to know whether these manoeuvers are satisfying patient's information needs, as this chapter discusses, we need to know what these needs are and how to measure them.

* Correspondence concerning this article should be addressed to: Professor Robert Thomas, Department of Oncology, The Primrose Oncology Research Unit, Bedford Hospital, Kempston Road, Bedford. MK42 9DJ.

# Introduction

In order for patients to be empowered to share decisions with their medical teams, they need to truly understand their options. They therefore, have to transgress from normal members of society, to a cancer expert in a mater of weeks and at the same time cope with the emotional trauma of a diagnosis of cancer. The quality and level of information they require at this point after diagnosis and for that matter critical stages in the cancer management cancer is high [9-13]. As this is often higher than many physicians appreciate or have facilities to provide [9-11], it is not surprising that a number of large retrospective surveys have previously demonstrated high levels of dissatisfaction among patients and their relatives [9,14-17].

## What are the Consequences of Poor Information Provision?

The unpleasant feeling of being inadequately informed has been linked with more sinister psychological and physical consequences. It can lead to frustration at the ability to make a proper decision, thus preventing patients to fully exercise their autonomy [18]. Lerman et al in 1993 demonstrated a link with anger, confusion and poor adjustment to illness [11]. Other observational studies have also demonstrated an inverse relationship between post treatment anxiety, depression and self-care during radiotherapy and initial satisfaction with information given pre-treatment [1,7,19,20]. Patients with less knowledge before surgery have demonstrated higher anxiety, recovered more slowly from their anaesthetic and were less ambulant post-operatively [21,22]. Dissatisfied patients are more likely to turn away from the clinic and look for information from uncontrolled, and often inappropriate, sources elsewhere [23,24]. Furthermore, failures in provision of relevant information are among the most common reasons for official complaints by patients and relatives [25] which can involve hours of medical and managerial time, and legal expenses [26].

## What are the Benefits of Good Information Provision?

Providing higher levels of information and involving patients in their own treatment decisions has been shown to have a protective effect on patient's wellbeing. In both randomized [1-5] and prospective observational studies [6-8] patients with a variety of cancer types offered higher levels of information were significantly more satisfied and had better psychological adjustment to their illness. In another prospective, but non-randomised study, patients offered a choice in their management had lower levels of anxiety and depression, better adjustment of work and attitudes towards the future [19]. Furthermore, children of parents with cancer coped better when informed of the diagnosis [4,27,28] and had lower levels of anxiety when given more complete information.

### What Level of Information do Cancer Patients Need?

In two separate UK studies, an information needs questionnaire was used to estimate the level of information patients wanted after their diagnosis of cancer [12,13]. Nearly 80% indicated that they wanted as much information as possible. Only 20% wished to have only positive information or wanted to let the doctor make decisions for them without informed input [12,13]. Measurements of anxiety levels in one of these studies indicated that the group of patients who wanted to let the doctor decide had very low anxiety. The old saying "ignorance is bliss" therefore stands, and should be respected. For example, Franz Ingelfinger, formerly editor of the New England Journal of Medicine, who himself died of carcinoma of the oesophagus, sensed "immediate and immense relief" when he abrogated responsibility to his doctor [29]. This tells us that it is probably unwise to force information on this small but significant group of patients, and research is underway to identify patient's level of information requirements at the outset [7,30]. For the majority of patients, time pressures and patient numbers mean that consultations are often short. Combined with the tendency of many health professionals to overestimate patient's understanding of their treatment options [9-13] and to underestimate the level of information they require [31,32], results in some patient's feeling inadequately powered to take an active role in their own treatment decisions [9,15,16].

Most oncology units around the world are now investing time, money and effort in improving their information strategies and in general patient satisfaction is improving. At the same time, however, patient's expectations have also increased in terms of quantity and diversity, and in order not to lag behind, even more sophisticated and individualized information strategies are required.

## Developing a Multifaceted, Evidence Based Information Strategy

These included:-

- Communication training for medical staff
- A separate consultation with the nurse re-enforcing the main consultation
- A comprehensive range of written materials
- A hand-held file containing information only relevant to that individual's case
- An information video on chemotherapy and radiotherapy (CancerBACUP)
- A designated website hosting the information materials (cancernet.co.uk).

### Communication Training

Face-to-face communication with skilled health and social care professionals who are able to *'engage with patients on an emotional level, to listen to them, assess how much information a patient wants to know, and to convey information with clarity and sympathy'*, is highly valued by patients and carers [33]. It is the preferred mode of information-giving at critical points in the patient pathway [33,34]. Interpersonal communication is underpinned and enhanced by mutual understanding, respect and awareness of individual's roles and functions, and is a vital process through which patients and carers are helped to explore issues and arrive at decisions. Some professionals, however, have reported feeling inadequately trained in aspects of communication such as listening, communicating significant news, explaining complex treatment options, exploring uncertainty (particularly in relation to prognosis) and discussing end-of-life issues. They may lack the necessary skills to be able to communicate effectively with the children and grandchildren of people with cancer, people with hearing, sight or combined sensory disabilities, those with learning disabilities, people who do not speak or understand English, and those from minority ethnic backgrounds and traditions. In addition, they may also lack skills in eliciting patient's needs for information and their desire for involvement in decision making. Communications skills training programmes have been demonstrated to improve senior doctor's communication behaviours [33,35,36].

The first stage in developing and improving a multifaceted information strategy was to ensure that all staff were up-to-date in their communications skills. The next step was to arm the staff with the suitable tools.

## Written Materials

The benefits of additional information booklets, for example, have been demonstrated in a number of randomised controlled trials. In two of these trials, where patients received radiotherapy, the patients had a higher level of self-care and greater satisfaction compared with the control groups [7,11]. In two other prospective trials, a preparatory booklet significantly reduced anxiety in patients about to undergo surgical procedures [37,38].

Although numerous patient advocacy and support groups exist, it is important to have a local panel which preferably involves patients, to ensure materials are relevant and of a suitable policy. Local materials are also inevitably required by patients, and there are various guidelines published to help write materials to a standard which will provide optimal information in a concise, clear way. Good examples of these include; The King's Fund *Promoting Patient Choice* initiative, involving a comprehensive set of guidelines for producing quality evidence-based information for patients [39]; The POPPI Guide (the practicalities of producing patient information), harnessing the expertise of the Plain English Forum and the Centre for Health Information Quality (CHiQ), has been drawn up in a collaborative publication by the BMA and the King's Fund [40].

## A Hand Held File

The lack of control of written materials still makes it difficult for patients to sort the wheat from the chaff, and many patients and relatives remain confused [9,15,16]. Although a relatively simple procedure, giving patients an individualised folder such as a filofax, which pools the relevant literature together, is a concept welcomed by patients [41]. It can be made up with general and site-specific documents, as well as those giving practical information such as directions to the hospital, appointment times, etc. The relevant sheets can be inserted at the appropriate time during the treatment pathway, so patients receive relevant and timely information. The system introduced in our centre is designed to integrate with a designated website (cancernet.co.uk) which allows patients and professionals to down load the relevant advice sheets into the folder at the appropriate stages in their management [42].

## Information Films

DVD/video can be used to present pre-formatted information and have the advantage of combining vision, sound and the written word. This is a communication medium that is becoming cheaper and commonplace in most households. In one study of patients with cancer, 89% owned or had easy access to a video player [17]. The concept of filmed information appears to be welcomed by patients, as nearly 90% of patients when asked, felt receiving this medium in their management would have been helpful or very helpful [17]. Some oncology departments have commissioned their own films, whilst others have chosen those available commercially. Most films have a tendency to concentrate on idiosyncrasies within individual departments. The target audience is not defined and neither is the stage of treatment management, as to when patients should watch it. Few have invested sufficient money to involve professional film companies. They tend to overprotect viewers from information instead of giving patients what they want [9,12,16] - a crisp, comprehensive description of therapy, with a clear idea of the risk of the various treatment options.

There have been a number of published trials evaluating the effectiveness of videocassettes dating back 20 years. For example, Moldofsky et al (1979) showed that patients retained more information in subsequent consultations if video was included in their information package after their diagnosis [43]. This work has subsequently been confirmed in a number of randomised trials in a variety of procedures and specialties, including ambulatory day surgery [44], surgery for breast cancer [45,46] colonoscopy for malignant disease [47], coronary angiography [48-50], tooth extraction [51] and genetic counseling [52].

In addition to videocassettes helping the retention of knowledge, two of these trials have also showed an improvement in treatment-associated anxiety and satisfaction in patients having cardiac catheterization [49,50]. Not all subsequent trials, however, have had consistent results. Although none of them showed any increased anxiety in the video groups, a randomised trial of patients undergoing colonoscopy reported increased knowledge and satisfaction, but failed to demonstrate a reduction in anxiety [47]. A similar study of patients receiving genetic counseling reported similar benefits and shorter consultation times, but again no reduction in anxiety [52]. Two further randomised trials, the first in patients having breast surgery and the second in patients undergoing coronary angioplasty, failed to show any improvement in satisfaction or anxiety [46,48].

The variation in these trial results suggests that, like all educational materials, the quality of the content is paramount and how it is used is vital to success [27]. For example, the latter two trials failed to utilise the main benefit of film by insisting patients watched it in the clinic, missing the opportunity to continue the learning process at home. Ideally films should be given to patients before treatment, but after their routine consultation, and then taken home and watched alone or in the company of friends, relatives or community health workers who may not have attended the original oncology consultation - educating all parties simultaneously. This gives patients the control to watch it as often as they wish, with whom they wish, thus ensuring that one individual has the opportunity to retain the same level of information as another.

The largest randomised trial evaluating preparatory information on video used precisely this strategy, but also invested sufficient resources to ensure the opinions of patients themselves were presented in a clear and skillful production. Professional help was gained from established film directors, and a commercial film company specialising in the production of medical documentaries (HEP©). Patients themselves described the common side effects of chemotherapy and radiotherapy, and explained ways to alleviate them. Two hundred and twenty newly diagnosed patients with cancer were randomized to receive the video 'Chemotherapy & Radiotherapy', or not as part of their information package at that time. Satisfaction to the information received, and anxiety and depression levels (HAD Score), were measured throughout their subsequent oncology management. There was a significant correlation between satisfaction and reduced treatment related anxiety overall. In the Video Group the mean HAD anxiety score was significantly lower during treatment compared to the Non-Video Group (4.6 v 7.4, Chi square test $p=0.001$). Likewise, the mean HAD depression scores where also significantly lower in the patients prepared for the side effects of treatment with the video (2.9 v 5.3 Chi square test $p=0.001$). Furthermore, 87% of patients felt the film contained just the right amount of information, was very helpful for the whole family and no patient felt that it was misleading [5,17].

These highly statistically significant results suggest a clear role for patient information in a film format. It is also clear that quality and method of giving the film has a vital influence in its effectiveness. If further disease specific films are to be made, considerable time, patient involvement, co-ordination and expense are required. Departments would need to stock sufficient quantities of these films, allowing each patient a copy to take home, and to justify the development costs, the emphasis should be directed at an international rather than local level.

## The Internet

The attraction for patients and their relatives or close friends is considerable; electronic mailing lists, online support groups and websites devoted to their specific cancers can provide valuable information as well as a degree of emotional support [53,54]. The internet improves patient's sense of control, as well as their ability to participate actively in health care decisions [53-55]. Some American authors have suggested that it could also improve skills for self-help and reduce the financial burden of their care [56].

The ability for anyone in the world to freely and easily add information onto a website is clearly the secret of its success, but likewise it is the key to its dangers. As there is no control over quality and quantity, much of the information is inaccurate or misleading, and it is difficult for patients to make judgements on the relevance of the advice [57-59]. Inaccurate information could have serious consequences. An over optimistic view of medical treatment could foster demand for inappropriate intervention, leading to iatrogenic harm, increased dissatisfaction and unnecessary cost [58]. Furthermore, there is no protection from unscrupulous or bogus websites preying on the vulnerability of newly diagnosed and terminally ill patients - persuading them to buy "remedies" of unproven benefit.

With the complexity, variability and dynamism of the information on the internet, any attempt to evaluate its effectiveness is likely to be futile [58]. Some authors advocate taming the beast by using tools such as internet directories, indexes and specific search engines which review and rate the quality of the registered websites [60]. Theoretically, by relying on these ratings, consumers can easily identify valuable information sites. Unfortunately, current rating systems remain flawed by excessive commercial bias and promote sites which sell specific products, rather than those providing good quality information. A study in 2007, from Birmingham UK, evaluated patients attitudes to the information they received from the internet. It also looked at their patterns of use and how it influences the decisions they made on a daily basis. A major finding was the lack of trust in internet information, and again an inability to sort fact from fiction. The majority of patients still wanted a sanction from their own healthcare team that what they were looking at was sensible and genuine [34]. At Bedford Hospital we have attempted to overcome these problems by providing a website (cancernet.co.uk). It acts as a useful bulletin board for local facilities and information leaflets. It also provides a list and gateway to well prepared, reliable websites such government organisations, major universities and charities, which are all free from commercial bias.

## PATIENT FEEDBACK

### Developing a Patient Information Satisfaction Questionnaire

In order to enhance an established information strategy, it is vital to gain further feedback from patients. The initial step in this feedback process is to unearth the specific issues which concern patients, and then measure whether these concerns are being met within routine clinical practice. A number of questionnaires have been developed and have successfully be used to measure global satisfaction such as that used in the recent UK Department of Health survey [61]. These do not particularly separate satisfaction for the information they received from other general issues of satisfaction. It is also important, to evaluate subcategories of information from each other. A questionnaire specifically addressing information issues, however, had not previously been available. To address this deficit, we designed a simple study in 2003 which aimed to unearth the specific information issues which are of most concern to patients with cancer.

Seventy seven consecutive patients with a diagnosis of cancer, attending the oncology outpatients department were asked to annotate the most important aspects of information which helped them during their illness and subsequent therapies. Patients were required to have had a histological diagnosis of cancer and had completed an active treatment for cancer within the last six months, to ensure that issues were still fresh in their minds. They were approached by the clinic nurses whilst waiting for a consultation, within six consecutive outpatient clinics at the Primrose Oncology Unit, Bedford Hospital, over a two-week period. Following a verbal and written explanation of the project, patients were then given a blank sheet of paper and asked to write five or more of the most important categories of information which either helped them, or would have helped them, following their diagnosis, during their treatment and follow-up. The nurse also recorded on the same page the sex, age, diagnosis and treatments the patient received. Four patients declined (2 male, 2 female), the remaining 73 (95%) patients returned the questionnaire before they left the clinic or returned it later by post. Twenty-four were male, 49 female, aged between 26-78 years (mean 55 yrs), 38% had breast cancer, 28% bowel, 12% had ovarian or lymphomas. Each of the 303 answers were read by a multidisciplinary panel of nurses, doctors and patients and categorised into 9 main groups of similar themes based on order of frequency.

For example, "*I would have liked more information on transport and parking*", was categorised into the logistical issues section. "*I wasn't sure if I could exercise*" into the lifestyle section. "*Information on how would feel and side effects during chemotherapy*" into the side effects of treatments, "*Would the treatment work?*" into the outcome section.

**Table 1. Categories of information which most concerned patients with cancer (combined and equally weighted into 5 sections)**

| Combined categories | No.(% patients) |
|---|---|
| Side effects of treatment /How will I feel | 65 (87%) |
| Explanation of illness / Prognosis / Genetic risks | 64 (83%) |
| Logistical issues /Follow up arrangements | 60 (82%) |
| Treatment options /Clinical trials | 58 (75%) |
| Lifestyle issues /Support groups /complementary Rx | 56 (77%) |
| | **303 (100%)** |

The score for each section was then determined by a standard 5-point Likert Scale [62]. An additional question was also included to give patients the opportunity to provide a score for overall performance. Patients demographics were included to allow the questionnaire to be used in audits which look for deficits between patient types, including age, sex, ethnic groups, tumour diagnosis or whether in a clinical trial. Finally, three questions ask patients level of information requirements were added based on our previous adaptation of an original information needs questionnaire developed for a West of Scotland Survey [12,20]. The completed one A4 page Information Satisfaction Questionnaire ISQ questionnaire is freely available on www.cancernet.co.uk in a variety of languages, is now used routinely to measure patient's satisfaction to information across a large UK cancer network (West Anglia).

## Feed Back from the ISQ

The questionnaire has been used as a fundamental tool to gather feedback for the development of an integrated patients information programme across a large UK cancer network. First used in clinic in 2003, the ISQ was given to a hundred consecutive patients at the Primrose Oncology Unit, Bedford over a 3-week period within fifteen clinics. The overall score was gratifyingly high (92% satisfied or very satisfied), and an enormous improvement to a similar audit two years earlier using a rudimentary previous satisfaction questionnaire (23% satisfied or very satisfied). Although, not directly comparable, it reassured us that the information strategies instigated over this time were having a benefit. Despite these manoeuvres, and this high overall score, the questionnaire was still able to spot limitations in the information provision service particularly amongst patients indicating that they were from ethnic minorities. They had lower scores (68% satisfied or very satisfied) in keeping with findings from previous studies [5]. Patients from ethnic groups were also less frequently entered into clinical studies, also suggesting a lack of trust in the service. To address these issues, thanks to sponsorship from the UK Department of Health New Opportunities Fund, preparatory information films were made in the 5 most common ethnic UK languages - Urdu, Hindi, Gujarati, Bengali and Italian. In a previous study, ethnic subgroups had demonstrated a particularly strong preference for information in a video format [5]. The emphasis is diverted away from the spoken and written word into vision and movement which may be an attraction to patients whose first language is not English [63]. Films were made with patients from these language groups and were designed to sensitive to their cultural and educational needs. Like the English film, it was then given to all patients before chemotherapy or radiotherapy. They provide an overview of treatment, risks of side effects and methods used to alleviate them, and show patients describing their own experiences.

The ISQ was then used in a similar audit in 2006. Reassuringly, patients from ethnic groups then scored the same as others (84% v 89% satisfied or very satisfied). There were however some other concerns (table 2):

- Advice on logistical issues and follow-up arrangements scored low (73% satisfied).
- Lifestyle advice appeared to be insufficient (69% satisfied).
- Patients not in clinical trials scored significantly less satisfied than those in trials.

### *Logistical Advice:*

Confusion with the practical arrangements relating to the complexities of cancer therapies leads to anger and frustration. These emotions distract patients from clear thought and may lead to inappropriate decision-making. In response to this audit, a practical issues and logistics panel was established to gather practical information on transport, travel, clinic times and parking and money was raised to buy extra cars bolstering the transport services, etc. The audit has also stressed the importance of there being adequate levels of good quality clerical staff.

*Lifestyle Advice:*

There is now persuasive evidence that a healthy lifestyle after cancer is associated with a number of significant advantages for the patient [64-66] and these can be summarised as following:-

- Can slow the progression of an established cancer
- Reduce the risk of relapse of a treated cancer.
- Reduces risks of side effects *during* cancer therapies. In particular:-
  - — Reduces fatigue and tiredness
  - — Improves mood, reduces the risk of anxiety and depression
  - — Improves appetite, reduces sickness and vomiting
  - — Improves digestion (avoiding diarrhoea, constipation and indigestion)
  - — Avoids deep and superficial vein thrombosis
  - — Improves skin care
- Reduces the *long term* risks and speeds recovery from cancer therapies such as surgery, radiotherapy, hormones and biological therapies. In particular lifestyle helps long term:-
  - — Psychological wellbeing
  - — Speeds recovery from post-treatment fatigue
  - — Enhances body constitution (more muscle, less fat)
  - — Can help urinary function and sexual wellbeing
  - — Diminished bowel problems (adhesions, constipation, indigestion)
  - — Helps skin tone, breast tenderness and joint pains
  - — Helps hot flushes and bone health
  - — Reduces the risk of second cancers
  - — Improves intellectual capacity and cognitive skills

The decisions patients make regarding the activities of daily living such as nutrition, exercise, smoking and supplement intake are now as important as those related to conventional areas of oncology management. What's more, these are decisions which allow patients to exert their greatest autonomy. Despite the enormous expanse of lifestyle information available on the internet, television, books and magazines, patients feel more reassurance of their credibility if guidance has the sanction of their medical institution [34,64-66]. Unfortunately, further in-depth interviews with the patients in our network discovered patients all too often either felt embarrassed to ask their clinicians about everyday nutritional and exercise activities, or felt they were taking up too much of their limited clinic time. Of more concern, some patients or their relatives felt they either did not have the confidence in their clinician's abilities on this subject, or were rebuked by a paternalistic retort [64,66].

In an attempt to correct this lag between patient's expectations for lifestyle guidance and what they had been receiving, a number of measures have been initiated based on a review of the Worlds published literature [64-66].

A series of lifestyle advice sheets have been written and published on the internet (cancernet.co.uk/lifestyle), ready to be printed out at appropriate times during a patient's management, to be included in their hand-held file if required. The most notable examples of these include guidance on:

- Exercise; finding local gyms, dance, yoga, Pilates classes, swimming pools, sports
- Personal fitness instructors
- Diet and cancer
- Quitting smoking
- Fertility issues and cancer
- Sexual issues and cancer
- Complementary therapies
- Carcinogens in common food
- ORAC ratings of food
- Psychological counseling
- Alcohol dependence
- Drug dependence
- Financial advice and Insurance
- Traveling and cancer

Staff have also been alerted to the desire of patients to receive lifestyle advice. A government grant has been requested to establish a specific lifestyle clinic within our institution. Finally a manual has been written, entitled "lifestyle after cancer" and is available to patients as well as health care professional that are in contact with patients during their management.

**Table 2. Comparison of satisfaction for patients in trials to those not in trials**

| | Patients recording unsatisfied or very unsatisfied scores | | | |
|---|---|---|---|---|
| | All (n:200) No. (%) | Trial (n:83) No. (%) | Non-trial (n:117) No. (%) | Difference (% difference) |
| Explanation of illness | 19 (9.5%) | 5 (6%) | 14 (12%) | 6% (50%) |
| Types of treatments | 28 (14%) | 9 (11%) | 19 (16%) | 5% (31%) |
| Logistics | 53 (27%) | 20 (24%) | 33 (28%) | 4% (14%) |
| Side effects | 30 (15%) | 11 (13%) | 19 (16%) | 3% (19%) |
| Lifestyle | 61 (31%) | 27 (32%) | 34 (29%) | 3% (10%) |
| Overall | 24 (12%) | 6 (7.2%) | 18 (15.4%) | 8.2% (53%) $Chi^2$ $p<0.01$ |

### *Clinical Trial Information*

It is reassuring that patients within clinical trials are generally very satisfied with the information they have received, with the exception of lifestyle advice (Table.2). This may be because patients in clinical trials are fitter and deemed by their clinicians to be easier to communicate with, but nevertheless trial literature is clearly an example of best practice. There was, however, concern that 27% of patients, not in trials, were uncertain as to whether they were in a clinical trial or not. Paradoxically this implies that more trial information is required for the majority of patients not in a clinical trial, than those who are. This has been addressed with new explanatory posters displayed in patients' areas, trial information included in the standard information sheets and staff have been briefed to specifically mention to patients that they are not in a clinical study.

## Conclusions

In order for patients and their relatives to make informed decisions concerning their own management, they need to be adequately informed. The anger and frustration associated with an inability to understand their treatment options can lead to anxiety, depression, poor compliance and poor co-operation with strategies to reduce treatment related side effects. More recently published evidence has highlighted that patients who decide to improve their lifestyle will have major benefits in terms of their quality of life and improved cancer outcomes.

Oncology units, around the world, have universally accepted these data and have established patient information services with varying degrees of enthusiasm. Providing information however is not a 'one-off' procedure, and there are still on going challenges for medical teams. They have to keep up to speed with the growing expectations from patients and the rapid technological advances in oncology practice. A regular, formal patients feedback programme, using questionnaires such as the ISQ will ensure that unforeseen deficits in information provision can be corrected before they impinge on the decision making process.

## References

[1] Dodd MJ, Efficacy of proactive information on self-care in radiation therapy patients. *Heart and Lung*, 1987. 16: p. 538-544.

[2] Eardley A, Patients' worries about radiotherapy: evaluation of a preparatory booklet. *Psychology and Health*, 1988. 2: p. 79-89.

[3] McHugh P, Lewis S, and Ford S, The efficacy of audiotapes in promoting psychological well-being in cancer patients: a randomised controlled trial. *British Journal of Cancer*, 1995(71): p. 388-392.

[4] Reynolds PM, et al., Cancer and Communication: Information-giving in an Oncology Clinic. *BMJ*, 1981. 282: p. 1449-1451.

[5] Thomas R, et al., Preparatory information on video significantly improves treatment associated anxiety, depression and satisfaction - a multicentre study. *JCO*, 1999. Supp 8 (ASCO): p. 1570.

[6] Deustch G, Improving communication with oncology patients: taping the consultation. *Clinical Oncology*, 1992. 4: p. 46-47.

[7] Fallowfield LJ, et al., Psychological effects of being offered choice of surgery for breast cancer. *BMJ*, 1994. 309: p. 448.

[8] Hogbin B and Fallowfield LJ, Getting it taped: the bad news consultation with cancer patients. *British Journal of Hospital Medicine*, 1989. 41: p. 330.

[9] Audit Commission, What seems to be the matter: communication between hospitals and patients. 1993, HMSO LONDON.

[10] Ford S, Can oncologists detect distress in their outpatients and how satisfied are they with their performance during bad news consultation? *Breast Cancer Journal*, 1994. 70: p. 767-770.

[11] Lerman C, Daly M, and Walsh WP, Communication between patients with breast cancer and health care providers. Determinants and implications. *Cancer*, 1993. 72: p. 2612-2620.

[12] Meredith C, et al., Information needs of cancer patients in the west of Scotland: cross-sectional survey of patients' views. *BMJ*, 1996. 313: p. 724-6.

[13] Thomas R, et al., Anxiety and Depression - Effect on patients' preferences for information following a diagnosis of cancer. *Annals of Oncology (ESMO)*, 1998. 9(4): p. 141.

[14] GIVIO, Interdisciplinary Group for Cancer care Evaluation. What doctors tell patients with cancer about diagnosis and treatment: findings from a study in general hospitals. *British Journal of Cancer*, 1986. 54: p. 319-326.

[15] Mosconi P, et al., Disclosure of breast cancer diagnosis: Patient and Physician reports. GIVIO (interdisciplinary Group for Cancer Care Evaluation). *Annals of Oncology*, 1991. 2: p. 273-280.

[16] National Cancer Alliance, Patient-centred cancer services? What patients say. National Cancer Alliance, 1996.

[17] Thomas R, Stockton D, and Akass K, Patients preferences for video directed information. Effects of age, sex and ethnic group. *European Journal of Cancer Care*, 1999. 8: p. 81-86.

[18] Thornton H, Breast Cancer Trials: a patients' viewpoint. *The Lancet*, 1992. 339: p. 44-45.

[19] Neuling SJ and Winefield HR, Social support and recovery after surgery for breast cancer: Frequency and currulates of social behaviour by family friends and surgeons. *Soc Sci Med*, 1988. 27: p. 385-392.

[20] Rainey LC, Effects of preparatory patient education for radiation oncology patients. *Cancer*, 1985. 56: p. 1056-1061.

[21] Elsass B, E.B., Junge J, Lykke J, Staun P, Feldt-Rasmussen M., Psychological effect of detailed preanesthetic information. *Acta Anaesthesiol Scand*, 1987. 31: p. 579-583.

[22] Kulik JA and Mahler HM, Effects of pre-operative room-mate assignment on pre-operative anxiety and recovery from coronary-bypass surgery. *Health Psychology*, 1987. 6: p. 525-543.

[23] Coulter A, Entwistle V, and Gilbert D, Sharing decisions with patients: is the information good enough? *BMJ*, 1999. 318: p. 318-322.

[24] Shingler G, Bulusu R, and Thomas R, Where do patients seek additional information after a diagnosis of cancer - a multicentre survey. *European Journal of Cancer*, 1996. 33(8): p. 1426.

[25] Ombudsman, Report of the Health service Ombudsman. 1995, HMSO: London.

[26] Black N, Medical litigation and the quality of care. *The Lancet*, 1990. 335: p. 35-37.

[27] Kroll L, et al., Cancer in parents: telling children. *BMJ*, 1998. 316: p. 880.

[28] Welch AS, Wandsworth ME, and Compas BE, Adjustment of children and adolescents to parental cancer. *CANCER*, 1996. 77: p. 1409-18.

[29] Ingelfinger FJ, Arrogance. New England Journal of Medicine, 1980. 303: p. 1507-1511.

[30] Fallowfield L, Giving sad and bad news. *The Lancet*, 1993. 341: p. 476-478.

[31] Coulter A, Partnerships with patients:the pros and cons of shared clinical decision-making. *Jornal Health Service Res Policy*, 1997. 1997(2): p. 112-21.

[32] Lloyd AJ, et al., Patients' ability to recall risk associated with treatment options. *The Lancet*, 1999. 353: p. 645.

[33] Bristol Royal Infirmary Inquiry, Learning from Bristol: The report of the public inquiry into children's heart surgery at the Bristol Roay Infirmary 1984-1995. Command Paper: CM5207, 2001.

[34] James N, Patients attitude to web-based information. *Clinical Oncology*, 2007. In press.

[35] NHS Centre for Reviews and Dissemination, Informing, communicating and sharing decisions with people who have cancer. *Effective Healthcare Bulletin*, 2000. 6(6): p. 1-8.

[36] NICE Committee, Supportive and Palliative Care Clinical Guidelines. 2002.

[37] Kerrigan DD, et al., Who's afraid of informed consent? *BMJ*, 1993. 306: p. 298-300.

[38] Marteau T, et al., Reducing anxiety in women referred for colposcopy using an information booklet. *British Journal of Health Psychology*, 1996. 1: p. 181-189.

[39] Duman M, Promoting patients choice. Some Do's for producing quality evidenced based patient choice information. The Kings Fund, 1998.

[40] Duman M and Farrell C, The practicalities of producing patient information - The POPPI guide. In press, 1999.

[41] Kaminski E, DeZeeuz N, and Thomas R, Patients attitudes towards an individualised filofax information system. *European Journal of Cancer*, 1997. 33(Supplement 8): p. 1401.

[42] DeZueew N, Balusu R, and Thomas R, Cancer patient education and information: development of a new structured information package. *European Journal of Cancer*, 1997. 33(Supplement 8): p. 1401.

[43] Moldofsky H, et al., Videotape education programme for people with cancer: more knowledge in the clinic. *Canadian Medical Association Jo*urnal, 1979. 120: p. 669 - 72.

[44] Done ML and Lee A, The use of video to convey pre-anaesthetic information to patients undergoing ambulatory surgery. *Anaesthesia & Analgesia*, 1998. 87(3): p. 531-6.

[45] Chapman GB, Elstein AS, and Huches KK, Effects of patient education on decisions about breast cancer treatments:a preliminary report. *Medical Decision Making*, 1995. 15(3): p. 231-9.

[46] Street RL, et al., Increasing patient involvement in choosing treatment for early breast cancer. *Cancer*, 1995. 76: p. 2275-2285.

[47] Agre P, Kurtz RC, and K. BJ., A randomised trial using videotape to present consent information for colonoscopy. *Gastrointest Endosc*, 1994. 40: p. 271-276.

[48] Bernstein S, et al., A randomised controlled trial of information-giving to patients referred for coronary angiography: effects on outcomes of care. *Health Expectations*, 1998. 1: p. 50-61.

[49] Herrmann KS and Kreuzer H, A randomised prospective study on anxiety reduction by preparatory disclosure with and without video film show about a planned heart catheterization. *European Heart Journal*, 1989. 10: p. 753-757.

[50] Uzark K, et al., Use of videotape in the preparation of children for cardiac catheterization. *Ped Cardiol*, 1982. 3: p. 287-291.

[51] Adler DN, et al., Information seeking and interactive video disc preparation for third molar extraction. *Journal of Oral Maxillofacial Surgery*, 1992. 50: p. 27-32.

[52] Cull A, et al., The use of videotaped information in cancer genetic counselling: A randomised evaluation study. *British Journal of Cancer*, 1998. 77(5): p. 830-837.

[53] Ferguson T, Consumer health informatics. Health Forum Journal, 1995(January): p. 28-33.

[54] Vaitones V, Protocol 'shopping' on the internet. *Cancer Practice*, 1995. 3: p. 274-278.

[55] Wyatt JC, Measuring quality and impact of the world wide web. *British Medical Journal*, 1997. 314: p. 1879-1881.

[56] Bennett-Clark J, Wher health information is byte-size: online advise can help you manage health costs. Kiplinger's Personal Finance, 1996(June): p. 96-97.

[57] Impicciatore P, et al., Reliability of health information for the public on the world wide web: Systematic survey of advise on managing fever in children at home. *British Medical Journal*, 1997. 314: p. 1875-1881.

[58] Jadad AR and Gagliardi A, Rating health information on the internet: navigating to knowledge or to Babel? *JAMA*, 1998. 279: p. 611-614.

[59] Silberg WM, L. GM, and Musacchio RA, Assessing controlling and assuring the quality of medical information on the internet. *JAMA,* 1997. 277: p. 1244-1245.

[60] Kim P, et al., Publishing criteria for evaluating health related websites: review. *British Medical Journal*, 1999. 318: p. 647-649.

[61] Annomynous, The National Patients Survey, in *www.doh.gov.uk/nhspatients/ ancersurvey*. 2002.

[62] Likert R, A Technique for the Measurement of Attitudes. *Archives of Psychology*, 1932. 140: p. 55.

[63] Williams MV, Parker RM, and Baker DW, Inadequate funtional health literacy among patients at two public hospitals. *JAMA*, 1995. 274: p. 1677-82.

[64] Thomas R, Blades M, and Williams M, Can dietary intervention alter prostate cancer progression? *Nutrition & Food Science*, 2007. 37(1): p. 24-36.

[65] Thomas R, et al., Dietary advice combined with a salicylate, mineral and vitamin supplement (CV247) has some tumour static properties: a phase II study. *Nutrition & Food Science*, 2005. 35(6): p. 436-451.

[66] Thomas R, Woodward C, and Williams P, Diet, salicylates and their effect on prostate cancer. *British Journal of Cancer Management*, 2006. 3: p. 5-9.

In: Decision Making in Medicine and Health Care
Editor: P. C. Tolana, pp. 185-199
ISBN: 978-1-60021-870-5


*Chapter X*

# Why are Primary Care Physicians Avoiding Rationing Decisions and What Can Be Done About It? The Case of Norway

***Benedicte Carlsen*** *
Stein Rokkan Centre for Social Studies, University of Bergen, Norway.

## Abstract

This chapter gives an overview of the literature regarding the ethical dilemmas that are debated in relation to primary care physicians' gatekeeper role. Theories and experiences of policy measures aiming at motivating rationing decisions in primary care are presented with the empirical case of the Norwegian health care system and policy.

Gatekeeping systems are health care systems where access to secondary care is filtered through primary care, as is the case in Norway, the UK, the Netherlands, Denmark, France and within managed care in the USA. One of the dilemmas often referred to in studies of primary care physicians' rationing decisions is how to balance the needs of the individual patient against the needs of the population while securing patient involvement in decision making.

Recent research gives several indications that primary care physicians are avoiding the rationing task. The Norwegian health care sector is one of the most expensive health care systems in the world, and it is almost entirely covered by universal insurance which means that it is practically free at the point of service. While the system is increasingly dependent on the primary care physicians' gatekeeper function for cost containment and fair and effective resource allocation, professional freedom of primary care physicians is extensive.

---

* Correspondence concerning this article should be addressed to: Benedicte Carlsen, Stein Rokkan Centre for Social Studies, University of Bergen, Norway. E-mail: Benedicte.carlsen@rokkan.uib.no.

Finally, the chapter suggests and discusses policy measures to motivate rationing in gatekeeping systems.

## Introduction

Rationing of health care is inevitable. Health care is rationed in all health care systems, either as a haphazard consequence of resource allocation or deliberately, according to a plan for priority setting. Rationing in the latter sense is receiving increased attention both in affluent and poor countries because of a growing gap between resources and demand for health care. This situation is caused by a combination of factors such as ageing populations, increasing possibilities for screening, new treatment technology, increasing consumer power and as some would argue; the increasing media driven anxiety about illness and death.

To promote deliberate rationing, several health care systems restrict access to secondary care. Access is filtered through the primary care system, placing the primary care physician in a central role as gatekeeper. Gatekeeping systems are incorporated in the health care sector of among others Norway, the UK, the Netherlands, Denmark, France and within managed care in the USA.

Recent research gives several indications that primary care physicians are avoiding the rationing task, both in Norway and in other countries [1-4]. The Norwegian health care sector is one of the most expensive health care systems in the world, and it is almost entirely covered by universal insurance which means that it is practically free at the point of service. While the system is increasingly dependent on the primary care physicians' gatekeeper function for cost containment and fair and effective resource allocation, professional freedom of primary care physicians is extremely high and there is practically no monitoring of practices, neither are physicians held responsible for failure to ration health care.

Part of the reason for the concern with rationing in Norway is that while Norway, together with Germany, have the world's highest public sector health expenditure as a proportion of GDP, Norway is only ranked as no 11 in the world in terms of life expectancy [5]. Thus these statistics indicate that while Norway spends large amounts on health care, it apparently gets less out of it's health care spending than for example, the UK or Canada, while the US spends even more on health care as compared to life expectancy.

## Studies of Rationing

Rationing occurs when a health care system denies people scarce resources which would have been of benefit to them [6]. Questions of rationing are inevitably connected to questions of power relations, patient involvement and ethical dimensions of health care delivery. A key question is whether to include patient preferences in the understanding of the concept of benefit. Should for instance services that are desired by the patient but unwarranted in the biomedical sense be rationed?

In short there are two main reasons for why it is seen as necessary to ration health care:

1) Because experience shows that demand exceeds available resources

2) To secure distributional justice and efficiency, and to ensure that resources are allocated as intended according to valid principles for priority setting.

We distinguish between several types of rationing. Firstly, health care can be limited directly through means directed at the public, for instance by limiting the number of doctors, by regulating waiting times or through different forms of co-payments. Secondly, health care can be limited indirectly through incentives directed at decision-makers thereby making them responsible of rationing decisions.

Some authors use the concept of priority setting to describe allocative decisions at the macro-level and limit the concept of rationing to implementation of priority setting at the micro-level [7].

Priority setting on the micro-level, in face to face encounters with individual patients, is characteristic of rationing in the primary care sector. This is also referred to as second order prioritising decisions as opposed to first order decisions that affect groups of patients. Benefits that are rationed through doctors include: Access to specialist care, medical treatment, check ups, tests, time and effort and different kinds of certificates. If resources are to be distributed according to politically agreed-upon principles this requires that decision makers at lower levels fulfil their gatekeeper role by rationing according to these principles. However, rationing decisions at the individual level are more affected by medical uncertainty than is priority setting at the macro-level.

It has proven difficult to operationalise rationing in empirical studies. One reason for this is the inherent uncertainty of most clinical decisions coupled with lack of guidelines and professional independence of doctors. Another complicating dimension is that rationing decisions in practice often are less clear then in theory. A common example is rationing by dilution: offering less intensive care, spending less time with the patients or exerting less effort to diagnose the patient. Hence the empirical knowledge of primary care rationing is limited. What is possible to measure is the degree to which patients get what they want from the doctor. Another alternative in empirical research is to ask doctors how often they abstain from giving into patients' demands because of health care costs. As primary care doctors' main rationing task in many countries is to limit unnecessary use of higher levels of care, referral rate is also a much applied indicator for level of rationing.

## FOCUS OF THIS CHAPTER

The present chapter elaborates on the ethical dilemma of rationing versus patient involvement and discusses possible policy measures to motivate rationing in gatekeeping systems. The focus is mainly on prioritising on the micro-level regarding individual patients in the primary care sector, which means that important issues regarding the political game at the macro level such as the influence of the Medical Association or the pharmaceutical industry will not be elaborated on. Further the discussion will concentrate on indirect rationing; which means measures directed towards professional decision makers. Hence measures directed at patients, such as out of pocket payments, will not be discussed.

## ETHICAL DILEMMAS OF RATIONING

Although there is broad agreement among policy makers, doctors and the public that patient involvement in medical decision making is the ideal, there has been considerable debate about the relative value of explicit and implicit rationing. Explicit rationing is a transparent process; the doctor is open about rationing and the reasons behind these decisions are revealed to the patient. The opposite, implicit rationing, means that the doctor does not reveal all treatment alternatives and does not offer any explanation for why an intervention is not offered.

There is as yet no consensus on whether and how patients should be involved in health care rationing. Recent research suggests that opinion is divided on the need to be explicit and that there is some dissonance between health workers and the public. In a study of the views of UK citizens, a majority wanted to know about rationing of their health care and to be given an explanation for the decisions that had been reached [8].

It has been argued that rationing might violate two fundamental principles of medical ethics regarding the individual patient [9,10]. This might explain why there is a certain resistance to rationing among both policy makers, health care workers and the public: Firstly, rationing limits the personal autonomy of the patient. Secondly, rationing might be in conflict with legal or moral rights to health care. The understanding that rationing is in conflict with underlying ethical principles sheds some light on the resistance to rationing which is found both in policy makers, health care workers and the public. These limitations need to be balanced against the ethical principle and policy aim of distributive justice, which states that the autonomy and rights of one patient must be weighted against the needs and claims of other patients. However, patient autonomy is not an absolute principle. It has been argued that autonomy requires a degree of understanding and freedom from controlling influences. Hence in empirical studies one usually speaks of a continuum of autonomy. The practical consequences of this line of thought would be that patients may be too influential in medical decision-making. From this follows that it can be ethically valid to restrict patient involvement in medical decision making for the sake of the common good. Health authorities may decide upon a level of adequate health care and set criteria for prioritising within this limit.

Within British health services research there has been some opposition to the idea of transparency in rationing decisions. Several authors have argued for the inevitability and usefulness of implicit rationing [11-15]. One repeated argument is that implicit rationing is inevitable in practice since there are no clear criteria on which to base explicit rationing. Indeed, in a recent British study, Ian Rees Jones and colleagues find that the ideal of explicit rationing is not adhered to in practice [16]. Another weighty argument is that professional discretion is more suitable and flexible than principles and guidelines to incorporate individual needs. It has also been argued that implicit rationing makes the administrative processes of healthcare provision run more smoothly. This argument focuses on the bureaucratic and political difficulties that are said to accompany explicit rationing. A further argument against explicit rationing emphasises that patients will be distressed if they are told that they are denied potentially beneficial treatments because of costs and not because of lack of effects. This argument is countered by those who argue that if the patient discovers this deceit, such a discovery could again lead to considerable unhappiness. Of course, if we take seriously the patients' right to protest against rationing decisions then such deception would be unjustifiable in any case.

The realisation that there is no consensus among stakeholders about how to solve the conflicting principles for priority setting has led to a shift in focus from principles to fair procedures. It is argued that an open and shared process is both a sound ethical solution and a practical tool for the implementation of priority setting. Norman Daniels's model of *Accountability for reasonableness* has received much attention [10,17]. Daniels proposes four conditions that need to be fulfilled for a fair, accountable and transparent process of explicit rationing:

- Publicity: Decisions and their rationale should be transparent to the public.
- Reasonableness: Decisions should be made on the basis of reasons that "fair-minded" people can agree are relevant when pursuing appropriate patient care under the necessary resource constraints.
- Appeals and revision: There should be mechanisms whereby limit-setting decisions can be disputed.
- Enforcement: There should be regulation of the process to ensure that the other three conditions are met.

It is, however, not given that accountability for reasonableness is applicable to rationing in primary care. While there is considerable literature on prioritisation at a macro level, there has been limited research on the way in which funding constraints influence the decisions of doctors in primary care, and *Accountability for reasonableness* has yet to be explored empirically with respect to rationing in primary care. If you visit the doctor because of something you fear may be cancer and your request for referral is declined with a reference to distributive justice by the primary care physician because she considers it unlikely to be cancer, you might prefer to play it safe and insist on a referral, even though you under other circumstances would argue for distributive justice. A transparent process takes time and is socially unpleasant. What if, after going through the whole meticulous procedure of explicit rationing, the doctor ends up with a decision the patient disagrees with? Then the patient could appeal, which would further increase the workload of the doctor. It may seem doubtful whether *Accountability for reasonableness* is a feasible procedure for the daily, undramatic rationing decisions of primary care. This is not an argument against *Accountability for reasonableness* however. Transparency in rationing decisions supports patient involvement, which is an aim in most health care systems, but, as Steven Pearson puts it, still, rationing is time consuming and the risk of losing patients is not eliminated by a transparent decision procedure, so why should primary care physicians bother to ration? [18]. *Accountability for reasonableness* is a tool, but not a motivating factor in itself and it is difficult to see that it will be used if motivation is lacking.

# Policy Measures

How do we get from these procedures to policy recommendations that will influence general practitioners' rationing behaviour? Today hardly any country has succeeded in eliminating the gap between priority setting at the macro-level and the pattern of health care resource distribution, which is largely a product of the thousands of daily decisions at the micro-level.

Let us have a look at some of the different policy measures used to motivate primary care physicians' behaviour:

Clinicians' behaviour could be governed through *laws and regulations* such as evidence based guidelines, monitoring or audit and feedback (the latter means that the clinician gets an overview of her own practice style as compared to the average or best practice.)

There are also a range of *economic incentives* in use: Three main types of payment systems are commonly used in primary care. These are salaried payment, capitation, and fee for service. Capitation means that the primary care physician is reimbursed according to the number of patients registered in the practice, and fee-for-service means that the reimbursements are activity-based. Negative incentives such as restrictions on re-imbursement are also used. One example is Denmark, where physicians' activities are monitored and if the activity level surpasses best practice, reimbursements are restricted accordingly.

Then there are *organisational incentives* such as budget responsibilities and different kinds of enrolment systems. Examples of the former would be fundholding in the UK or managed care in the US.

Finally health authorities may motivate doctors through medical *education*, continuous educational groups, *information* attached to new guidelines, medical congresses etc

Below I highlight experiences with the use of clinical practice guidelines and economic incentives and discuss whether they could encourage rationing while ensuring adequate quality in primary care:

## Guidelines and Audit and Feedback

Empirical research shows that most primary care physicians are positive to clinical practice guidelines and find them useful [19]. Still, several studies confirm that guidelines mostly are not adhered to and audit and feedback has had limited effect [20-22]. Guidelines seem to change clinical behaviour only when the doctors responsible for implementing them agree with their contents [23]. In addition extensive use of rules and regulations, coupled with monitoring has been claimed to be a danger to professionalism and undermine professional ethics [24,25]. Nevertheless, a recent OECD report finds that the Danish experience with restrictions on reimbursements has contributed to restraining expenditure [26]. And a few studies also indicate that guidelines and regulations can be used as support when physicians have to make rationing decisions [27,28]. However, the cost side of implementing clinical practice guidelines is seldom included in evaluations of their effectiveness [22].

## Economic Incentives

Some evidence shows that salaried doctors have lower activity levels than doctors in the other payments systems, and their patients complain about long waiting times and poor service [29,30]. Somewhat in contrast, a recent study from New England found that when presented with proposed compensation models for doctors, patients expressed most discomfort with capitation, and least discomfort with salaried payment [31]. The effects of capitation depend on competition. The system gives doctors incentives to compete for patients and thereby to satisfy patients. Economic theory and empirical studies suggest that if there is a surplus of doctors, and patients are free to change doctor, capitation leads to more activities within the practice. In the opposite case, when patients are locked in, there are more referrals [29,30]. In general fee for service payment leads to a higher activity level in the consultation and less referrals than in a pure capitation system [29,30].

Mark that a limitation of these studies is that the patient is not included as an actor in the models. The patient might also have an agenda and it is not given that the patient prefers to be treated in the primary care physician's practice in stead of being referred to a specialist.

There are two main problems connected to the use of economic incentives for doctors [32,33]:

1. Some economic literature warns that monetary incentives may backfire and ruin professional discretion. The argument is that when society uses incentives to promote changes in clinical behaviour, it sends a signal that doctors should consider their self interest when making medical decisions. This may lead to better practice in the short run. However, encouraging the self interest of doctors compromises a professional ethos that is central to good medical practice. The argument is that no compensation system will produce the results we want if it undermines the ethos that is necessary for professionalism.
2. If the behaviour of doctors is motivated primarily by self interest we will need to monitor their behaviour carefully and adjust incentives precisely. Several studies demonstrate that to monitor details of complicated work tasks is difficult and may even be counterproductive.

Experiences with budget responsibilities from UK-fundholding, and US-managed care are mixed [20,34]. The British experience shows that primary care physicians are able to ration if they are motivated or forced to, but an adverse effect seem to be that rationing decisions are made implicitly. Effects on quality are largely unknown but problems of distributive injustice have been reported as the system seems to secure treatment to fund-holdning members at the cost of other patients. However, there are indications that budget-responsibility curbs expenses to a moderate degree, with for example less referrals to secondary care.

### Challenges to Rationing Health Care

To ration health care while ensuring high quality of care is a challenge to health care insurers across countries and health care systems. The dilemmas regarding primary care physicians' gatekeeper role can be summarised as three main challenges:

- Rationing is inevitable but uncomfortable, thus the gatekeeper role is often avoided.
- Patient involvement is defined as an important aspect of quality in modern health care systems, but this ideal is not always compatible with the primary care physician's gatekeeper role.
- Primary care physicians hold a central role in rationing in several countries, but it has proven difficult to make doctors ration health care explicitly.

The policymaker's dilemma is to decide to which degree we should rely on primary care physicians' professional discretion to secure rationing and quality of health care. Should we follow the Danish model, where economic incentives and monitoring of physicians characterises the system? Then professional ethics could be undermined and a long term effects could be need for detailed, bureaucratic and expensive monitoring in the future. Or should we follow the model used in the UK, and grant more clinical freedom to primary care physicians and rely on their professional discretion by giving them budget responsibilities, which could mean that we risks implicit rationing and inequity?

## THE NORWEGIAN EXPERIENCE

The Norwegian health care sector is affluent, but also expensive. Health care is practically free at the point of service. Secondary care is under the responsibility of the central authorities, while primary care is under the responsibility of the municipalities.

Professional freedom of general practitioners is extremely high; there is practically no monitoring of practices. For all practical purposes primary care physicians are not held responsible for failure to ration health care. Still, there is an ongoing political struggle to bend costs of health care in Norway. Several factors have provoked the authorities' efforts to promote rationing of health care: Firstly, also in Norway demand exceeds resources. But equally important is the concern with fair distribution of services; there are some disturbing signs of inequity in health and health care utilisation. Additionally, there are tendencies towards defensive practice and overuse of services, and finally the health care budget has to be balanced against expenses in other sectors that are increasing: such as care for the elderly, disability pensions and sickness benefits.

In 1997 a White Paper established the basic criteria for priority setting in the Norwegian health sector [35].

The four criteria were:

- The seriousness of the disease.

- The effectiveness of the intervention
- The cost–benefit ratio of the intervention
- The quality of the documentation of the effects

Stricter control and tighter regulations of Norwegian primary care has been announced and the Directorate for Health and Social Affairs has initiated the process of developing mandatory principles for priority setting within primary care.

In 2001 a comprehensive reform was carried out in primary care. The new scheme, which is called "The regular general practitioner scheme", is an enrolment system ensuring every citizen's right to a regular primary care physician. The stated aims of the reform were to enhance patient involvement, improve the quality and accessibility of the services, and to strengthen the gatekeeper function of primary care [36]. These goals were to be achieved through the organisational changes as well as through economic incentives aimed at the primary care physicians: a new capitation based component in the primary care physician's income was introduced, which constitutes 30% of the payment, while the other 70% are fee-for-service based. In addition the new system accentuates the primary care physician's clinical responsibility and gatekeeper role as the primary care physician is supposed to co-ordinate all care their patients receive.

Lately, the reform has been assessed [37-39] and a national evaluation of the scheme shows that accessibility has been somewhat increased, primary care physicians seem to be offering better service, and patients have gained negotiating power. However, at the same time expenses have increased because of raised reimbursement fees to the primary care physicians, and increased number of activities per physician. Also the gatekeeper role seems to have been weakened and the intended monitoring and controls by the health authorities have not been effectuated.

**Table 1. Reasons why Norwegian primary care physicians avoid rationing health care**

| |
|---|
| • Lack of motivation |
| - Traditionally responsible only for the individual patient |
| - Increased competition and patient power (consumerism) |
| - Ideal of patient involvement in medical decision making |
| - High level of professional freedom from health authorities |
| - No budget responsibility |
| - Increased clinical responsibility |
| - Time consuming |
| - Socially uncomfortable |
| - Risks losing patients |
| - High activity level pays off |
| • Lack of instruments |
| - Lack of guidelines |
| - Lack of competence to negotiate with patients |

Do Norwegian primary care physicians ration health care? Our knowledge about Norwegian primary care physicians rationing decisions is very limited. In a study from 1995, 68% of the primary care physicians reported that they sometimes or often refrained from giving the best treatment to patients because it was too expensive [40]. In contrast two later surveys as well as an interview study conducted by this author find that the primary care physicians' willingness to ration is declining. Simultaneously referral rates have increased after the list reform [4,39,41,42]. This evidence could indicate that Norwegian primary care physicians have been rationing, but that the willingness to ration has declined.

Carlsen and Norheim have revealed a number of reasons why Norwegian primary care physicians avoid rationing health care (Table 1) [39,43]. In short the primary care physicians fail to ration to avoid conflict with patients because of a lack of motivation, increased patient negotiating power and lack of instruments for rationing.

## How to Motivate Rationing in Gatekeeping Systems

What measures can policymakers in Norwegian health care and other gatekeeping systems take to enhance rationing and secure that the principles for priority setting are adhered to? Let us look at some suggestions based on the limited evidence of the effects of policy measures on rationing and patient involvement in primary care.

### 1. Information

It seems to bee vital that evidence based practice and more extensive guidelines are implemented in order to support rationing decisions. To achieve this, physicians need to be informed and updated about current evidence. Such information must be presented in a short and flexible format that is possible to incorporate in practice situations of medical decision making.

Also health services research should be strengthened. Particularly, there is a need for more empirical knowledge about decision making in primary care. In connection with this it is important that central registration of journal and activity-data from general practice is practiced. A broader evidence base would make a better basis for developing practice guidelines.

### 2. Monitoring

Some restrictions on primary care physicians' professional freedom by monitoring, feedback and economic sanctions are necessary. By introducing national clinical standards and monitoring of journal data, restrictions on reimbursements could be activated when a primary care physician deviates from the national standard. However, following the Danish experience, for such a system to be accepted by the primary care physicians, it is important that the assessment of the practice is managed by a group of peers.

This system must also be coupled with more elaborated and evidence based guidelines.

A downside of this policy could be increased costs of bureaucracy, but still it may be worthwhile if it leads to better quality, less unnecessary interventions and more just distribution of services.

Not surprisingly, The Norwegian Medical Association is arguing for preservation of professional freedom. However, as of today Norwegian primary care physicians have more freedom than most of their colleagues working in a hospital setting, hence there should be a certain margin to work within.

## 3. Motivation

Through medical education, information and awareness of both respect for patient autonomy and the need for rationing could be promoted. Also the tension between these ideals should be debated. To promote adherence to guidelines, the process of developing guidelines should be transparent to the primary care physician through information attached to new guidelines. If we could make primary care physicians include concerns about resource allocation as well as clinical benefits in their ideals of what it is to be a good doctor, much would have been accomplished.

## 4. Pragmatism

Primary care physicians' negotiation competence could be increased by means of for example teaching conflict resolution or accountability for reasonableness, during education and later. One could promote shared decision–making perhaps without always aiming at letting the patients have the final word. There are some indications that doctors who focus on shared decision making and take time to negotiate with patients generate less cost and have more satisfied patients [44-47]. Also, both doctors and politicians should be reminded that patient satisfaction is not always the same as high quality.

A controversial, but pragmatic argument is that that policymakers should steer a middle course between explicit and implicit rationing, recognising that primary care doctors have to find pragmatic solutions to the unsolved dilemma of patients' rights to be involved and the need to ration, without using too much time to negotiate with each patient. Perhaps it must be left to professional judgement to deem when it is not necessary to be explicit about rationing?

Finally, there are some indications in the empirical literature that policy makers could be more cautious with the use of monetary incentives. It could be argued that a system of salaried payment has many advantages over the current scheme of mixed capitation and fee for service. Absence of activity based economic incentives underscores professional responsibility and clinical judgements in decision making. Curiously, our empirical investigations suggests that primary care physicians are able to say no when it comes to addiction–inducing drugs, demonstrating that primary care physicians withhold services that patients desire when motivated by clinical reasons [39]. Besides, as mentioned earlier, salaried primary care physicians generate fewer costs. Hence, in a salaried system primary care physicians would probably user more time per consultation without over-treating patients.

A drawback of a salaried system is that patients tend to be less satisfied with service attitude, waiting time and accessibility. In that respect consumer influence would be weaker than today, but simultaneously patient influence through shared decision-making within the consultation as well as the doctor's inclination to listen to patients could even be enhanced. There is broad evidence that an important concern of the general practitioner, besides the clinical concern, is to preserve the doctor-patient relationship and the social and professional incentives to keep patients satisfied would still apply in a salaried system.

## Conclusion

There is reason to argue that to overcome barriers to fulfilment of the primary care physicians' gatekeeper role in Norwegian primary care and other gatekeeping systems, policymakers need to intervene at several fronts. There is a need for motivation, enforcement and tools. The arenas of potential efforts are:

1) Strengthen the evidence base
2) Monitoring and economic sanctions
3) Motivation of primary care physicians
4) Negotiations and pragmatism
5) Less intensive economic incentives

The central challenge would be how to moderately increase monitoring of primary care without risking the primary care physicians' professional attitude, especially if the activity based economic incentives were to be relaxed. Also the individual patient's influence could be restricted somewhat to contain costs and ensure a fair and efficient distribution of services.

## References

[1] Forrest CB. Primary care in the United States: Primary care gatekeeping and referrals: effective filter or failed experiment? *BMJ* 2003;326(7391):692-695.

[2] Ayres PJ. Rationing health care: Views from general practice. *Social Science & Medicine* 1996;42(7):1021-1025.

[3] Bindman AB, Majeed A. Primary care in the United States: Organisation of primary care in the United States. *BMJ* 2003;326(7390):631-634.

[4] Gulbrandsen P, Førde R, Aasland OG. Hvordan har legen det som portvakt? *Tidsskrift for Den norske lægeforening* 2002;122:1874-1879.

[5] OECD Health Data; 2003.

[6] Light DW, Hughes D. Introduction: A sociological perspective on rationing: power, rhetoric and situated practices. *Sociol Health & Illness* 2001;23(5):551-569.

[7] Klein R. Priorities and rationing: pragmatism or principles? *BMJ* 1995;311(7008):761-762.

[8] Coast J. Who wants to know if their care is rationed? Views of citizens and service informants doi:10.1046/j.1369-6513.2001.00147.x. *Health Expectations* 2001;4(4):243-252.

[9] Daniels N. Meeting the challenges of justice & rationing. *Hastings Center Report* 1994;24(4):27-29.

[10] Daniels N, Sabin J. Limits to health care: Fair procedures, democratic deliberation, and the legitimacy problem for insurers. *Philosophy & Public Affairs* 1997;26(4):303-350.

[11] Coast J. The case against. *BMJ* 1997;314(7087):1118-.

[12] Doyal L. The rationing debate: Rationing within the NHS should be explicit: The case for. *BMJ* 1997;314(7087):1114-.

[13] Klein R. The case against. *BMJ* 1997;314(7079):503-.

[14] Mechanic D. Dilemmas in rationing health care services: the case for implicit rationing. *BMJ* (Clinical Research Ed.) 1995;310(6995 SU -):1655-1659.

[15] Mechanic D. Muddling through elegantly: finding the proper balance in rationing. *Health Aff* 1997;16(5):83-92.

[16] Jones IR, Berney L, Kelly M, Doyal L, Griffiths C, Feder G, et al. Is patient involvement possible when decisions involve scarce resources? A qualitative study of decision-making in primary care. *Social Science & Medicine* 2004;59(1):93-102.

[17] Daniels N. Accountability for reasonableness. *BMJ* 2000;321(7272):1300-1301.

[18] Pearson SD. Caring and cost: the challenge for physician advocacy. *Ann Intern Med* 2000;133(2):148-53.

[19] Farquhar CM, Kofa EW, Slutsky JR. Clinicians' attitudes to clinical practice guidelines: a systematic review. *The Medical Journal of Australia* 2002; 177(9):502-506.

[20] Coulter A. Managing demand at the interface between primary and secondary care. *British Medical Journal* 1998;316:1974-1976.

[21] Treweek S, Flottorp S, Fretheim A, Håvelsrud K, Kristoffersen DT, Oxman A, et al. Retningslinjer for allmennpraksis - blir de lest og blir de brukt? (Guidelines in general practice: are they read and are they used?). *Tidsskr Nor Laegeforen* 2005;125:300-3.

[22] Grimshaw JM, Thomas RE, MacLennan G, Fraser C, Ramsay CR, Vale L, et al. Effectiveness and efficiency of guideline dissemination and implementation strategies. *Health Technology Assessment* 2004;8(6).

[23] Grol R, Dalhuijsen J, Thomas S, Veld Cit, Rutten G, Mokkink H. Attributes of clinical guidelines that influence use of guidelines in general practice: observational study. *BMJ* 1998;317(7162):858-861.

[24] Kassirer JP. Managed care and the morality of the marketplace. *N Engl J Med* 1995;333(1):50-2.

[25] Lian AS, Røttingen J-A. Legen - homo economicus eller homo sociologicus? *Tidsskr Nor Laegeforen* 2002;122:1682-5.

[26] OECD. Enhancing expenditure control with a decentralised public sector in Denmark. Paris: OECD; 2002.

[27] Pollock K, Grime J. The cost and cost-effectiveness of PPIs: GP perspectives and responses to a prescribing dilemma and their implications for the development of

patient-centred healthcare. *European Journal of General Practice* 2003;9(4):126-133+140.

[28] Venn S, Edwards A. Assessing the awareness of and attitude to NICE guidance within GP partnerships in one PCO in Wales: a qualitative study using focus group interviews. *Quality in Primary Care* 2003;11:123-8.

[29] McGuire TG. Physician agency. In: Culyer AJ, Newhouse JP, editors. *Handbook of Health Economics*. Amsterdam: Elsevier; 2000. p. Chapter 9.

[30] Scott A. Economics of General Practice. In: Culyer AJ, Newhouse JP, editors. *Handbook of Health Economics*. First edition ed. Amsterdam: Elsevier Science B.V.; 2000. p. 1175-1200.

[31] Pereira AG, Pearson SD. Patient attitudes toward physician financial incentives. *Archives of Internal Medicine* 2001;161(10):1313-1317.

[32] Fehr E, Falk A. Psychological foundations of incentives. *European Economic Review* 2002;46(4-5):687-724.

[33] Holmstrom B, Milgrom P. Multitask Principal Agent Analyses - Incentive Contracts, Asset Ownership, and Job Design. *Journal of Law Economics & Organization* 1991;7:24-52.

[34] Dixon J, Glennerster H. What do we know about fundholding in general practice? *BMJ* 1995;311(7007):727-730.

[35] NOU 1997:18. *Prioritering på ny (Priority setting revised)*. Oslo: Sosial- og helsedepartementet; 1997.

[36] Regulation relating to a Municipal Regular GP Scheme. In. *Oslo: Ministry of Health and Social Services*; 2000.

[37] Sandvik H. Evaluering av fastlegereformen 2001-2005 (Evaluation of the Regular general practitioner scheme 2001-2005). Oslo: Norges forskningsråd. (The research council of Norway); 2006.

[38] Riksrevisjonen. [The Office of the Auditor General]. Riksrevisjonens undersøkelse om forvaltning av og måloppnåelse av fastlegeordningen [The Office of the Auditor General's report regarding the management and achievements of the goals of the Regular General Practitioner Scheme.] Report No. 1 2005. Oslo: Riksrevisjonen; 2005.

[39] Carlsen B, Norheim OF. Introduction of the Patient-list System in General Practice: Changes in Norwegian Physicians' Perception of their Gatekeeper Role. *Scandinavian journal of primary health care* 2003;21(4):209-213.

[40] Arnesen T, Fredriksen S. Coping with obligations towards patient and society: an empirical study of attitudes and practice among Norwegian physicians. *Journal of medical ethics* 1995;21:158-161.

[41] Sandvik H. Fastlegeordningen - forventninger og erfaringer. *Tidsskr Nor Laegeforen* 2003;123(10):1319-21.

[42] Iversen T, Kopperud GS. Regulation versus practice - the impact of accessibility on the use of specialist health care in Norway. *Health Economics* 2005;14(12):1231-1238.

[43] Carlsen B, Norheim OF. "Saying no is no easy matter". A qualitative study of competing concerns in rationing decisions in general practice. *BMC Health Services Research* 2005;5(70).

[44] Little P, Everitt H, Williamson I, Warner G, Moore M, Gould C, et al. Observational study of effect of patient centredness and positive approach on outcomes of general practice consultations. *BMJ* 2001;323(7318):908-911.

[45] Benbassat J, Pilpel D, Tidhar M. Patients' preferences for participation in clinical decision making: A review of published surveys. *Behavioral Medicine* 1998;24(2):81-8.

[46] Cecil D, Killeen I. Control, compliance and satisfaction in the family practice encounter. *Family Medicine* 1997;29:653-657.

[47] Grol R, Maeseneer Jd, Whitfield M, Mokkink H. Disease-centred versus patient-centred attitudes: comparison of general practitioners in Belgium, Britain and The Netherlands. *Family Practice* 1990;7(2):100-103.

# INDEX

## A

## B



## C

## D



## E

## F

## G



## H



## I

## J



## K



## L

## Q



## R

## S

## T



## U



## V

## W



## X



## Y